S0-ARF-434

THE PHYSICIAN'S GUIDE TO

Avoiding Financial Blunders

To Kelly:
It's great knowing you as
neighbors! Hope you like
this!

Sincerely,

Carl

10-7-11

THE PHYSICIAN'S GUIDE TO

Avoiding Financial Blunders

Kenneth W. Rudzinski, CFP®, CRPC®, CLU, ChFC, CASL, CAP®

The America Group

Wilmington, Delaware

www.slackbooks.com

ISBN: 978-1-55642-875-3

Copyright © 2010 by SLACK Incorporated

The following degrees are registered: CFP, CLU, CRPC, ChFC, and CAP.

All rights reserved. No part of this book may be reproduced, stored in a retrieval system or transmitted in any form or by any means, electronic, mechanical, photocopying, recording or otherwise, without written permission from the publisher, except for brief quotations embodied in critical articles and reviews.

The procedures and practices described in this book should be implemented in a manner consistent with the professional standards set for the circumstances that apply in each specific situation. Every effort has been made to confirm the accuracy of the information presented and to correctly relate generally accepted practices. The authors, editor, and publisher cannot accept responsibility for errors or exclusions or for the outcome of the material presented herein. There is no expressed or implied warranty of this book or information imparted by it. Care has been taken to ensure that drug selection and dosages are in accordance with currently accepted/recommended practice. Due to continuing research, changes in government policy and regulations, and various effects of drug reactions and interactions, it is recommended that the reader carefully review all materials and literature provided for each drug, especially those that are new or not frequently used. Any review or mention of specific companies or products is not intended as an endorsement by the author or publisher.

SLACK Incorporated uses a review process to evaluate submitted material. Prior to publication, educators or clinicians provide important feedback on the content that we publish. We welcome feedback on this work.

Published by: SLACK Incorporated
                6900 Grove Road
                Thorofare, NJ 08086 USA
                Telephone: 856-848-1000
                Fax: 856-853-5991
                www.slackbooks.com

Contact SLACK Incorporated for more information about other books in this field or about the availability of our books from distributors outside the United States.

Library of Congress Cataloging-in-Publication Data

Rudzinski, Kenneth W.
  The physician's guide to avoiding financial blunders / Kenneth W. Rudzinski.
     p. ; cm.
  Includes bibliographical references and index.
  ISBN 978-1-55642-875-3 (alk. paper)
  1. Physicians--Finance, Personal. I. Title.
  [DNLM: 1. Income. 2. Physicians--economics. 3. Investments. W 79 R917p 2010]
  R728.5R83 2010
  610.68'1--dc22
                         2009029116

For permission to reprint material in another publication, contact SLACK Incorporated. Authorization to photocopy items for internal, personal, or academic use is granted by SLACK Incorporated provided that the appropriate fee is paid directly to Copyright Clearance Center. Prior to photocopying items, please contact the Copyright Clearance Center at 222 Rosewood Drive, Danvers, MA 01923 USA; phone: 978-750-8400; web site: www.copyright.com; email: info@copyright.com

Last digit is print number: 10   9   8   7   6   5   4   3   2   1

DEDICATION

This book is dedicated to the memory of Stanley K. Brockman, MD, who first introduced me in 1978 to the medical profession and who would have been thrilled with this project.

CONTENTS

ACKNOWLEDGMENTS

I could not have written the pages that appear in this book, or the hundreds that just didn't make it (a sequel, maybe?), as a solo project. Many capable and dedicated people are lined up just behind me, like all those people in the ever-present cell phone commercials we see on TV.

First and foremost, I'd like to thank my spouse of 40 years, Mary Jane, who has always been supportive of any independent project I've undertaken. As the song goes, "I met her on a Monday and my heart stood still..."

It goes without saying (but I'll say it anyway) that without Beth Murphy, my right hand in this project from the beginning, I would have just produced a lot of words. Both she and Lori Rutkowski, both from my office (The America Group), helped me get it all together in its final form. While we were doing that, the rest of my staff—Antonia Mullen and Christina Croall—held down the fort. My partner, Brent C. Fuchs, CFP, ChFC, CLU, CRPC, filled in for me with clients on many occasions as I concentrated on the completion of this project. My hearty thanks go out to all of them.

Several willing volunteers read parts of this book as I was writing it, and all gave me honest and helpful feedback. Among these were Dr. Harvey Rosenwasser, OD (whose many suggestions made it into the final version), David Schiller, Esq. (sorry about the clichés), Doug Cranage (Chapter 7 bears your imprint), and Nasser Ali, CFA, CFP, CRPC, AAMS, CMFC (my investment mentor and friend despite his being an ice hockey player).

At SLACK Incorporated, my publisher, I owe a tremendous debt of gratitude to Nancy Hemphill who was the first to give me a chance in 1988 to write articles in *Primary Care Optometry News*. I've gotten ongoing support of my articles from my editors-in-chief, Joan-Marie Stiglich and Kathy Holliman. For this book, Jennifer Briggs served as my acquisitions editor and John Bond, my boss-man (your book on how to write a book was invaluable!). I sincerely appreciate all of you and your never-ending support for my literary efforts, be they articles or this book (and maybe the next one).

Professionally, my gratitude and my respect go out to Stephan R. Leimberg, Esq. for his early suggestions on book writing and his continued excellence in providing the best online source of information on all things financial at www.leimbergservices. com; my friend Peter S. Gordon, Esq. who always took time from his busy schedule to answer my technical questions; and Brandon Buckingham, JD who first spoke about a retirement timeline concept that I turned into Chapter 8. Additionally, thanks to Ed Slott, CPA and Natalie B. Choate who provided the valuable technical data where and when needed.

Thanks to my dear friend, Mike McFeeley, who showed me by his example how to write a book and lent me the peace and quiet of his lake house to work. And to Yvonne K. Brockman whose farm and nearby cows formed the backdrop (and sound effects) for several chapters that I wrote (as you said, "Stanley would be proud of this project.").

Lastly, to all of my friends and clients who, in one way or another, made it into this book, I am grateful for your continued support and I hope you will be as proud of this book as I am. Thanks especially to Dr. C. whose unfortunate disability inspired the opening of Chapter 4. Enjoy your retirement—you worked hard to get there!

ABOUT THE AUTHOR

Kenneth W. Rudzinski, CFP, CLU, ChFC, CASL, CRPC, CAP, has been a financial planner and wealth manager for over 35 years. He received his undergraduate degree at Villanova University in 1969 then completed his Master's degree in French at the University of Delaware in 1972. He taught French for 3 years before entering the financial services industry in June, 1973. For over a dozen years, Ken used his teaching skills in a management capacity at Lincoln National Sales Corporation and Aetna Life & Casualty. In 1988, he founded The America Group, a fee-based financial planning and investment management firm in Wilmington, Delaware. By that time, Ken had already spent over a dozen years working with many doctors in the critical areas of risk management, retirement, investment, and estate planning.

Ken's knowledge and experience have been recognized locally as well as on a national level. As a former contributing writer for the *Wilmington NewsJournal*, and a member of the *NewsJournal's* "Ask the Experts" panel, he has authored numerous articles on various financial planning topics. He has also been published nationally in various medical specialty publications, including a total of over 60 articles featured in *Orthopedics Today, Cardiology Today, Ocular Surgery News, Primary Care Optometry News, Endocrine Today, Infectious Diseases in Children, Hem/Onc Today,* and others.

Ken has lectured nationally on such topics as "Avoiding The Big Mistake in Investing," "Fundamental Financial Concepts," and "Retirement Planning Obstacles." He serves as the financial consultant for two national Web sites for doctors, "POP" (Proactive Optometric Physicians [www.proactod.org]) and ODWire.org (www.odwire.org/forum). He has been cited in *MONEY* magazine and has been listed in the Marquis Edition of *Who's Who in Finance and Industry* and *Who's Who in the East.*

Besides over 35 years of practical field experience, which has found its way into Ken's articles, lectures, and now into this book, Ken has a substantial educational pedigree, receiving the following professional degrees:

- Chartered Life Underwriter (CLU)—1983
- CERTIFIED FINANCIAL PLANNER™ (CFP)—1985
- Chartered Financial Consultant (ChFC)—1986
- Chartered Advisor for Senior Living (CASL)—2005
- Chartered Advisor in Philanthropy (CAP)—2007
- Chartered Retirement Planning Counselor SM (CRPC)—2008

Ken is a Life and Qualifying Member of the nationally-recognized Million Dollar Round Table. Additionally, he is a member of the Society of Financial Service Professionals, The National Association of Insurance and Financial Advisors, and the prestigious Chairman's Council and Resource Group at Lincoln Financial Advisors.

Ken has spent his career serving the people of the Delaware Valley and beyond. His financial planning and investment management practice is national in scope. He and his spouse, Mary Jane, have been residents of Wilmington, Delaware since 1970. He has served as a photographer for the Wilmington Blue Rocks minor league baseball team, and his hobbies consist of golf, baseball (he attended Villanova University on a full baseball scholarship), and collecting rock 'n' roll music. He has two sons, Matt and Alex.

INTRODUCTION

The genesis of this book occurred in 1998, when Nancy Hemphill, editor of the newest SLACK Incorporated publication, *Primary Care Optometry News*, informed me that she would publish articles of mine in its "Practice Management" section. Sixty or so articles later, I began to feel that other doctors and physicians might benefit from the subject matter of those articles, many of which did not appear in other SLACK Incorporated medical specialty publications until much later. I came to that conclusion as I received volumes of e-mail feedback from doctors all over the United States.

I first learned that readership of my articles exceeded 500,000 medical professionals as more specialty publications such as *Cardiology Today, Ocular Surgery News, Infectious Diseases in Children, Orthopedics Today,* etc printed them. Readers expressed gratitude for the content of my articles, but most of all, they told me over and over again that they appreciated the "call to action" my writing instilled in them. They said that while they felt educated by my column, they came away with the distinct message that whatever they needed to do, or not do, as suggested in the article, they should take care of it ASAP. I recall one doctor even wrote that he drove home "white knuckled" after reading what I wrote about disability insurance, but he finally took care of that risk exposure.

In the final analysis, I strongly believe in that old adage, taken from a book title by Joe Gandolfo back in the 1970s, "Ideas are a dime a dozen but the man who puts them into practice is worth a million." That goes as well for all you women out there too. So, if you read this book and fail to take action in areas that need attention, then I have failed you as an author. But I don't think that is going to happen. There are just too many facets of your financial plan for life that are impacted here, and it would be a very rare reader who has all the bases covered. My job is to prompt you to cover those.

This book is designed to challenge you to take action in those financial planning areas where action is needed. This book is not the *Encyclopedia Britannica* of financial planning by any stretch. On the contrary, it is both a stimulus to make you seriously consider various aspects of your financial plan for life and a catalyst and guide for you to take the actions necessary to correct what needs correcting. As a result, I will be asking you many times throughout, "If you don't do this, who will?" So, expect to be challenged.

Whether you are a 30-year-old cardiologist, a 75-year-old ophthalmologist, or any age in between, I am certain you will derive ideas from these chapters that you can adopt immediately. I suggest planning "fire drills" throughout as the means to accomplish those things you know you must do—or avoid.

You live and work in a busy world. We all do. That's why I divided the chapters into pieces you could digest bite by bite. Most of you will probably not read this book all the way through from Chapter 1 to Chapter 10. You will most likely read the subject matter out of turn based on your personal priorities. I suppose Chapters 5 and 6 will interest many of you since they deal with simple-to-complex methods to protect your assets from "predators and creditors." Those of you who are losing sleep at night thinking about your retirement will gravitate to Chapter 8 where I discuss the timeline to prepare for "the longest vacation of your life." When I wrote about that in a two-part article a few years ago, I received over 500 responses from doctors throughout the country about the benefits they derived from thinking along the "timeline," wherever they found themselves in their pursuit of a successful retirement.

I am conscious of my job to help you make the best use of your time reading this book as well as helping you make money or prevent you from losing money from its ideas and concepts. With those thoughts in mind, you will find the material in Chapters 2 and 9 on investing more geared toward your emotional approach to your portfolio than its detailed elements.

In my 35+ years of working with clients of all means, I have seen client behavior short-circuit portfolio success more often than the specific stocks or mutual funds contained within those same portfolios. Never was that more evident than in October and November 2008 when the markets plummeted seemingly out of control. What investors did or didn't do during that crisis period will dictate their investment success moving forward. I try to make readers aware of the emotional content that goes into making those instant decisions and how to avoid the worst of repercussions. It's with a deep appreciation of market history that I guide you through the tough times hoping to keep you from making "the Big Mistake." You will have several opportunities to contact me for additional information that can supplement the material in this book. Please feel free to send requests to my attention at bookspublishing@slackinc.com.

What I write about in my articles, and in this book, comes from more than 3 decades of experience counseling doctors, business owners, and others as a financial advisor. In my everyday dealings with the financial world of my clients and other individuals, I have seen and heard almost everything imaginable, from people who became incapacitated and, unprepared for this financial calamity, died penniless, to doctors (like Brad in Chapter 4), who successfully weathered a devastating disability. I've seen people try to time the markets and fail. I've seen investors buy and hold and succeed. Many of their stories populate this book since they are the best evidence of the principles I am advocating.

Throughout the book I have attempted to keep the same writing style that is the trademark of my financial articles, although I found making the transition from article to book format is easier said than done. So while the skeleton of the articles that inspired these chapters remains, the details have been greatly expanded, updated, and improved. In other words, if you read the original articles as published, you have much to gain by the substantive new material added here to those original articles. Additionally, Chapter 10 and the connective material in Chapter 9 are brand new, never having been previously published. Lastly, the coverage of my articles when written did not appear uniformly in all the SLACK Incorporated publications. For example, ODs have not seen the two-part article on "Longest Vacation"; DOs only ever got to see a few articles, almost none that are contained in this book. The bottom line is that much of the material here should be fresh and new for all readers of my past columns.

In the end, this book will not make you a better doctor. But what it WILL do is to help you understand why actions you take or do not take may make or break your financial plan for life. It will help you create and maintain both a financial map to reach your goals and an investment policy statement to guide your portfolio decisions. It will suggest ways to build a moat around your castle to keep out unwanted creditors. It will shed light on those estate documents you need to pass on your financial legacy to your children and grandchildren. Finally, it will serve as a future resource for you to dust off from time to time when you need a reminder about the meaning and fulfillment of your financial plan for life.

1

Avoiding the Most Common Financial Planning Mistakes

"The journey of a mile starts with a single step."
Lao Tzu

When was the last time you checked your financial plan for leaks? Have you been under the "hood" recently to make sure it's still a realistic and viable plan? Or maybe you've been putting off an organized, determined approach for your retirement and estate planning, for your children's college expenses, for your practice succession plan, all the while thinking that you can start such planning on another unspecified day sometime in the future. If this is you, then you might be guilty of one or more of the most common financial planning mistakes discussed next, as outlined by fellow financial writer Stephan R. Leimberg (www.leimbergservices.com).[1] My task here is to help you avoid them.

MISTAKE #1:
YOU DON'T KNOW WHERE TO START—SO YOU DON'T

Planning for your future can be a daunting task, so many people just don't do it repeatedly and systematically. Some do and that might be you. But most never really start at all. We've all heard the famous saying, "People don't plan to fail; they just fail to plan." In developing a financial plan for your family's future, it happens to be true.

Right from the outset, you need to remember that you can't get to where you're going unless you first know where you are. For example, to get to Chicago, I go west from Delaware, but Californians go east instead! Sounds basic, right? However, most people skip this very important first step. Knowing where you are is key to knowing the direction your planning process must take to succeed. Where you are is where you start, which is by sitting down with your checkbook and credit card statements or visiting your online banking to view spending levels and patterns.

Rudzinski K. *The Physician's Guide to Avoiding Financial Blunders (pp 1-20)*
© 2009 SLACK Incorporated

The reason why many people do not start the planning process properly is that this opening step is by far the most difficult, unless you've been keeping close score with software like Quicken or Microsoft Money. Why? Keeping track is tedious, time-consuming, and often so spotty as to present an inaccurate picture of your true spending. Many people with good intentions just stop the process right here. However, this fundamental data gathering is arguably the most necessary step to achieving financial freedom, and the earlier you start to make it an unshakable habit, the easier it will be to create the map for your financial future.

It helps to have a good data sheet to organize your expenditures into groupings divided generally into your fixed expenses (needs) and your discretionary expenses (wants). I've provided a sample "Annual Expense Summary" at the end of this chapter, which you can recreate as your guide through your expenditure maze. E-mail me at bookspublishing@slackinc.com if you do not have Quicken or Microsoft Money and I'll send you an EXCEL (Microsoft Corp) spreadsheet to use for multiple months expense input.

When you work with any data sheet to itemize your normal expenditures, you'll find that listing certain expenditures like mortgage payments, auto loans, cable TV, etc is fairly simple because these are recurring expenses and remain relatively unchanged month to month. But discretionary expenditures like food, eating out, and cash for personal use, vacations, and travel are tougher to quantify because they fluctuate according to your whims and daily appetite. This is why keeping track of those expenses via a data sheet or program is so important. Many other expenditures are nonrecurring expenses such as landscaping, a new roof, or basement remodeling and can be either ignored or minimized for future budgeting.

To get off square one, you need to come up with a pretty good—not necessarily perfect—accounting of your ordinary monthly expenditures. Emergencies can be planned for separately with a cash emergency fund. Just do the best you can. If you can get within 5% of your true after-tax expendable cash, then that's a great start. I suggest you add an expense called "buffer" expense equaling about 5% to 10% of your after-tax income to account for those expenditures you just can't track. As a result, you can now feel confident that you've captured the vast majority of your outflow and can then begin to sort out what excess money, if any, you might have on hand to save for goals such as retirement, education, debt repayment, etc.

Planning Pointer

Getting a realistic handle on paper of what you regularly spend is the best and most important first step you can take.

The next step is to list your income from all sources (salary, bonus, commissions, rental income, investment income, etc) along with the various taxes that serve to diminish that income. Now you can realistically compare your total expenditures against sources of recurring income. This is your "cash flow" statement, and it's extremely revealing, just like it is for big businesses. An obvious conclusion you can draw is that positive cash flow (income exceeds expenses) means you've got a surplus to further consume or to save. Negative cash flow means you either need to decrease expenditures, increase income (moonlighting?), or dip into your savings/net worth to plug the gap. With negative cash flow, you need to implement a "budget" to avoid depleting your net worth and incurring unwanted, unnecessary, and unsupportable debt. Deficit spending—whether emotional, binge, or just plain unregulated—can lead to personal bankruptcy (in the worst case) and/or to fits of depression worrying about money and the deep financial hole you've dug for yourself and your family.

I pose this question to you: Do you have a firm grasp of your cash flow bottom line or do you experience too much month and not enough paycheck? If you were retiring next month or next year, can you state with near certainty what your retirement standard of living (budget) needs to be? If you don't know this vital data, when will you? Work with the data sheet and start now.

The next step is to compile your assets, such as cash, savings, retirement plans (IRAs, and 401(k)s, 403(b)s, etc), real estate, personal items, business interests, etc. Separate liquid (those easily converted to cash) from illiquid assets (house, furniture, etc). Now list your debts, indicating those coming due within the next few months (short term) and those not payable for 1 year or more (long term). This difference between what assets you own and what debts you owe is your "personal net worth." "If you stop right here, you've come a long way," asserts Steve Leimberg.[1]

What can you do with this information? First, if you plan to seek help from a certified financial planner (CFP) or other planning professional, you would now have an objective snapshot of where you are, financially speaking.

Second, you would have the raw data to begin tracking your future income and expenses, paying special attention to the growth or depletion of your net worth. This allows you to convert each future snapshot of your net worth and cash flow into a motion picture of your family's financial direction. When you watch your money grow by comparing your net worth statements over time, you give yourself the psychological stroking you need to keep harnessing present gratification for the benefit of future consumption (ie, at retirement). On the other hand, seeing your net worth plummet from unbridled spending deficits and/or market declines can be an immediate wake-up call to get your expenditures under control and to extinguish ongoing deficits before they overwhelm you. Hiring a financial planner in the latter case can get you the accountability you need, especially if you can't do it yourself.

Finally, does anyone else, such as your spouse and/or grown children, know where your important papers are or where a summary of your financial assets might be, including account numbers and location, advisor contacts, computer passwords, etc? You might want to make others aware of such issues in case you can't at a crucial time.

Planning Pointer

If you want to get a meaningful head start toward controlling your financial future, start today by itemizing your income and outflows, assets, and liabilities. This is the hard data that forms the map to guide you forward.

MISTAKE #2:
YOU HAVE A DREAM RATHER THAN A GOAL

This mistake occurs when people confuse a dream ("secure lifestyle" during retirement) with a goal (income of $50,000 per year at age 65, growing at 3% per year until at least age 95). The former is vague (dream), while the latter is specific (goal).

Your goals include not just financial objectives, but also personal ones as well. The former might include such specific goals as planning a special family vacation (budget of $8500) this year, purchasing a house ($750,000) in a certain geographic area before age "X," providing a quality education ($35,000 per year with inflation) for each of your children, or planning a date or age when you will retire and the income you will need to support your retirement standard of living.

An even better example was a doctor-client of mine in his very early 30s who had as his goal to accumulate $1,000,000 by the time he turned 40 so he could consider retiring at an early age. He could see it, taste it, feel it. He woke up to that goal in the morning, and it was the last thing he thought about at night. You know what? He did it, reaching just over $1,050,000 the day he hit age 40. That was a clearly definable goal, not just a dream.

Examples of personal goals might be getting a specific advanced degree by "X" age, joining the Rotary, volunteering your free time to your favorite charity, and coaching your son's little league baseball team. When was the last time you wrote down a list of your goals—short (next 12 months), intermediate (1 to 3 years), and long term (beyond 3 years)? Have you ever done this? If not, would you commit to doing so?

Ask yourself this question: What has to happen in the next year, or in 3 and 5 years, to enable you to declare those time frames "successful?" Write out your answers and keep them visible. Make sure those financial goals are clear and precise as to time and dollar amount. Share them with your spouse and, if applicable, with your children. Get them involved. Hold yourself accountable to them and measure your success (or dare I say, lack of success) along the way. Ask them to do the same for their own personal and/or financial goals. Build in rewards for specific goals reached along the way.

Why do I stress the need for specificity in setting goals? Because, for example, as a financial planner I cannot help someone who tells me he wants to retire, but doesn't have the faintest idea when and/or doesn't have a clue about how much he is spending now. A budget you say—what's that? Far fetched? I see people like this more often than you'd think, maybe 40% of the pre-retirees and early-retirees who come to me seeking some miracle answers to their ill-defined goal-setting questions. What about you? Have you put the specifics of your financial roadmap to paper? If not, when will you?

On the other hand, if you tell me that you want to provide $30,000 a year (in today's dollars) for the education of your 2 children, for 4 years of college, and have all monies saved by their freshman year, beginning in 2020 and 2022, as a financial planner, I can help you. The goal is specific as to time and quantity (how much).

But all is not lost if you haven't been able to discover and define the specific route(s) you must take on your financial roadmap to success. Don't let uncertainty stop you from at least beginning the process. Seek help if this step eludes you.

That said, be flexible with your goals and have fallback positions in case life intrudes on your well-intentioned goal setting. Sickness, economic conditions, political interference, family issues, etc can force you to alter even the best-laid plans. Most importantly, start early, both defining and working toward your goals—especially your financial goals—as the time value of money works in your favor the earlier you begin.

Planning Pointer

Take time to write down your personal and financial goals. Make them as specific as possible as to amount and time frame. Have family members do the same.

MISTAKE #3:
YOU'RE AFRAID TO TAKE RISKS—SO YOU RISK IT ALL

As they say, "No risk, no reward!" It just doesn't happen; you need to anticipate and prepare for future risks today. Most people, to avoid risk, do nothing and that can be the greatest risk of all.

There are many forms of "risk" associated with financial and other assets. In most cases, it's almost impossible to avoid all forms of risk in the marketplace as the extinguishing of one form of risk may initiate or escalate another. Some risks are obvious, while some are hidden or simply overlooked. Some can wreck your portfolio, and others can subject your retirement income to a slow death by depletion. Just what are these risks? The list below cites those most common to investors.

Inflation Risk

This is the risk that causes your dollars to buy less and less as prices go up. It works in tandem with "purchasing power risk," which is the actual risk associated with losing buying power from the deleterious impact of inflation.

Investors fearful of the volatility of the equity markets ordinarily maintain or switch to CDs, money markets, or other "safe" investments (ie, no risk of principal loss). But earning a 4% fixed rate of return in a 3% inflation environment after first subjecting the yield to a 30% or higher combined tax bracket means you are systematically losing purchasing power. Taxes cut your 4% fixed rate to a 2.8% after-tax yield. A 3% inflation rate leaves a -0.2% in purchasing power. Every year then is a downhill slide.

Same thing with a fixed pension or other static payment. Imagine retiring in 1980 on a fixed $40,000 pension with no inflation adjustments. Fast forward to the present. What amount of goods and services can that $40,000 buy now? $30,000? $20,000? At a 3% annual assumed inflation rate, it would buy less than $17,000 today. That's a 57% loss of purchasing power. Taken another way, at 3% inflation, it would take today over $94,000 annually to buy what $40,000 could buy in 1980.

Inherently, inflation is the silent killer of fixed but "safe" investments, bond yields, level pensions, etc. Inflation-indexed US Treasuries (I-Bonds or TIPS) are one way to cope with this insidious risk in the fixed income portion of your portfolio, or gold or real estate elsewhere in your portfolio, but in the long run, exposure to equities is among the best ways to counter the damage of inflation and lost purchasing power over the long run, meaning 5 to 10 years and beyond.

Planning Pointer

Does your portfolio contain hedges against inflation? If none, then seriously consider I-Bonds or TIPS (such as Vanguard's Inflation Securities Fund [VIPSX] or PIMCO Real Return [PRRDX]). TIPS can also be purchased individually in brokerage accounts. Consider adding gold but no more than 5% to 10% of the portfolio. Inflation-adjusted fixed annuities may work well too if you are at the stage where you've begun or will soon begin taking income from your portfolio. If you've removed equities from your portfolio, reconsider adding them back but only to the degree you remain comfortable with the risk level and where you'd not lose sleep in a market decline. Think maybe 20% to 30% equities if you are squeamish, no more.

Interest Rate Risk

Throughout most of the 1980s and 1990s, bonds experienced a record period of price appreciation as interest rates fell from record highs to record lows. This rapid rate decline occurred again in the aftermath of 9/11. But rising rates, as we've seen recently, cause bond prices to fall, especially those bonds with longer maturities. Briefly, bond prices move inversely to interest rates. As interest rates in the marketplace fall, for example, bond prices rally (rise); as interest rates rise, bond prices fall. Many investors fleeing to bonds for "safety" fail to realize that bonds are not the automatic safe haven from equity volatility, as they can produce volatility of their own brought about by interest rate movements. This is especially true if you select mutual fund bond positions as the share price of the fund can and does fluctuate daily.

Buying individual bonds and stashing them into your safety deposit box until maturity seems to eliminate that volatility. Out of sight, out of mind. When mature, they are cashed in for their face amount. Simple! But beware along the way that if you choose to sell the bonds before they mature, you would become very much aware of the bond price fluctuation as you cash out at market value, either at a premium or discount to the bond face amount.

Choosing shorter maturities, or shorter duration in bond funds, can help dampen the effect of rising interest rates on your fixed income portfolio. Think of it this way: remember jumping rope as a child? Suppose you grasped one end of the rope and started swinging your hand up and down in front of you. What happens to the rope ends closest to your hand and farthest from you? The rope near your hand moves about as far up and down as your hand. The farthest end though oscillates wildly up and down the farther away the rope gets from your hand. That's how bonds and bond maturities work. The shortest maturities—like the rope nearest to your hand—reduce the volatility of bond prices, while at the longer maturities—the farther you go out on the rope to its endpoint—the more violent the swing in bond prices.

However, the longer maturities typically produce the highest yields all things being equal. Thus, investors seeking higher bond yield resort to longer maturities and therefore increase the risk—often unknowingly—that they will lose money if the bonds are surrendered in a period of rising interest rates.

Planning Pointer

The term duration is used to express the volatility of a bond fund as interest rates rise or fall 1%. A fund with a 3.5-year duration means that the share price should move 3.5% up or down relative to a 1% movement in prevailing market interest rates. The shorter the duration, the less the price fluctuation as interest rates move in the marketplace. So, you can ladder bond mutual funds by selecting them based on their varying duration. To look up this handy statistic for bond mutual funds, go to www.morningstar.com.

Economic Risk

Economic slowdowns such as those the United States and other global economies inevitably experience can and do affect smaller, highly leveraged companies more than larger companies. Junk bonds, for example, take it on the chin in a market slowdown as investors seek safety in government issues and higher quality corporate bonds. Therefore, in such a market decline, being diversified in both high yield bonds as well as high quality corporate bonds and US Treasuries of varying maturities can help prevent drastic slides in your fixed income portfolio. The same holds true with your position in equity asset classes. Generally, diversifying among small-cap, mid-cap, and large-cap stocks or mutual funds, as well as domestic and foreign holdings and "growth" (new economy) and value (old economy) equity styles can help mitigate economic risk. This process of diversifying by asset class is known as asset allocation.

Planning Pointer

Most admit that asset allocation all by itself is not necessarily a guarantee against extreme market volatility. This was never more evident than during the autumn of 2008 when the threat (and actuality) of global recession along with the near-panic in the world credit markets made asset allocation ineffective in reducing economic risk. Almost every major asset class fell dramatically, including most bond funds (except short-term US Treasuries), and many well-allocated portfolios fell more than 35% to 45% despite the diversification that asset allocation provides. That said, the market and economic declines in 2008 were rare in their intensity and scope. Asset allocation in the past has generally worked to help reduce economic risk.

Market Risk

This is the risk to your portfolio as various equity sectors/markets fall separately or in tandem. It is risk in many cases that you cannot avoid because it is innate with equities. Many times market risk can overpower even stocks with excellent fundamentals. For example, in 2008, many stocks in the financial sector fell precipitously even though they might have been relatively unexposed to the subprime problem that other more highly-leveraged firms incurred. The whole financial sector was punished due to the sins of a few. If you held financials, they all got hammered even if you had cherry picked the sector and owned only the best firms. The bottom line is that sometimes there's just nowhere to hide.

As stated earlier in discussing economic risk, diversification among various equity asset classes like growth (new economy) and value (old economy); large, mid, and small caps; etc can reduce but not necessarily eliminate market risk. Finally, included in this type of risk are international developments, both economic and political, and currency risks.

Specific Risk

Sometimes called "business risk," specific risk is inherent in the particular stock you own, such as General Electric, IBM, etc. Specific risk means that the value of your investment in a specific company may be affected by the growth performance (or lack of it) of that company alone. Take Fannie Mae, for example, or Enron. If you owned those stocks in your portfolio, you took it on the chin.

If you are purchasing stocks on your own, you cannot avoid specific risk. Unless you can develop and implement your own plan for selling those stocks at the right time, you may want to diversify your holdings into quality equity mutual funds that you or your financial pro have researched. Fear and greed do take their toll.

> ### Planning Pointer
>
> To reduce risk, you need to understand it. With that understanding, you can diversify your portfolio properly to eliminate many, but not all, of those dangers. In investing, ignorance is not bliss. It can be counter-productive and destructive to your short-term and long-term goals such as retirement, education funding, etc. Get to know these risks, but especially get to know how you react to them as it's your behavior that can influence the success (or lack of it) of your portfolio over time. If your reactions are too emotional and unpredictable, think about working with an objective and unemotional financial planner or professional investment advisor to guide you through the maze of risk.

MISTAKE #4:
YOU WANT IT ALL—AT NO COST—
AND IN 10 MINUTES

Never was this mistake more apparent than in the late 1990s when people of all financial means flocked to the dot.com stocks for instant gratification and then sold the carcasses of those dead issues at the market bottom in September to October, 2002. The media fed us constantly with these images, stoking our emotions of fear, greed, and jealousy.

In response, ordinarily conservative investors dumped their CDs, money market funds, and even their old economy stocks like GM and Exxon-Mobil. They followed the media-driven pied piper toward dot.com riches and "permanently-ascending" stock markets, all to be achieved in mere weeks or months. I remember when teenage grandchildren were advising grandmom and grandpop about which of the latest dot.com wonders to buy. What did you do back then? Did you fall prey to the tech frenzy? Did you lose your shirt or did you sit by amused? Did your time frame for portfolio success progressively shrink from years to months to days to minutes?

We see this as well in the younger generations who wish to have everything mom and dad have "right here, right now." What they don't understand is how those same parents struggled financially in their early years of marriage. They only see the later years when financial success has been achieved. This is not a social or political statement; it's a recognition of a certain level of expectation in our culture today that is the fuel for driving people to make this prevalent mistake.

So, if you are tempted to spend way over your head for a house, car, or vacation home, step back and ask whether this "thing" you're considering—which might set you back significantly financially—is really necessary at this time. If you find yourself reaching anyway because you just have to have this now, but you sense this decision may come back to haunt you, ask your financial planner to quantify the effect of this acquisition on your comprehensive financial plan for life.

In November 2005, I received an email from an optometrist who read an article I wrote on investing. What she wrote was both gratifying and enlightening. She commented, "Luckily I had a father...who taught all six of his kids delayed gratification, saving strategies and the general ins and outs of investing in the stock market. At present, my...husband and I live below our means, preferring to sock savings away for retirement and for the kids' college education. Your article reinforces our choice *not* (italics not mine) to buy the boat, wave runner, or opulent vacations, but to continue on the investing 'journey.' After 12 years of marriage, we can see that it has paid off very nicely for future security."

I wish I could quote the entire letter here, but it's obvious this doctor clearly "gets it." What about you? Are you house, car, and jewelry poor because you just have to have these things even as your monthly budget strains under their collective weight? Or, like this well-positioned doctor, have you avoided the Madison Avenue lure of the moment, thus avoiding this tempting mistake?

In the area of investing, avoiding this mistake means investing for the long haul, with a time horizon of at least 5 years or more. If your time horizon is much shorter, then reduce or completely eliminate equity exposure. Don't run to the newspaper the day after you purchase an equity mutual fund to see if it has turned up sharply. Recognize that with compound interest and compound returns, "nothing happens early." The biggest gains come at the back end when your money doubles that last time before you retire. So be patient and watch your money grow over the time it needs to grow.

> *If you expect to be a net saver during the next five years, should you hope for a higher or lower stock market during that period? Many investors get this one wrong. Even though they are going to be net buyers of stocks for years to come, they are elated when stock prices rise and depressed when they fall. This reaction makes no sense. Only those who will be sellers of stocks in the near future should be happy at seeing stocks rise. Prospective purchasers should much prefer sinking prices.* —Warren Buffet

Finally, expect market declines. They're healthy and normal though they don't seem that way as they happen. Declines occur maybe every 4 out of 10 years so don't invest like market drops are a surprise. When markets fall, keep investing in 401(k)s, 403(b)s, and systematic monthly savings plans through the market lows because your money buys more shares at cheaper prices. Investing at or near market lows requires patience and is the exact opposite of instant gratification. Invest over time for the long term and stay the course. Avoid the mistake of wanting it all right now.

Planning Pointer

Remember how you felt emotionally when the equity markets were searching for the bottom as they did in late 2008? Were you hesitant? Scared? Fearful? Panicked? Well, that was what it felt like to buy low. What did you do then?

MISTAKE #5:
YOU HAVEN'T PROTECTED YOUR ASSETS

This is the area of risk management, or insurance and asset protection. It comes in many sizes and shapes. In its most common forms, risk management is protecting your loved ones against financial bankruptcy at your premature death. It's providing cash to replace your lifetime of lost earnings; paying off debts; providing for the education of your children if you die (life insurance); insuring your most valuable resource, your income, against total or partial loss (disability); replacing your home and its contents against all forms of disaster (homeowner's); and shielding significant portions of your net worth from medical catastrophe (adequate health insurance), identity theft, as well as liability from personal lawsuits (umbrella coverage), professional liability (malpractice insurance and asset protection strategies), and the threat of long-term care. It's a big list that demands your attention.

When was the last time you performed a risk management "fire drill" where you met with your brokers to make certain you had no gaps in your various coverages? Are you guilty of scrimping on any of these plans to save money? Maybe you even dropped coverages or failed to initiate them to cut down on premium outlay?

After a claim arises, your permanent disability begins, or you receive the bad health news that may shorten your life, it may be too late and that $250 you saved by purchasing less-than-adequate policy limits will seem painfully unimportant.

Imagine you had died yesterday. What would your family's financial future look like today? If the summons was served to you yesterday, how much of your hard-earned assets are at risk today? If the mild shaking in your hands became tremors yesterday, where would your replacement income come from today and for how long?

I daresay the meager amount you might save by eliminating or reducing important personal and professional risk management lines of coverage would seem insignificant the day after the tragedy strikes. I know because I've worked with people who lived to regret it like a pediatrician-client in Philadelphia who, against all advice, dropped his business overhead disability coverage to save money, became disabled a year later, then lost his staff and his office lease because he couldn't pay them. What about you? Have your risk management exposures been bulletproofed, or will the serious gaps become evident only after the claim reaches your doorstep? If you haven't checked recently, how will you know?

If you're not yet convinced, stop reading and take a moment to imagine yourself AFTER a claim (malpractice lawsuit; serious health reversal; your daughter uses your business car, drinks up a storm, and causes head-on collision; etc) to fully understand the implications of decisions you make in this vitally important area of your financial plan for life. Don't kid yourself by thinking that "it's not going to happen to me." Hospitals, courtrooms, and cemeteries are full of people who assumed it would happen to someone else, not them. If you've let this slide, I hope you're agitated because you should be. Stop, pick up the phone, call your broker(s) and attorney, and arrange for that important "fire drill." You'll feel better having taken that critical first step.

One area you probably review almost by requirement is your professional liability coverage. Have you covered all the bases with your malpractice broker as to those coverages you need? Have you made sure, absolutely sure, that your malpractice carrier is in good standing and financially sound? Have you tried cutting costs by moving your malpractice insurance to a "substandard" carrier, taking the chance that come time of claim, that carrier may have gone bankrupt? Have you made the switch without making sure your "tail" was covered or informing both carriers, new and old, that a patient "event" has occurred? If so, you may be out in the cold as both carriers may be able to duck responsibility in that claim situation.[2] Have you visited with your attorney to determine what asset protection strategies (see Chapter 5) you can implement to protect each and every one of your hard-earned assets? Remember, to avoid what is referred to as "fraudulent conveyance," you must finalize your plan of asset protection well before any potential liability incident occurs. Otherwise, your assets may remain fully exposed to liability claims.

Often forgotten in recent years, incapacity has become a pressing financial issue as average life expectancies lengthen. Yet despite progress in this area, a large percentage of the population—approximately one-third—will face debilitating health conditions that can lead to months, perhaps years, of extended home health care or nursing care.

Most doctors will not ever qualify for government aid (Medicaid) under such circumstances (too much in accumulated assets), so your assets may be at risk against a $75,000 to $90,000 annual long-term care drain, rising at 5% or greater due to medical and wage inflation. If you've done nothing to plan for this possibility, you are in essence self-insuring. Does your spouse know that some or most of your retirement assets are at risk then? What can you do? Long-term care insurance may be the answer. During your risk management "fire drill," ask your broker for a quote. Check it out if you don't already have the coverage. Rule it in or rule it out, but at least get information to make an informed decision. Your retirement security or that of your spouse may depend on it.

If your medical practice involves more than one doctor, have you adequately protected yourselves from the loss of a partner or partners? What succession plan have you implemented to preserve the value of the practice for all concerned? How much and for how long will you be paid under your employment contract with the practice, or with the hospital where you work, if you cannot work due to a disabling injury or sickness?

There are many risk management issues to address within a medical practice, and a separate "fire drill" needs to be arranged where all partners sit down to face the implications of all potential exposures before they occur. Death, disability, liability, termination, retirement, bankruptcy—they all happen. But you're too busy, you say, to get the gang together in the same room. Busy or not, the "stuff" of life happens often when you least expect it. As with your personal risk management, imagine the state of your professional practice today if your partner died yesterday, you became permanently disabled last evening, or your computerized patient records were stolen or destroyed. What would your world look and feel like today?

Lastly, what have you done to protect yourself against the newest form of asset loss—identity theft? Have you purchased a shredder to destroy personal information no longer needed? Do you destroy old credit cards? Why not dump out the contents of your wallet on your copier and make copies of all your credit cards (front and back), medical cards, drivers license, etc. Having photo records when your wallet is stolen or misplaced is priceless. Imagine just trying to remember what was in that wallet if it is stolen. For more information, type in "identity theft" at www.Google.com and check out all the free information you can examine to shut down this potential asset grab. If you can't do it, assign a family member or practice administrator to do so and report back.

Planning Pointer

If your assets are so important that you spend perhaps your entire working lifetime accumulating them, then make sure you protect them against the various risks that could separate you forever from those hard-earned assets. Will you do this? If you don't, who will?

MISTAKE #6:
YOU'RE NOT WILLING TO STAY ON A FINANCIAL DIET

Have you ever experienced a span of time when you know you made a lot of money—your pay stub says so—but you have no idea where the money went? Everything you earned (and sometimes more) was consumed with nothing saved. You say to yourself that you can always start saving another day, maybe next month, next year. But educating the kids, owning the latest model car, or adding the new landscaping to the house always seem to take priority over the education savings account or the 401(k) plan. Is this you? Do you try saving but just never get around to it? Or do you simply procrastinate with everything?

To seriously and deliberately avoid this recurring mistake, you must "pay yourself first." That means you need to save before you spend. The only higher priority is taxes withheld from your pay. Why not hire yourself? Put yourself on your payroll, then save from your pay automatically. First, make sure you have money set aside for emergencies, perhaps between 3 and 6 months' expenditures. Then begin auto-funding for retirement, education, or for your first house if you are a young physician. The "auto" part is the key. Anyone who puts money aside in a 401(k) plan or a 403(b) program knows the inherent truth of the old saying, "Out of sight, out of mind." The more your spending patterns are erratic and impulsive, the more you need to save first. Decide how much you need to save, then plan your discretionary expenditures afterward. If done in conjunction with your financial goals set earlier, you'll be on track and on autopilot.

Why not take it even one step further? Increase your savings rate each year so that you direct more and more toward your net worth and less and less to impulse consumables. Lastly, never go backward. Don't ever decrease your automatic savings amount. Keep plugging away. Remember, out of sight, out of mind.

MISTAKE #7:
YOU LOSE SIGHT OF THE BOTTOM LINE

A wise person once said, "It's not what you make that counts; it's what you get to keep that matters." In other words, it's the bottom line that amplifies your financial success. Anytime we can reduce or remove the Internal Revenue Service (IRS) or other drain on our portfolio performance, we should seek to do so.

Briefly, examine the fees and other costs of your investments, then seek to lower transaction costs without losing quality of service or performance. Investments that automatically reinvest earnings/dividends at no cost to you are preferable over those that do not. Dividend Re-Investment Plans (DRIPs) allow investors to buy additional stock shares from quarterly dividends free of charge. They're great! Cross-investing of mutual funds dividends can be done at no cost (eg, using dividends from bond funds to buy shares in stock funds of the same fund family—a mild form of "dollar cost averaging").

Contrary to popular media beliefs, low fees and costs are not the sole guiding criteria for investment success. Performance matters, and no-load index funds are not automatically the best performers despite the lower fees. In some instances, load funds may sometimes outperform their equivalent no-load brothers over time. Here's where you need to do your research. Mutual fund information can be obtained at www.morningstar.com and other popular Web sites. Stock information is available through Standard & Poor's and from just about any brokerage Web site like www.etrade.com or www.tdameritrade.com. But data without meaning or perspective or context is only data that can be confusing and contradictory for many investors, especially for beginners. Consider hiring an investment professional to assist you if you don't have the time, inclination, or emotional constitution to research and manage your own portfolio.

Consider the effect of taxes on your bottom line. With equity mutual funds, for example, some asset classes like small caps or emerging markets are extremely tax inefficient. They have very high turnover in their portfolios, generating high transaction costs, especially short-term gains, which are taxed as ordinary income. Better to put them in tax-deferred accounts like retirement plans and annuities where their high annual gains are sheltered by the tax deferral of earnings within these plans.

For bonds, tax-free municipals are not always the best choice to lower the tax cost of bond interest. For example, a taxable bond fund yields a 5% taxable dividend and you are in a 35% combined tax bracket. The after-tax yield then is 3.25% (5% x [1-35%]) = 3.35%). If the equivalent tax-exempt fund yields 3.00% net of any local taxes, then the taxable bond fund could be better for you. However, you may need to re-examine this yield comparison often as yields fluctuate constantly.

Have you considered tax-free or tax-deferred investments? Are you maximizing contributions to qualified plans, including the "catch-up" contributions for those of you age 50 and older? The new variable annuity products with living benefits riders enable you to postpone taxes on the growth within the annuity until needed. Some even permit tax-favored annuity payout (principal and interest/return) without giving up control of the invested funds as happens with an immediate annuity or income annuity.

Exchange-traded funds (ETFs) are the latest rage in tax-efficient investing. Like index funds, ETFs usually track an index like the Standard & Poor's 500 Index or the EAFE (International) Index. Currently, there are hundreds of ETFs and their numbers are growing. Unlike mutual funds that create turnover, and therefore potential capital gains, ETFs trade like stocks so that gains (or losses) are only applicable at the time shares are sold. As the number of ETFs explodes, there appear to be some that are tax inefficient and therefore produce gains like mutual funds. If you favor old-fashioned mutual funds, then consider funds with low turnover rates because these reduce annual capital gains exposure. Use your retirement plan to hold high turnover mutual funds. Consider investing in ETFs for some of your overall nonqualified, taxable portfolio.

Finally, when was the last time you checked your estate documents? Do you even have them? If not, then instead of giving your assets to your kids, you may be shipping them out to the IRS. That's a tax effect you can and should avoid. Besides, the IRS won't even send you a thank-you note. See Chapter 10 for more details.

MISTAKE #8:
YOU'RE WILLING TO
REPEAT THE MISTAKES OF THE PAST

Do you have money sitting in a bank savings account earning a mere 2.0% (taxable) while at the same time carrying credit card debt at 15% or 18% (nondeductible)?

Why? This is reverse leverage and the credit card finance companies love it! When did you last count how many credit cards you carry? I've heard it said that the average American owns 16 credit cards. How about you?

Get rid of the credit cards, except for one universal card. If you don't, you'll be tempted to use them again and again, repeating this same mistake over and over. If you are a parent, remember that one day your children will follow your example, not your advice. If you are a credit card junkie, your children are watching.

Always consider using OPM whenever you can, as Steve Leimberg is fond of calling it. What's OPM? It's "other people's money." A good example is buying a car at 0% financing rather than leasing (although leasing may make sense for other reasons). You can put your money for the car in a simple money market earning 3%, perhaps 2% net after taxes, and pull out the monthly payments from the account to pay for the car. You'd be ahead by all the interest you earn over the time you must make the payments. You can always change your mind and pay off the car at any time from the cash in the money market account. The bottom line is when you can safely earn more investing your own money (after taxes) than you'd need to pay to use OPM money (financing), taking into consideration possible tax savings on the financing and the risk of investing, then use OPM. It's surprising how many people get this one wrong.

When your income goes up, do you spend the increase twice? You see, we feel good when our income rises and many of us want to go out and immediately reward ourselves. The problem is, we lose track of our impulsive spending as we buy things. We forget that we've already spent the raise on the new furniture, and we spend it again on that new flat screen TV. Does this happen to you? Have you done this more than once? If so, you are not alone.

Why not consider saving your raise instead? Stash it into a college savings plan for your kids, like a Section 529 plan, or maybe increase the size of your emergency fund. Increase your monthly 401(k) or 403(b) contribution, then use the raise to replenish your monthly cash flow outlay, thus replacing the extra money set aside for retirement. If you insist on managing your tax withholding to get an income tax refund every April so you can splurge, try breaking that cycle of planned consumption by substituting a new cycle of saving. Sock the tax refund away! Your child's education fund, your savings account, or your IRA will be the better for it!

As Steve Leimberg suggests, "Resist the temptation to do dumb things." Tear up credit cards you don't use. If you must pay interest on consumer debt, substitute tax-deductible interest (home equity loan or line of credit) for nondeductible interest (credit cards). But never, ever pay for something you've purchased for any time longer than the life of that product. Wrapping a 3-year car loan into a refinanced 30-year mortgage means that you'll be paying for the car for maybe 25 years after you've trashed it.

Planning Pointer

If you are just starting your medical practice, you are probably faced with 6-figure student loans, the expense of a family with children, and no cash on hand to cushion against emergency needs. Here you must really work to control spending impulses to avoid that infamous $300+ pizza ($20 on your credit card today compounded at 18% over 16 years). With surplus in your budget, if any, try to extinguish your highest cost debt first among debts, but don't do so to the exclusion of adding even small amounts to your emergency fund and saving for retirement if your employer has a 401(k)-matching program. This is easier said than done, but with a disciplined mind-set toward expenditures and a commitment to the principles of saving early, you can accomplish all 3 goals, though not to the same degree for each. The bottom line is to triangulate your budget surplus, if any, into past debt reduction, current emergency funds, and future spending for retirement or education.

MISTAKE #9:
YOU THROW UP YOUR HANDS
WHEN YOU SEE WHAT IT TAKES

How many times have you put off even starting a big project because you just couldn't imagine doing all that work? Instead of breaking the project down into smaller, workable parts, you just never get started at all.

Most people cannot satisfy all of their financial goals at once, so instead they do nothing. I find it helpful in working with clients with overwhelming and overlapping financial goals to create a family "timeline" for them (Figure 1-1) that starts with today and ends with normal life expectancy.

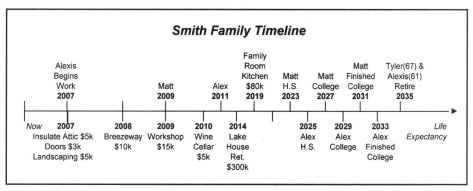

Figure 1-1. Sample family timeline.

Take out a piece of paper, and draw a horizontal line. At the left end, mark "Now." At the right end mark "Life expectancy (year)." Now start filling in all the major financial happenings, chronologically, along the line. For example, in 2027, you may write in "Matt starts college," and for 2031, "Matt finishes college." Put in the year you wish to retire, the year you wish to buy a vacation home, etc. It doesn't have to be perfect, and some dates along the line may not be certain, but list them as best you can.

As you do this, you will feel better almost immediately. You see, when these objectives roll around in your mind, along with the known or perceived financial obligations they carry, you can't get a handle on them, and they become larger than life, causing anxiety and sleepless nights. But when you export them from your brain to paper, the act of writing them down in an organized and chronological fashion can help you see them for what they are—time-weighted financial requirements that sometimes overlap, sometimes precede or follow, but all with some discernible beginning and end.

As you study your family timeline, you'll notice that retirement might be lurking out there in, say, 25 years. But the timeline clearly illustrates that there are also education bills due much sooner. Your conclusion may be that you need to rob Peter to pay Paul temporarily by funding education needs first, then retirement later. Or perhaps you can partially fund education while at the same time funding retirement, especially if your 401(k) or your employer's retirement plan provides a matching contribution, which you should always try to grab. In other words, you don't have to do it all now, but at least do something. Having 50% of your child's tuition for college saved is better than having nothing at all because you were too overwhelmed to start saving. Remember, the journey starts with that first step.

In the investment world, time is your ally. It has a way of wringing risk from the markets, but only if you stay invested. That is easier said than done, as you may need patience and perspective when the markets tank, like they did in 2008 and early 2009. On the other hand, you need courage to sell when a specific investment requires it. If you get caught in the emotional "sell dilemma," ask yourself, "Considering the entire range of investment possibilities, would I buy that investment today if presented the opportunity?" If you honestly say "No!" then sell it and don't look back.

Remember that with compound interest, nothing happens early. It takes time to make compound interest work and work effectively. In Chapter 2, we'll examine this money miracle, which immensely fascinated even the great mathematician, Albert Einstein.

Above all, don't panic when you figure out what it takes. Avoid the temptation of doing nothing because you can't do it all. Draw out your timeline and set priorities.

MISTAKE #10:
YOU WANT SOMEONE ELSE TO MAKE YOU RICH

Are you the type who can't wait to meet your golf buddies each weekend to get the latest stock tip? Then, on Monday, you buy without questioning why. Zombie-like, you watch the cable financial news shows regularly to get the latest "skinny" on what to do with your money. All these pundits and talking heads tell you what to do, then forget what they said tomorrow, next week, or next month. In other words, the daily shows operate in a proverbial vacuum. Today they say "buy" but tomorrow they say "sell." There's generally no philosophical, financial continuity except the same pundits and talking heads show up every day telling you today to do the opposite of what they espoused yesterday. You are left holding the investment bag that nobody cares about but you.

Make a resolution to do your own thinking. Who cares more about your money than you do? Nobody! Repeat, nobody! If you don't have the time or inclination to manage your money properly, find a competent wealth manager or financial planner (make sure the planner is a CFP or ChFC) to do so for you, as well as a tax advisor to guide you. But don't ever relinquish the final responsibility for your own financial affairs. Always require a say-so for any action taken—never give discretionary control to anyone, ever! Stay in charge—remember, it's your money.

The most eloquent, and perhaps tragic, example of making Mistake #10 occurred late in 2008 when the Ponzi scheme perpetrated by Bernard Madoff was fully and finally exposed. It illustrated how people can be mesmerized by the fame of a "star" and anesthetized by the herd mentality. Investors turned a blind eye toward the markets as a whole, reveling in their good fortune to be included in Mr. Madoff's investment circle and the consistent "results" that seemed to defy the odds even as the markets tumbled. Average investors, banks, charities, and hedge funds all fell prey to this treacherous pied piper. When they gave away their right of oversight and refusal by signing over to Madoff complete control of their money—allegedly $50 billion in total—they sadly became guilty of making Mistake #10.

So, above all, educate yourself. Make time to read at least one financial newspaper (perhaps the Wall Street Journal) and at least one financial magazine like Forbes, Barrons, etc. Ask questions of your advisors, and if you don't understand the answer, ask again. If the answer's still not clear, then don't do what they are telling you to do. If they cannot explain their suggestions in simple, understandable language, don't automatically give your approval. Be skeptical until you fully comprehend what you're being told.

Steve Leimberg summarizes the 10 mistakes by suggesting the following:

"With the help of competent financial planning professionals, you should annually: 1) measure your needs, 2) establish a priority of needs, and 3) give preference to those goals most important to you. Develop and work a plan to make certain that you're on target to meet your financial independence objectives. Remember that the finest plan is worthless until it is put into place. Establish a written timetable of what is to be done, who will do it and when each stage is to be implemented."[1]

In other words, get under the "hood" of your financial plan for life and make sure all the parts are working properly and efficiently (Figure 1-2). If you don't, who will?

Planning Pointer

From what you've learned in this chapter, what action or actions are you now motivated to take? Write them down and assign a deadline to each action. Do the same for anyone else like your spouse or partners who need to take any action or actions. How will you remind yourself about your deadlines? If you do not take action now, when will you? If you do not take action now, who will?

REFERENCES

1. Leimberg SR. The 10 most common financial planning mistakes. Available at http://www.leimbergservices.com. Accessed May 7, 2009.
2. Gassman A. Creditor protection for physicians' most common mistakes. *Steve Leimberg's Asset Protection Newsletter.* 2006;86.

INCOME/EXPENSE DATA SHEET

Client _____

Advisor _____

Spouse _____

Date _____

	Monthly	Annual
INCOME SOURCES		
Salary (C):		
Salary (S):		
Bonus		
Self Employment (C):		
Self Employment (S):		
Social Security (C):		
Social Security (S):		
Pensions:		
Rental Income:		
Investment Income:		
Other Income_____		
Other Income_____		
TAXES		
Fed Inc/Soc Sec/Med (C):		
Fed Inc/Soc Sec/Med (S):		
State Income (C):		
State Income (S):		
Other Taxes_____		
Other Taxes_____		
SAVINGS*		
Retirement Plan (C):		
Retirement Plan (S):		
Investment Savings:		
Other Savings_____		
Other Savings_____		
INSURANCE**		
Life (C):		
Life (S):		
Disability (C):		
Disability (S):		
Health:		
Long Term Care:		
DEBT		
Mortgage:		
Home Equity Loan:		
Credit Card Debt:		
Student Loan:		
Other Debt_____		

	Monthly	Annual
HOUSING EXPENSES		
Mortgage/Rent:		
Homeowners Insurance:		
Property Taxes:		
Maintenance/Repairs:		
Cleaning/Yard:		
Utilities		
Electric/Gas/Oil:		
Cable TV		
Telephone:		
Water/Sewer:		
Other Housing_____		
TRANSPORTATION		
Car Payments/Lease:		
Fuel:		
Car Insurance:		
Tax/Reg/License:		
Repairs/Maintenance:		
Other Car:_____		
LIVING EXPENSES		
Groceries:		
Childcare:		
Child Support/Alimony:		
Clothing:		
Education:		
Medical/Dental:		
Other Required: _____		
DISCRETIONARY EXPENSES:		
Charity:		
Personal Care:		
Club Dues:		
Dining Out:		
Gifts:		
Pets:		
Recreation:		
Subscriptions:		
Vacation:		
Other Discretionary:_____		
Other Discretionary:_____		

* Indicate monthly/annual savings amounts
** Indicate monthly/annual insurance costs

Figure 1-2. Annual expense summary.

2

Avoiding the Big Mistake in Investing

"The only people who get hurt on roller coasters are the jumpers."

An October 2002 e-mail: "Please let's go to cash…! Got my 401(k) statement today and my brokerage account statements, and I'm so tired of losing money. Can we sell everything and put it in my money market!" (from anonymous business client)

Readers often ask me where I've gotten my ideas for the 60 or more articles I've written in various medical specialty publications. Well, most actually come from real-life situations, especially those relating to the series of articles I've written on avoiding the BIG mistakes in investing. These range from clients panicked about sudden and significant market drops to clients hearing pundits like Cramer speak about investment doomsday (or nirvana) on cable TV channels to clients expressing absolute certainty about a stock tip they heard from a total stranger at last Friday's cocktail party. You get the idea. Those cards, letters, and e-mails just keep coming in!

Since I entered the financial services industry in 1973—just in time to witness the 1973 to 1974 market plunge—I've seen or heard just about every mistake investors can make. I've concluded that most of those mistakes could easily have been avoided if there had been some form of an investment plan in place to guide the often-emotional behavior of the average investor.

Financial writer Nick Murray was the first person I heard call these "The Big Mistake(s)," which I adopted into the series of investment articles I started.[1] What I have found interesting in observing investor behavior is that many investors, left to their own devices, seem to make the Big Mistake not just once, but over and over, not learning a bit from prior experience. I believe they realize deep down that such behavior is counter-productive, but they do it anyway. It's what happens every time emotions like fear and greed overpower reason, logic, and a deep-rooted sense of market history.

Nick Murray has written that, "…financial success is not driven by the performance of investments, but by the behavior of investors."[1] I could not agree with him more. With hammer in hand, Nick drives the nail in even further when he adds, "The enemy of successful investing isn't 'underperformance'; it's the big mistake!"

Rudzinski K. *The Physician's Guide to Avoiding Financial Blunders (pp 21-42)*
© 2009 SLACK Incorporated

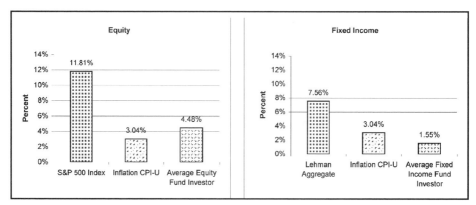

Figure 2-1. This represents the average annual compound return of the equity and bond indices versus equity and bond mutual fund investors. It is based on the length of time shareholders actually invested in a fund against the historic performance of the fund's appropriate index for the time period. Past performance is no guarantee of future results. Investors cannot invest directly into an index.

Like the classic study that demonstrated that stock picking and timing were almost irrelevant to portfolio success compared to a proper asset allocation strategy (see Figure 2-3), Nick Murray has concluded that perhaps even the very best selection of stocks and/or mutual funds won't matter if the investor selecting those can't or won't avoid making the Big Mistake.

Exactly what is the Big Mistake? It's not just one thing or one action. It is a multitude of errors that lead to the same result—preventing long-term portfolio success. We'll expose those along the way. But first let's examine recent empirical evidence that enables us to reach the same conclusions Nick Murray did and has written about—the famous Dalbar study (Figure 2-1).

You may sense that investor behavior can affect investment results, but really, how much can it be? To determine that, the Dalbar Institute decided to collect and examine market performance data from 1987 through 2007 to see if any empirical evidence existed that could point to a disparity between the measure of portfolio success the market achieved and that of the "average" investor over the exact same period of time. What they discovered was in some ways truly surprising yet in other ways totally predictable. The study found that during the 1987 to 2007 time period where the average annual return of the S&P 500 Index was 11.81%, the return for the "average" equity fund investor was a paltry 4.48%. You may conclude that such results are certainly not yours. Probably they are not. But if the client who wrote me the e-mail reproduced at the beginning of this chapter was on his own, he might turn out to be the "average investor" cited by the Dalbar study The reason is that his expressed sentiments put him on the verge of making the Big Mistake.

I remember in 1973 hearing from a client about his father who had retired a millionaire from Sears & Roebuck because he automatically invested a little bit of money from every paycheck over 35 years in the Sears stock purchase program. Funny thing was he never really paid much attention to the statements he got, which itemized his number of shares and their value. He became a millionaire almost by accident, and he didn't even know it.

Some people buy on euphoria, some—maybe the same people—sell out of panic and fear. Others, like my client's father, adopt almost a benign neglect approach, investing systematically and selling rarely if ever. These 2 exactly opposite investor behaviors almost always lead to contrasting portfolio results. Where do you see yourself?

My articles on investor behavior so far have not been about rocket science, betas, alphas, efficient frontier, etc. They have been more about avoiding the kneejerk reactions and ill-advised portfolio planning that can and will most likely prevent you as the average investor from making those repetitive mistakes that short circuit your portfolio success. The mistakes I have recounted are ones I've seen in the course of working with new and existing clients. Many times these clients just can't help but be human in their emotional and spontaneous reactions to the US economy. They react similarly to the various equity markets and most importantly to the headlines they read and the financial news shows they watch so faithfully.

Though each of the prior articles was written at a specific time with references to what was happening then, the investor behavior—and the mistakes it engenders—is mostly timeless. Clients expressed the same fear and panic in October 2008 that I heard in the summer and autumn of 2002. Why? Because it is human behavior above all laced with the flood of emotions that surface when one's own money is at stake and the markets seem bottomless. With this in mind, let's list some of those mistakes to avoid in the spirit of the articles that raised them.

Planning Pointer

As you read through this chapter, examine your past behavior during market stress periods like 2000 to 2002 and 2008 to 2009. If you were calm and focused on the long run (though maybe concerned), then you are more likely to see better long-term portfolio results than if you became fearful and sold out at or near market lows, remaining on the sidelines indefinitely.

MISTAKE #1:
FAILING TO ESTABLISH A
WRITTEN INVESTMENT POLICY STATEMENT

Why are you investing? What is your time frame? What is your risk tolerance? What asset allocation should you maintain? What about tax consequences?

Think about this. If you were planning a journey around the world, do you think you'd take some maps to guide you, or would you just wing it? Would you select the best route or the most scenic route, though much slower? Would you figure out what hotels to stay in, where to rent the cars you'll need, who to call in an emergency? Certainly you would, right?

Yet, it's interesting that while most people will plan trips or vacations in minute detail, those same people fail to plot the course of the very assets that will give them the freedom and the money to take those trips and vacations. If you are saving for retirement, for a house, for your kids' education, or for whatever, does your investment plan to accumulate assets toward those ends conform to the goals themselves? For example, if you'll need $50,000 from your portfolio in a year for a house down payment or for your son's wedding, are you taking chances by leaving the money invested in equity assets, or have you gone to cash to avoid getting blindsided from another market swoon? Likewise, if you have 30 years until retirement, are you stuck in cash or money markets or short-term taxable CDs because you fear losing some or all of your principal at some unknown time in the future?

I raise these questions because, without a detailed investment roadmap, you may find yourself making kneejerk subjective decisions at just the wrong time. Why? Because you default to your human emotions of fear and greed as the guiding principals for your portfolio decisions. Many of you may admit to doing just this, and maybe even repeatedly.

Instead, I propose that you take a few moments and think through both your financial goals and objectives—short and long term—as well as the time frames necessary to achieve those goals. Having that basic information in writing where you can see it, like seeing the various stops on your roadmap of the world, helps you select the kinds of investments that best suit those financial goals. For example, college funds for your newborn should not be in the money market account of your baby's 529 Plan. Nor should retirement funds needed decades away.

Does your investment direction look like this?

Certainly other aspects of risk tolerance and time horizons come into play, and we'll cover those in other mistakes to avoid. But after plotting your goals and their time frames, you can develop a basic "investment policy statement" (IPS) to guide your investment decisions. At the end of this chapter, I've included a sample completed IPS for you to review. Create your own IPS based on how you think your portfolio ought to be invested, keeping in mind that you may want or need objective, professional help to do so. It doesn't have to be supremely analytical or detailed or I suspect you will never finish it. My sample IPS is basic. Yours can be as simple as wanting your portfolio to remain "80% in equities, 15% in fixed income, and 5% in cash, with annual rebalancing and representation of large-cap, mid-cap, and small-cap per the Wilshire 5000 index, with a 20% allocation to international equities." The most important thing about this exercise is simply that you do it. Most people don't, which is why they fail and why the average investor doesn't come close to the average market returns, per Dalbar, Inc.

Action Step

To avoid making this first mistake, create an IPS roadmap to help guide your portfolio decisions objectively and unemotionally. If you send an email request to bookspublishing@slackinc.com, I will send you a blank IPS template for your use.

MISTAKE #2:
WAITING TOO LONG TO BEGIN SAVING

There is a high cost to procrastinating in investing. Let's say you are a 30-year-old cardiologist just getting started. Despite a mountain of student loan debt to repay, perhaps a spouse and a baby or two to feed, and other financial burdens to bear, you manage to save $4000 a year for 10 years, then stop completely. You've saved $40,000 in total.

Your best friend Dr. Pete, the orthopedic surgeon, stayed true to his lavish college habits and bought a Porsche at age 25, the 6000-sq ft house at 28, and the Aspen vacations each winter, saving nothing in the meantime. Then, at age 40 the lightning bolt hits and Pete decides he needs to start socking away money for retirement. So he sets up a brokerage account and deposits $4000 a year, let's say, all the way out to age 65. He's in the game for $100,000.

Assuming you both earn 8% annually, which of you would have the bigger account balance at age 65? You with your $40,000 invested, or Pete with his $100,000?

Now you know this is a loaded question! You would have $428,591 at age 65 while your buddy Pete would have only $315,818. Your dollar gain is $388,591, while Pete's is merely $215,818. The big difference is TIME and the magic of compounding. You started early and he started late. Even if Pete saved at the same rate till age 100, he still wouldn't catch up to you.

The moral of this story is the earlier you start investing, the less of your own money you'll need to reach your goals. I've included a chart (Figure 2-2) that shows the amount of monthly savings needed to accumulate $1 million by age 65 at various ages. A 25 year old needs only $308 in monthly savings while a 45 year old must save $1746 to hit the $1-million mark. More importantly, the 25 year old only needs to invest $147,840 of his own money; the balance, or $852,160 comes from compound returns at 8% annually. By extreme contrast, the 55 year old must come up with $661,192 from savings garnering only $338,808 from compound returns.

None other than Albert Einstein believed that the law of compound interest was one of the greatest inventions of mankind. That's because he could visualize the end result. You see, the problem with compound interest is that nothing happens early, so it's relatively boring.

Suppose you save $100 today in a 5% CD and next year it's worth $105. Big deal! But if you do that faithfully for 40 years (all you 25-year old doctors!), you've got $148,856. At 8%, you'd have $324,180. Just $100 per month—perhaps equal to just one nice dinner out!

With compound interest, nothing happens early! Burn those words into your mind. Getting back to you and your friend, Dr. Pete, your big advantage over Pete occurred in the last 9 years when your account doubled in value from $214,295 to $428,591. It wasn't until then that your patience was rewarded. Einstein was no dummy!

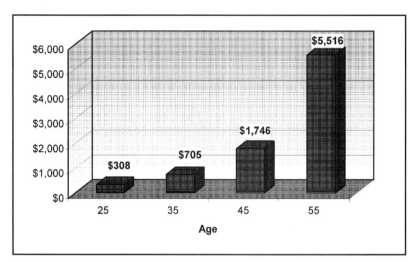

Figure 2-2. Monthly investment at 8% to accumulate $1 million by age 65.

Planning Pointer

Avoid Mistake #2 by recognizing that the earlier you start to save, the less of your own money you'll need. Make the power of compound interest work in your favor. Check your discretionary spending for expensive dinners or $5 cups of coffee and shift a portion of those to long-term savings and watch what happens. Nothing early, but an avalanche from a snowball later on.

MISTAKE #3:
BUYING HIGH…SELLING LOW!

What's wrong with this picture? Every day I drive by 2 men's stores sitting side-by-side in a little shopping center. Let's call them Jim's and Bob's. Last Monday I noticed a sign in Jim's window that announced, "SALE—5% OFF!" I saw a similar sign in Bob's window, but instead it read, "BARGAIN—5% MARK-UP!" I squinted to make sure I was not imagining things. Mark-up? I did notice that people were going into both stores, so I drove on.

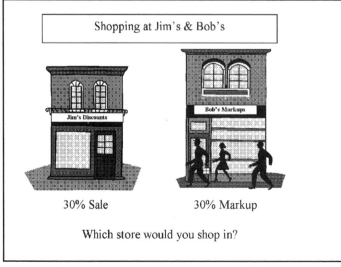

Shopping at Jim's & Bob's

Jim's Discounts

Bob's Markups

30% Sale   30% Markup

Which store would you shop in?

Next day, Jim's sign offered a 10% DISCOUNT while Bob, believe it or not, advertised 15% MARK-UP. Incredulously I watched more people heading into Bob's than Jim's.

Come Friday I pulled into the parking lot on my way home. Jim's new sign read, "30% OFF—FREE ALTERATIONS—WHY PAY MORE?" Bob's new sign boldly touted, "30% MARK-UP—BUY NOW

BEFORE PRICES GO UP EVEN MORE!" I was astounded to see no one heading to Jim's store while a whole horde of shoppers almost tore down Bob's door rushing to get in before any further mark-up could occur. Are you scratching your head in disbelief trying to understand this seemingly irrational and inexplicable shopping behavior? Or are you saying, "Ken, we always knew Delaware was strange!" Have you guessed how this little imaginary tale relates to investor behavior? If not, go back and reread it.

It's been said that the stock market is the only market where buyers wait till the price goes up to buy. This is the moral of the Jim and Bob analogy. It is not unusual for investors to flock to the equity markets just before those markets peak—remember late 1999, early 2000?—then avoid those same markets as they reach their troughs like in early October 2002.

There is almost a universal failure of average investors to overcome their fears of portfolio collapse and to recognize when markets decline as they did from 2000 to 2002, or more recently in 2008 and 2009, that a "sale" is occurring right before their eyes. Just like the buyers who avoided Jim's store even as his prices plunged, investors avoid the equity markets or actually bail out in droves just when major opportunities—maybe the best ones—present themselves.

Conversely, many of those same investors might have waited to invest just as the equity markets reached their highs during the last 5-year run-up (2003 to 2007), just like Bob's customers flocked to his store as his mark-up soared. Why? Investors act out of both fear and greed emotionally. It could be said that both sets of investors at Jim's and Bob's acted out of a basic fear emotion. Investors who bail fear the worst, a further spiraling out-of-control loss of their money, while those who wait until the markets are near their peak, although greedy for fast cash, also demonstrate fear that they will miss the boat full of investment riches, and so they board the overcrowded deck with friends and family. How about you? Where do you stand? Though you may say you shop at Jim's, do you really frequent Bob's instead?

Longtime readers of my articles know I do not believe in the concept of "market timing." Rather, I espouse the slow and steady, buy and hold asset allocation method. Yet I can't help but recognize a bargain when I see one, and I see one now as day by day the markets give up traction and move lower than the day before. (Note: original reference here was to markets of September to October 2008.) This is the time when mutual fund managers who are carrying large cash positions in their portfolios lick their chops at the near bargain-basement prices certain stocks present to them. For them, it's buying time, like shopping at Jim's. What is it for you? Are you buying or selling?

Here's a good example of a typical mistake investors make as markets decline. I received an e-mail recently from a business client who has a $400,000 401(k) balance. He invests monthly through payroll deduction and funds to the maximum allowable amount (ie, $16,500 [2009 limit] plus his catch-up amount). In his e-mail he wrote, "My account value is down $40,000 since before Christmas and I'm losing money even after putting in my monthly deposits. I'm thinking of stopping my deposits until the market looks better, and maybe moving some money to cash. What do you think? What should I do?" Some of you may be shaking your head thinking, "Yes, I understand; he should stop." Others are thinking, "No way, tough it out." Well, this client knows he'd be making the Big Mistake, which is why he asks. In fact, he'd be making 2 Big Mistakes. Problem was, he wanted me to bless his surrender! I didn't.

My first challenge was to point out to him one salient fact: he had been comfortable buying shares every month over the last 5 years as the markets were climbing. In other words, he was buying high and higher still, on average. Let's call it an average of $12.00 per share for his target retirement fund. Then why, I asked him, wouldn't he have been more attracted to buying shares monthly now that the price had fallen to $7.00 per share? In other words, this client felt better shopping at Bob's than at Jim's.

Has this ever happened to you where you got shaken by a down market and stopped investing in automatic investments like in a 401(k) or 403(b) plan? Well, buying shares at lower prices, when markets decline, is what balances off buying at higher prices. If we only buy high, like when it feels good to do so, we are doomed to suffer inferior portfolio results. In other words, we need to shop at BOTH Jim's and Bob's, at highs AND lows and the in-betweens.

The second mistake my client was seriously considering was selling low. Intellectually, we know that buying low and selling high is the way to portfolio success. But under fire, when fear is rife and doom and gloom dominates, many investors do the opposite. What do you do? Have you wanted to "feel better" by bailing out of the markets when they are down 20% or 40%, moving the proceeds to cash? My client admitted that his first choice for the $500,000 bailout (surrender?) was in fact to a money fund yielding only about 2%.

Here's the Big Mistake in action! First by selling out, my client would be turning a paper "decline" into a real "loss." Second, invested at 2%, assuming constant money rates, it would take him 15 years to recover the 30% loss he generated by selling out now, all things equal.

Interestingly, when I asked him if he thought the US economy would recover before the end of 10 years, he agreed, absolutely, that it would. So, in reality, he was actually bullish but had lost sight of that in his fear and panic.

Third, and maybe most importantly, I challenged him on just where the market levels needed to climb to signal his re-entry back into the equity markets. He had no clue. In other words, his sell strategy was irrational (sell low) and his buy-back strategy was nonexistent (probably buy high again). He was making 3 forms of the Big Mistake. Does this ever happen to you? Do you see similarities in your own behavior as the markets unravel?

If you ever begin to doubt your long-term investment objectives in the face of severe portfolio stress like we're seeing now, make sure you talk to your investment professional for guidance. If you invest on your own and you cannot control your emotional impulses in a volatile equity market environment, maybe you ought to seek objective, unemotional advice from a seasoned investment pro while you still have money to discuss. The biggest mistake you could make is to become the guy or gal who invested his or her money till it was all gone because you made the same mistake over and over again, selling low, buying high!

Planning Pointer

To avoid Mistake #3, shop at Jim's and Bob's consistently, not necessarily favoring one over the other, unless markets have fallen. Then visit Jim's a little more as prices are cheap and your money buys more.

MISTAKE #4:
FAILING TO UNDERSTAND THE
DIFFERENCE BETWEEN A "LOSS" AND A "DECLINE"

When in fact does a "loss" occur? Take, for instance, the following example. Your house is located in a fairly nice neighborhood. It is worth $500,000 today. But wait, you read in the morning paper that the Environmental Protection Agency (EPA) has discovered toxic waste exposures 3 blocks away. Suddenly the value of your house plunges. Have you experienced a "loss"? No, not at all. Rather you've been dealt a "decline," or as some call it, a "paper loss." It only becomes a "real loss" when in a panic you sell your house into the teeth of this isolated market downturn and move away. Once the EPA cleans up the toxic waste, your house value should recover. If you did not sell, you did not suffer a "loss" (except perhaps some inflation momentum).

Investors many times make the mistake of confusing a "loss" with a "decline" in their portfolios. I see this especially among clients with 401(k) account balances. I see e-mails like the following so frequently when markets decline that I can predict the next wave with ease. "I've lost $5000 in my account since 5 minutes ago and I've been putting money in every month. Why do I keep losing money?" Do you feel this way when your portfolio values suffer declines in down markets? If so, you are not alone.

I was purging a client's review file recently, and I found a copy of the Wall Street Journal's "Money and Investing" section with investment return summaries for September 30, 2002. You may remember that the year 2002 was the third year in a row where the markets declined, and the third quarter ending returns (September 30th) were especially dismal. Many investors simply gave up at that point, as evidenced by the e-mail I received and reproduced at the very beginning of this chapter. "Please, let's go to cash!" The S&P 500 Index had fallen by 28.99% and the NASDAQ Composite had plunged an astounding 47.21% through September 30th. Those were just the declines in 2002; markets had fallen in 2000 and 2001, as well.

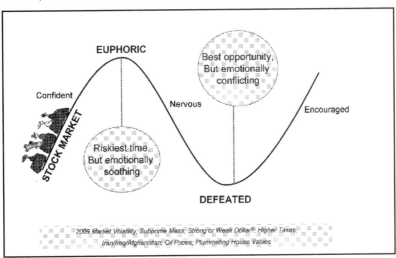

Do you remember, as you reviewed your statements back then, the knot tightening in your stomach again? Did you feel those "declines" were real "losses"? Yes, probably like most investors and probably like now in 2009. Unless you had sold out your equity positions in the face of that equity roller coaster ride of 2000 to 2002, you suffered a mere "decline" of values. By staying put and holding on tight, by the end of 2004 you may have regained your pre-2000 values and more. You survived the ride, perhaps battered and bruised emotionally but with gains instead of losses.

MISTAKE #5:
FAILING TO DISTINGUISH BETWEEN YOUR LEAD-OFF AND CLEAN-UP HITTERS

In the early fall 2006, I received a phone call from a client in New Jersey who was scanning his 401(k) account at work and 2 brokerage accounts through our office. The $200,000 401(k) account had large positions in the Fidelity Contrafund (FCNTX) and Growth Fund of America (GFAFX), 2 large-cap growth funds. His $250,000 brokerage account contained only a small holding in the Vanguard Index 500 Fund (VFINX) and a large position in Washington Mutual Investors Fund (WSHFX), the latter a core large-value fund. In the second brokerage account valued at $1,050,000 was a diversified portfolio containing domestic and international equities, about 30% in fixed income as well as large-, mid-, and small-cap equities with about equal amounts of growth and value investment styles.

My client commented on the widely varying results of the 3 accounts, also adding that none of the 3 accounts measured up to the DJIA performance for 2006. His solution: disband the diversified account. Why? Because it trailed both the 401(k) account and the value-oriented brokerage account. If left to his own devices, this client would have surely committed the Big Mistake by selling out the diversified portfolio solely by comparing its singular results with the performance of the other 2 accounts. Do you do this too? Do you maybe expect your singles-oriented lead-off hitter to compete with your clean-up hitter in terms of home-runs and RBIs?

Like my client, many investors forget that a well-diversified account should perform like Tony Gwynn, that is, lots of singles and doubles, some widely-scattered home runs, and an outstanding career batting average. With the game on the line and the winning run on second base, as a manager, don't you want someone like Tony up there at the plate because a good line drive single is all you need? That was Tony's specialty and why he's a Hall-of-Famer.

On the other hand, many investors think that over-weighted sector bets like technology or emerging markets should perform like Tony Gwynn's career batting average when, in reality, they perform more like the Ryan Howards of the world (ie, scattered tape measure home runs among a record number of strikeouts). Perhaps 40 of the former, but 200 of the latter.

My client failed to remember that, first, you don't compare your entire portfolio to one single index, especially the narrowly-focused 30-stock DJIA. The year 2002 was a good year for the DJIA, the first in several years compared to indices like the S&P 500 Index. Second, he grumbled that the "growth-oriented" account (FCNTX and GFAFX) also underperformed the "value-tilted" account, citing only the relative performance of the funds themselves, not their asset classes of "growth" and "value." Let's sell the growth funds he suggested and buy more of the WSHFX.

Blindly comparing fund performance can only lead to disastrous results. My client failed to understand that in 2002, "value" funds (old economy) outperformed "growth" funds (new economy) and that WSHFX, a core large value fund, should have outperformed the "growth" funds, which it did. But it also underperformed a lot of core value funds (ie, its peer group). Even so, both FCNTX and GFAFX were outperforming their peer group growth funds at the time. So in reality, they were the "heroes" of the portfolio that year, not the value fund, and he was insisting I sell the growth funds. He had it totally backwards.

Lastly, recall that he wanted me to liquidate the fully-diversified account. Here too his solution was ill-conceived and factually misguided. He had forgotten that this account contained 30% in fixed income funds. Therefore, it rightfully trailed fully-invested accounts in a year that equities dominated bonds. This seems obvious, but sometimes to investors looking only at relative performance, it is not.

Since my client was a big baseball fan, I was able to explain to him that the diversified account was his Tony Gwynn account and the 2 brokerage accounts were his Ryan Howard accounts. He finally grasped the subtle differences and felt relieved that he was predominantly positioned for the high batting average and not the home run-strikeout rat-race. Our discussion got him back on track and re-focused his expectations.

Planning Pointer

What are your expectations for your portfolio as a whole and for individual positions or specific accounts within that portfolio? Do you expect your lead-off hitter to hit 60 homeruns, or your clean-up hitter to bat .365 consistently? Being your own portfolio manager who can distinguish between them and apply the lesson to the various positions and accounts within your portfolio will help you avoid Mistake #5.

MISTAKE #6:
DRIVING HOME LOOKING
THROUGH THE REARVIEW MIRROR

Are you chasing yesterday's returns?

Sometimes clients will call to ask me to add the latest "hot" fund or "can't miss" stock to their "serious money" portfolio (as compared with their "play money"). I sometimes respond by suggesting that they may have forgotten what their long-term goals are, but if they really want me to do this, that they come to my office adhering to one specific rule—they must drive all the way looking solely through their rearview mirror. When they question my logic (and sanity), I tell them that's exactly what they are asking me to do. They want me to add a fund or stock to their portfolio based solely on looking at the "latest and greatest" short-term history of the fund or stock. In other words, they are letting immediate past history dominate their future view. Do you find yourself guilty of this investment mistake? Many, many investors are. It's what caused many portfolios to implode during the market decline of 2000-2002.

Remember then? Investors throughout the late 1990s sunk whole portfolios of serious money—in many cases lifetimes of savings accumulated for retirement security—into the universe of dot.com wonders, often based on recommendations from their teen-aged children.

Well, we all know now that the undisciplined craze reached its zenith in early 2000 as mutual fund results for 1999 were published. Those results showed not unexpectedly that growth funds, heavily laden with technology and dot.com stocks, sported astronomical 1-year and 3-year returns. At the opposite end, value-oriented, old-economy stocks pulled up the rear of the return spectrum. So what did countless investors do? Thinking that "...it's different this time..." and that technology stocks knew no upper price limit, they shifted enormous amounts of capital from value funds to growth funds. In other words, they made the mistake of moving forward by looking in the rearview mirror.

What happened? These investors watched in horror as their serious money melted like the wicked witch in the Wizard of Oz. I saw this over and over with my own eyes as 401(k) participants got their 1999 year-end statements, or worse yet their first quarter 2000 statements, perused the performance charts, then shifted their entire balance to yesterday's winners, just before those very markets began their 3-year plunge. Unfortunately, they decided to shop at Bob's store, buying in even at the last minute, fearing that they'd miss out on the inevitable and ever-sustainable technology market miracle.

Investor behavior such as this occurs as well at the bottom of the market cycle, when the plunge has become a rout. Many of those people who got in the technology boom just before the collapse waited until near the bottom to get out, finally disgusted with their original mistake, ready as ever to make their second Big Mistake. Seeing cash and bonds do well from 2000 to 2002 and seeing their sector-oriented equity positions dwindle, especially through the summer of 2002, they threw in the towel and abandoned the markets, moving to cash or money markets barely yielding 1%. Once again many investors relied on past history—the rearview mirror—to guide their emotional response to market performance. Unfortunately for those who yanked their money from their equity positions, this movement occurred in the last few months and weeks before the markets reversed in October 2002, to begin the next 5-year bull market.

So, as a worst case example, following this pattern, Doctor Mike starts out with a portfolio of $1 million in an allocated portfolio on January 1st, 2000. He decides to move the portfolio to tech stocks/funds, and lives through a 70% plunge in the market. His portfolio drops to $300,000, as Mike then moves back to cash earning 1% on October 7th after seeing his September 30th statement. He misses the market rebound of late 2002 and 2003, still too scared to re-enter the equity markets that so decimated his retirement dream. Dr. Mike is not a figment of my imagination. He told me his story at an industry meeting in 2006, as he was still—can you believe it?—sitting in cash. He was not alone. He and many others had stopped looking forward and relied solely on their rearview mirror for guidance.

So, when studying mutual funds, stocks, or ETFs to add to your portfolio, be conscious of relying only on immediate past history to explain and define your future expectations. Look to 5- and 10-year trends and check how the fund or stock did during past volatile markets, especially relative to its peer group. Is the fund manager who created the track record still managing the fund? Is the CEO of the top-performing stock still leading the company? Is the fund still investing based on the investment style with which it enjoyed prolonged success? For example, if a long-term small-cap growth fund has just grown into a mid-cap blend fund, as often happens, then all bets are off. The manager is now fishing in an alien universe of stocks with which he or she may have little or no experience.

The bottom line, though, is that selecting a clear asset allocation strategy to guide your portfolio decisions will also help to keep you from making Mistake #6. Such a strategy will help you avoid those emotional knee-jerk reactions to recent historical fund or stock data when it appears. In fact, when it's time to rebalance your portfolio according to the asset allocation formula you have adopted and which you committed to writing in your IPS, you may be forced to act in exactly the opposite way that your human instincts would tell you to act. For instance, when one sector of the market is up and one down, the human, undisciplined tendency is to want to buy more of what's up and less of what's down, a good example of driving forward looking through the rearview mirror.

On the contrary, correct rebalancing dictates that you reduce your exposure to what's up and increase your position in what's down. It's the classic sell high, buy low. While this involves a look at the past, it's actually a forward-looking portfolio action that understands you can never really know when a sector reaches its peak or hits rock bottom. Your rebalancing then may be premature, but it doesn't seek to imitate Ryan Howard—it seeks to avoid Howard's extremes of feast or famine.

In the final analysis, Mistake #6 can be overcome by a forward-looking asset allocation strategy that does not allow for human frailties and inconsistencies to govern the portfolio selection process. It may be a bit boring but it works over the long run. It keeps you from relying on your rearview mirror to drive your investment portfolio forward.

MISTAKE #7:
FAILING TO THINK AT THE PORTFOLIO LEVEL

I have an orthopedic surgeon client who had major parts of her total invested assets in different places. This is not unusual. She had 401(k) and 403(b) accounts with TIAA-CREF from various prior employment positions, both traditional and Roth IRAs, 2 brokerage accounts, 2 annuities, a 401(k) in her current practice, plus savings accounts, CDs, and so on. Lastly, she had joint accounts with her spouse, who also maintained separate accounts of his own. All in all, a major jumble of invested and noninvested assets clumped together with no rhyme or reason and many times totally out of control.

If this is you, do you have any rational method to determine your overall asset allocation? Do you know if you have any undue exposures to certain asset classes that seriously increase your risk levels? Are you being compensated for the risks you are taking within the overall portfolio? Do you pick investments in your retirement accounts without understanding the impact of those tactical investments on the whole strategic asset allocation of your portfolio? If you see yourself in this mirror, then you may be guilty of failing to think at the portfolio level.

This mistake, like many of the mistakes I've cited, seems to come back to basic asset allocation errors where improper allocation or lack of any allocation strategy can effectively reduce your long-term portfolio success.

My first suggestion is that you try to find help to organize your current assets into a snapshot that details the allocation and investment styles within your overall portfolio. If your assets consist of mainly mutual funds and annuities, you can go to the Morningstar database (www.morningstar.com) to help draw a picture of your entire pool of assets. If you want expertise from outside, consider hiring a financial planner or other investment professional whose first task would be to help you understand just what you own at the portfolio level. Only by looking at the big picture can you begin to understand whether you are being too conservative or too aggressive, whether you've inadvertently created serious over-weights in certain assets classes and maybe dangerously ignored others.

Perhaps your assets are not disorganized, yet you still have accounts in different places that you might think bear no relationship to one another. However, from an asset allocation standpoint, the combination of the accounts, taken together, does present a certain risk-reward profile whether you realize it or not. It's only when you think at the portfolio level that you begin to understand how the allocation of one account can and does affect the other accounts as well as the balance in the total combined portfolio.

Let's say you work in a hospital that has only a narrow choice of retirement plan investment options from which you can choose. But among these options are a really good large-cap growth fund and an excellent international fund. The rest of the choices are ho-hum at best. So rather than try to allocate your 401(k) account across various asset classes, many of which are represented by inferior investment choices, you might want to use only those 2 superior investment options—large growth and international—for your entire 401(k) account. You can then offset this over-weighting in the 401(k) by underweighting large growth and international in other accounts until you reach the allocation balance you desire.

Wilmington, DE financial planner Brent C. Fuchs, CFP, CLU, ChFC, CRPC states, "In my experience, investors usually have limited 401(k) choices, and many of them are inadequate. By blending the 401(k) or 403(b) accounts into the total portfolio allocation, the investor can pick the best from the available 401(k) choices, even if it's only one fund and balance the portfolio with non-401(k) investment accounts."[2]

In the next few years, most 401(k) and 403(b) investment options will include either target-age or lifestyle funds, or both, for participants to select so the lack of really good investment options within those plans will diminish. However, there will still be tens of thousands of smaller plans that will not contain the new auto-allocated accounts, so balancing at the portfolio level will still have its merit. Here, portfolio allocation will matter as knowledgeable participants seek to enhance their portfolios by adding the best investment options offered by the plan.

Planning Pointer

Think across your entire array of invested assets to achieve asset class balance. In that way you can achieve the desired result for the totality of your investments even though the separate parts (accounts) themselves lack proper balance. Without that portfolio overview, you might be falling prey to Mistake #7 where you try to balance each account unsuccessfully due to limited choices, thus arriving at no strategic portfolio balance at all.

MISTAKE #8:
A POTPOURRI OF MISTAKES TO AVOID

I find myself running out of space to list in detail several other "mistakes" that investors need to avoid, so Mistake #8 is a concise treatment of a few other investment gaffes.

Failing to Keep Perspective

Do you ever get caught up in the daily mayhem of the various market indices? If so, you are never going to be satisfied with your portfolio and I hasten to add that your retirement years will be miserable. Why? Because you will have a full-time opportunity to drive yourself crazy, from preopening futures to postmarket euphoria or dismay. I only need mention the extreme volatility—mostly negative—we all experienced in early October 2008 when the DJIA plunged 22% over 7 trading days. Watching the "tape" those days could have led to severe nosebleed!

If we allow our market focus to become too short, day by day maybe even hour by hour, we get overtaken by the speed and lack of clarity that any one day in the trenches dumps into our brain. It is in fact a nervous, anxious and agitating view of the markets. However, if we let our eyes focus on the distance, on the long-term perspective of the markets as they move through time, we see a much different and much clearer picture. The advance of the markets may be herky-jerky, but the overall trend is up. That perspective may have been extremely difficult to appreciate sitting day by day through the horrendous volatility of late 2008, just as it was hard for investors around 9/11 to see beyond the smoke of the fallen twin towers and the grimness of the markets immediately afterward.

Planning Pointer

My advice to clients who are especially hysterical about the markets is to avoid as many encounters with the markets as they can. Turn off the cable-TV pundits and screamers. That way you don't get caught up in its daily vagaries. Today's results hardly matter in the long-term scheme of things. The day's results of Black Monday in 1987, as bad as they were back then, are now a mere blip on the chart of market results over time.

Leaving Free Money on the Table

Americans fail to capture billions of dollars each year from employer-sponsored plans that offer matching contributions. Young doctors especially miss out on the opportunity to enhance their retirement accounts with the "boss's" money because they are in debt-repayment mode and have families with young children to support. As a result, they fail to contribute to their 401(k) plan.

In discussing Mistake #2, I alluded to how much of your own money you needed to save to reach $1 million at age 65 at an 8% compounded rate of return. For a 25 year old, that's only $308 per month. Now, suppose that $308 were being matched by your employer in a SIMPLE-IRA or a 401(k). Our young doctor would have $2 million at age

Figure 2-3. Factors that determine portfolio success. (Figure created by author with data from Brinson GP, Hood LR, Beebower GL. Determinants of portfolio performance. *Financial Analysts Journal.* 1986;42(4):39-48.)

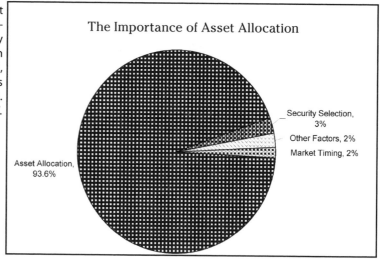

The Importance of Asset Allocation

Security Selection, 3%

Other Factors, 2%

Market Timing, 2%

Asset Allocation, 93.6%

65. Simple math tells us the total amount of his own dollars this 25-year-old doctor needs to save to reach $2 million is a mere $147,840 ($308 x 12 x 40). The combination of compound interest plus free money from the employer creates a dual investment pot of gold.

Look at it this way: when the employer matches retirement plan contributions, let's say only $0.50 for each $1.00 you save, that's like getting a 50% tax-free pay raise on the amount you contribute, or better yet, it's like getting a guaranteed 50% rate of return on your new savings dollars. I've met no money manager yet who could provide such a guarantee.

Smart Money Remains Fully Invested

Smart investors do not attempt to "time" the markets. That involves 2 correct decisions: when to get out and when to get in time and again. Even the very best managers cannot do this consistently. I remember when the manager of a very successful growth mutual fund tried to time the markets several years back. Fearing a market plunge, he went to cash for most of the fund's huge asset base just before the markets soared, then realizing his mistake later on, reinvested the fund's now mostly cash assets near when the markets declined. Two timing mistakes in a row, and this from a seasoned money manager who is immersed 24/7 in trying to maximize profits for his investors. I should add that his results since then have been much better.

Of all of the elements studied that can enhance the returns on a portfolio by decreasing volatility, asset allocation is by far the winner. Market timing, fund or stock selection, and other factors have much less bearing on the ultimate success of the portfolio as compared to top line asset allocation. Figure 2-3 illustrates this important fact.

Looking strictly at the performance of the S&P 500 Index from June 30, 1993 through June 30, 2003, if you remained fully invested throughout, you would have captured a 10.04% compounded annual rate of return. However, if you tried to time the market and missed out on the 10 best days during those 10 years, your rate of return would have dropped to only 4.95%. Worse yet, if you missed the 30 best days, you would have lost money, earning a -2.20% rate of return. This is why smart investors don't play the "timing" game.

> ### Planning Pointer
> Don't let yourself get caught up in the "thrill of victory" of one or two "timing" successes; those most certainly will be offset by many more "agonies of defeat." Successful portfolio management rests on the solid pillar of "staying the course."

I'd like to end this chapter of investment blunders with the exact text I used in August, 2005, closing the first article I wrote on investor mistakes. It was entitled In Investing, It's About Avoiding The Big Mistake, and it appeared in *Endocrine Today*,[3] as well as other medical specialty publications. Here's what I wrote then.

You'll recall what Nick Murray says about investing—"The enemy of successful investing is not under-performance; it's 'the big mistake.'" In its truest form, TBM is "buying high, selling low," sometimes over and over again. It's focusing on the here and now and not on the long-term. It's buying yesterday's high-flyer at its peak, then selling at its trough. It's abandoning your common sense and playing mouse to the financial media's pied piper. It's the act of balancing your portfolio by constantly selling the asset classes that have declined (selling low) in order to purchase more of the asset classes that have risen (buying high).

It's selling a flat Exxon-Mobil in late 1999 and then buying a bloated Intel... It's actually believing the ad that asked, "If your broker is so smart, why is he still working?" (like maybe trying to prevent you from making TBM). It's relying on the likes of CNBC and MSNBC and Money magazine and Barron's to act as your sole investment guides—not that they are bad in themselves—but they have awful memories from one issue or show to the next. Just think, some people actually count on a $2.50/month magazine to guide them in managing their $500,000 lifetime savings.

TBM is abandoning tried-and-true investment disciplines for the "quick buck." It's confusing "risk tolerance" with "loss avoidance."

TBM is each of these and all of these, and maybe some more. If golf is a game of opposites, then I contend that investing in many instances is the same. It's doing the opposite of what your inner, all-too-human, self is saying to do when that inner self is overwhelmed by fear at market lows and by greed at market highs.

Sometimes the cost of avoiding TBM is the cost of hiring a competent investment advisor or CFP to keep you on the straight and narrow toward realizing your long-term retirement goals.

I hope you have re-tooled your mind by reviewing the enduring investment principles I've itemized here. Remember Nick Murray's comment, "Financial success is driven not by performance of investments but by the behavior of investors." Above all, examine your own investor behavior to determine if it has caused you to make or helped you to avoid making the Big Mistake.[3]

REFERENCES

1. Murray N. *The New Financial Advisor*. Southold, NY: Author; 2001.
2. Rudzinski KR. Learn how to avoid making the "big mistake" with your investments. *Hem/Onc Today*. 2007;8(1).
3. Rudzinski KR. In investing, it's about avoiding the "big mistake." *Endocrine Today*. 2005;3(8).

Investment Policy Statement

Dr. and Mrs. Biff Beholden

The Investment Policy Statement (IPS) serves as a method to outline your financial objectives and to identify the guidelines by which your account will be managed. The IPS has been created specifically for your unique situation, and should be reviewed periodically to ensure that your goals and objectives have not changed in such a fashion to alter your investment approach. This IPS is not a contract. It is intended to summarize the investment philosophy which guides your account.

Portfolio Purpose

The portfolio will maintain an asset allocation strategy consistent with your risk tolerance and rate of return objectives (see below "Financial Objectives"). The primary purpose of the portfolio is to provide for retirement income for you and Mary Ann and for general savings for emergencies and lump sum needs.

➤ Your portfolio should be diversified among appropriate investments.
➤ It should provide for increases in your current lifestyle or standard of living.
➤ It should provide inflation protection over the long-term (your joint life expectancy).

Financial Objectives

➤ The primary objective of your strategic asset allocation model is to maximize the total return of the account consistent with your risk tolerance and time horizon.
➤ Due to your risk tolerance and time horizon as determined by your answers on your separate risk questionnaires, your additional needs stated above, and from our specific conversations regarding your risk-reward profile, your portfolio should maintain a conservative growth allocation. **This would be a strategic allocation of 45% in equities, 50% in fixed income and 5% in cash/cash equivalents. The expected (gross) average annual total return is 7.05% over the long-term, though there is no guarantee that this performance will be achieved. Unless changed, the portfolio will be maintained at this strategic allocation through ongoing re-balancing.**

Risk Considerations

➤ Your questionnaire exhibits that you classify yourself as a "somewhat" conservative investor. Due to the reliance on this portfolio to provide for living expenses around

1

the year 2015 and beyond (until the joint life expectancy of Dr. B and Mary Ann), it is important that the risk level on this portfolio be reduced. The goal would be to maintain a 3-year portfolio beta of 0.50 or lower

➤ The account should be diversified among various sub-asset classes (i.e. large cap stocks, small cap stocks, high yield bonds, etc.) to mitigate risks and returns associated with any particular sub-asset class. This also creates more consistent and predictable returns over time.

➤ The portfolio also needs to counter the effects of long-term inflation, so Treasury Indexed Bonds (TIPS), a small portion to gold and to other inflation-hedged investments ought to be added to the portfolio, as needed.

➤ To the extent that alternative investments can be added to reduce risk and therefore lower beta, the portfolio may use them in moderation (no more than 10% of total portfolio assets, taken from both equity and fixed income allocation)

Time Horizon

➤ The time horizon of 23 to 28 years should be considered for this portfolio.

Taxes

➤ This is primarily a non-qualified (taxable) portfolio; therefore income taxes are a factor. Use of tax-exempt bonds, tax-favored investments, ETF's, tax-deferred vehicles ought to be considered for use within this portfolio. Also, co-ordination of assets classes with tax-qualified accounts needs to be reviewed so that tax-inefficient asset classes and unavoidable taxable fixed income (i.e. TIPs) can be re-positioned inside qualified or tax-deferred accounts. AMT issues also need to be addressed with help from Bill S., CPA.

➤ Because of the above, this portfolio needs to blended with other accounts to maintain total portfolio allocation. A plan to do this will need to be developed and adapted.

Liquidity Needs

Liquidity refers to the ability to convert assets cash with no or little loss of principal.

➤ Since this portfolio is structured to provide income primarily as well as some long-term growth, cash/cash equivalents should be maintained at all times to provide for 24-months of income needs (expenditures) plus expected lump sum needs (to be determined from time to time but at least once per year – in December for following year). Dividends from fixed income and equity funds should be deposited to the cash account and not re-invested.

Legal Constraints

➤ You do not have any legal constraints for your portfolio.

2

Unique Circumstances

➢ You've indicated that a future contingency for this portfolio is the possible incapacity of Biff's mother, and the need to draw down some cash to assist her. No specific plans can be made at this time as the contingency is possible, though remote.

Security Guidelines

Based on your objectives and risk profile, as well as our discussions with you, the following preferences should be considered.

➢ The portfolio should avoid derivative transactions that are not designed as a hedge.
➢ Private equity should be avoided.
➢ A professionally-managed portfolio would be appropriate for this account.
➢ Alternative investments may be considered, other than private equity.

Control Procedures

➢ Investment reviews will be conducted on a semi-annual basis and review of the Investment Policy Statement will be conducted annually.
➢ Re-balancing will occur In January and July, as needed, unless otherwise decided sooner or more (or less) frequently.
➢ Investment managers will monitored on a continual basis to ensure proper and appropriate security selection.
➢ Performance reports will be available monthly via e-mail download
➢ Staff will be available to answer administrative questions regarding the portfolio.
➢ Phone calls to discuss portfolio can be arranged at any time.

Client Signature: _____

Date: _____

3

This chapter derives from the following previously published articles:

- Rudzinski K. In investing, it's about avoiding the "big mistake." *Endocrine Today.* 2005;3(8).
- Rudzinski K. Investing is all about avoiding "the big mistake." *Ocular Surgery News.* 2006;24(6).
- Rudzinski K. Learn how to avoid making "big mistake" with your investments. *Hem/Onc Today.* 2007;8(1).
- Rudzinski K. Avoiding the big mistake in investing. *Cardiology Today.* 2008;11(9).

3

Avoiding Common IRA Planning Disasters

"When was the last time you gave your IRAs a complete check-up?"

Are your IRAs becoming an ever-larger portion of your retirement asset pool? The answer is probably "yes." Despite stock market declines of recent times, larger and larger rollovers from qualified plans to IRAs as well as increased contribution limits for traditional and Roth IRAs, SEP-IRAs, and SIMPLE-IRAs have amplified the bottom line of most retirement portfolios. These accounts now serve as a taxpayer's most important source for retirement income production. Is this you?

Let me pose this question to you: Do you get under the "hood" of your IRAs as frequently as you change the oil in your car? When was the last time you gave your IRAs a complete check-up? If not recently, then you may be guilty of committing one or more of the most common mistakes in IRA planning.

Here's a list of IRA planning errors I see most often in my practice. They tend to dominate the landscape, and it's rare to find someone who is not guilty of at least one, and just one may be enough to sidetrack or derail your retirement success. Let's see how you fare.

MISTAKE #1:
FAILING TO TAKE ADVANTAGE OF INCREASED CONTRIBUTION LEVELS

For 2009, you can contribute up to the lesser of your earned income, or $5000. You can contribute an extra $1000, called a "catch-up contribution" if you are age 50 or older (Table 3-1). Beyond age 70 ½, you can still contribute to a Roth IRA, assuming continuing earned income, but not to a traditional IRA. Your $5000 or $6000 contribution can be made entirely to your traditional or Roth IRA, or to any combination of the two, as long as you don't exceed your dollar limit.

Rudzinski K. *The Physician's Guide to Avoiding Financial Blunders (pp 43-56)*
© 2009 SLACK Incorporated

TABLE 3-1

2009 IRA Limits

IRA CONTRIBUTION

Under age 50	$5000
Age 50 and over	$6000

PHASE OUT FOR DEDUCTING IRA CONTRIBUTION

Married, joint	$89,000 to $109,000 AGI
Single, head of household	$55,000 to $65,000 AGI
Married, separate	$0 to $10,000 AGI

PHASE OUT FOR DEDUCTING SPOUSAL IRA

	$166,000 to $176,000 AGI

PHASE OUT OF ROTH CONTRIBUTION ELIGIBILITY

Married, joint	$166,000 to $176,000 MAGI
Single, head of household	$105,000 to $120,000 MAGI
Married, separate	$0 to $10,000 MAGI
No Roth conversion if	$100,000+ MAGI

The availability to fund a Roth IRA phases out once your modified adjusted gross income (MAGI) exceeds $166,000 if you file jointly. MAGI equals AGI + tax-exempt interest and applies only to Roth IRAs. For MAGI above $176,000, no Roth IRA contribution is permitted. If you are single, the phase out is between $105,000 and $120,000 of MAGI, with no contribution allowed above $120,000 of MAGI. If you file married-separate, the phase out is particularly harsh—$0 to $10,000 of MAGI. For the rules regarding other income and funding limitations, such as IRA contribution limits when you are a participant in a qualified retirement plan at work, refer to Chapter 6.

If you exceed the income limits, you can still contribute to a "nondeductible IRA" in the same amounts you can put into a traditional or Roth IRA. There is no income phase-out for the nondeductible IRA. Deposits are made with after-tax dollars, but the growth until retirement is tax deferred. When you withdraw monies after age 59 ½, only that tax-deferred growth is taxable and at ordinary income tax rates.

Planning Pointer

Caveat: Withdrawing money at retirement from IRAs can get complicated, especially withdrawing from both traditional and nondeductible IRAs. My advice is to keep the 2 IRAs completely separate during the deposit and accumulation phase so as to lessen the record-keeping burden when withdrawals are made at retirement.

The Pension Protection Act of 2006 (PPA2006) added a wrinkle to benefit the funding of a nondeductible IRA. Ordinarily, taxpayers who desire to "convert" a portion or all of their traditional IRA to a Roth IRA may do so, except that such a conversion may not take place if in the year of the conversion their MAGI is $105,000 or greater. However, PPA2006 as written has removed this MAGI restriction for tax years 2010 and beyond.

Planning Pointer

If you fund a nondeductible IRA in 2009, or have funded one in prior years, you can convert it to a Roth IRA in 2010, paying income tax only on the growth of the account prior to January 1, 2010. The income tax can be spread over 2 tax years.

That prior growth may have been stunted by recent market declines with little or no growth to account for, or late 2009 funding may produce little or no growth on which to pay taxes. The bottom line is that once converted, the new Roth IRA grows tax free and permits tax-free withdrawals at retirement if you hold it until the later of 5 years or age 59 ½.

Planning Pointer

Always check with your tax counsel as to the availability of funding a traditional IRA, Roth IRA, or nondeductible IRA for yourself and/or nonworking spouse. This is true even if you are a participant in a qualified retirement plan at work.

The deadline for making contributions to your IRAs is April 15th. No extensions are permitted for the contributions even if you file an extension for your tax return.

MISTAKE #2:
FAILING TO FUND AN IRA
FOR YOUR NONWORKING SPOUSE

Ordinarily, you need earned income to fund an IRA. One exception, though, allows a nonworking spouse with no earned income to fully fund a traditional or Roth IRA. The annual contribution limits are the same (ie, $5000 + $1000 catch-up contribution in 2009). The AGI phase out for deducting contributions to a spousal traditional IRA is $166,000 to $176,000, with no deduction permitted above the $176,000 AGI limit. Roth contributions phase out at the same limits, except that MAGI is used (see Table 3-1).

Planning Pointer

If you are a young doctor with a family, paying off student loans, and you only have $5000 to begin investing in IRAs, whose IRA should you fund: yours or your spouse's? You could split the $5000 between your IRAs or, as many doctors opt to do, fund only the spousal IRA first as that provides a greater layer of asset protection over and above that provided by the IRA itself.

Don't miss out on this opportunity to sock away more dollars for retirement. Many stay-at-home moms or dads qualify as nonworking spouses under current IRA rules. As mentioned, assets growing in the name of your nonphysician spouse are assets not subject to professional liability claims against you. That could be valuable protection someday.

Mistake #3:
Paying Unnecessary Taxes
on Withdrawals Before Age 59 ½

It's been drilled into your head that you cannot take withdrawals from your IRA(s) prior to age 59 ½ without the threat of a 10% penalty. Some people liken this with taking the tag off your mattress—a lifetime no-no under any circumstances.

But what if circumstances dictate that you find money from somewhere, and your traditional IRA is the only place you can go? What action might you take that you want to avoid? You might err by simply removing the cash from your IRA, subjecting the amount withdrawn to both the 10% pre-age 59½ penalty and to ordinary income tax, effectively a tax on a tax. This is an expensive but avoidable mistake. What should you do instead?

Under Section 72(t) of the Internal Revenue Code (IRC), you can make pre-age 59 ½ withdrawals without the 10% penalty. How is that done? The rule says that you can take what are called "substantially equal periodic payments" (SEPPs) beginning at ANY AGE, so long as those same equal payments continue until the later of 5 years or age 59 ½. So, at age 48, the payments must continue until age 59 ½; at age 57, the payments must be made for 5 years.

The IRS provides for 3 calculation methods for determining how much the payments need to be. Your tax counsel or financial planner should have software to make those calculations for you, each of which produces a slightly different payment amount. You pick the one that best suits your needs. But remember, if the need for the money goes away quickly, you're still stuck with the 5-year-age 59½ rule, so tread lightly here before you take the plunge. Don't forget that IRA withdrawals—even under Section 72(t)—still require that ordinary income taxes be paid on the withdrawal. It's just the 10% penalty that Section 72(t) helps avoid.

As an example, for a 48 year old with an IRA balance of $1,000,000, using a 6% interest rate, and a beneficiary age of 48, the 72(t) level withdrawal amount is about $64,000 using the amortization method and about $62,000 using the annuity method.

What if you only need $20,000 a year, not $64,000 or $62,000? The way to solve the problem would be to first divide your IRA into 2 separate IRAs, one funded in the amount that produces the 72(t) payment amount that you desire ($312,500), the other funded with the balance ($687,500) from which no withdrawal is taken. That way, only the one IRA is affected. Later on, if you need more income than $20,000, you can again divide the remaining IRA ($687,500) to produce the additional 72(t) payment you need.

From an asset-allocation standpoint, when dividing up your IRA assets per the above example, make sure you keep cash equivalents in the 72(t) IRA, perhaps up to 18 to 36 months of distributions. This extra liquidity will enable you to avoid selling low in a severe market decline, the forced result if you only held equity positions in the 72(t) IRA.

> ### Planning Pointer
>
> Section 72(t) does not work well if you want a large single withdrawal from your IRA and you're under age 59 ½. In that situation, if your IRA is the only place you can go for emergency money, you could instead borrow money via a home equity loan or line or credit, if available, then use the 72(t) payment to pay off the loan. IRAs are not good places to go for nonretirement uses because of the income taxes due on withdrawals, which makes the use of that money very expensive, even without a 10% penalty.

MISTAKE #4:
NOT UPDATING IRA, SEP, SIMPLE BENEFICIARY DESIGNATIONS

This mistake unfortunately occurs so often and can result in disastrous consequences for your heirs, yet it can be avoided so easily. How does it happen?

Maybe you've just gotten your wills and trusts updated due to changes in the estate tax laws, you have a new addition to the family, or you've undergone a divorce or separation, among others. You file the documents away at the bank, go home, see patients the next day, and life goes on. But whose job was it to make sure your IRAs, annuities, retirement plans, etc all reflected the changes you made in your estate plan? Was it your responsibility to meet with your agent or broker? Or was the attorney's staff on board to do that? This is where communication often breaks down and the planning disaster is born. I see it more frequently than I care to.

More likely, though, you updated your legal documents but it was quite a while ago and the follow-up work was in fact properly done. You sense those documents need to be re-visited now, but you're so busy with your patient load that you can't find the time and time passes you by. Meanwhile, you've had a child by a second marriage at age 50, or your hard-working daughter is married to a do-nothing jerk who may divorce her and claim half her assets, including her share of your IRA if you happen to pass away before he skips town.

For these and other reasons—and there are countless life changes that require your attention—you need to make sure you review the beneficiary designations of all your retirement accounts, both personal and at work (401(k)s, 403(b)s, etc). Why? Because those beneficiary designations supersede anything you've established in your wills and/or trusts.

So, for example, you want to leave your entire estate to your trust, which divides up the assets perfectly according to your carefully-constructed wishes. But one of your IRAs somehow names your children equally as primary beneficiaries, excluding your spouse (real case I saw!), and another fails to name any beneficiary at all (goes to your estate with cousin Ernie lurking!). There's also a third one that still has your first wife (not your present wife) listed as primary beneficiary (another real case I saw—a prominent cardiologist who should have known better but was too busy to notice). Bad mistakes, bad results. You might say these are over-dramatized examples, and couldn't ever happen to you. Really? When did you last check?

In my 36 years in the financial services business, I've seen wives disinherited inadvertently. I've witnessed children and grandchildren left out in the financial cold, adopted children left penniless. In every one of those cases, the mistake was unintentional, yet painful. Nothing a few minutes of checking and a stroke of a pen couldn't have cured!

It's so vitally important to make sure your IRA beneficiary designations are as up-to-date as possible and coordinated with your overall estate plan. Be aware that life changes require review and review means taking the time to meet with those advisors who you rely on to keep you up-to-date. If you don't, you may fall prey unnecessarily to this dreadful planning mistake.

So what about you? When did you last look? Have you accounted for everyone—spouse, children, grandchildren (how about the newest ones?)? If you don't check this out, who will?

Planning Pointer

Schedule a beneficiary "fire drill" with your advisors every few years or sooner if family changes intervene. It's fairly routine in our practice. Remember, your beneficiaries are those you wish to receive your life's bounty; if they are not stated properly, or even omitted unintentionally, then your legacy plans may be fatally flawed.

MISTAKE #5:
FAILING TO ALLOCATE ASSETS
BETWEEN TAXABLE ACCOUNTS AND IRA ACCOUNTS

This mistake may become magnified as the full extent of the proposed Obama tax plan for individuals comes into play. Higher taxes on interest, dividends, and capital gains for certain individuals making above threshold income levels calls for a retooling of investment principles if you are in the targeted income range, however that is finally defined.

In my original 2005 article on IRA mistakes, I wrote the following, "Because equity assets are taxed at lower capital gains rates when sold (or when capital gains are declared in mutual funds), and because dividends (unless classified as "preferred" dividends) and interest are taxed at higher ordinary income tax rates, it is sometimes advisable to put income-producing assets in IRAs and equity assets in nonqualified brokerage accounts." This concept of tax allocation may well become more widespread as tax brackets increase.[1]

Writing in 2005, I added, "This (allocating between taxable and nontaxable accounts) may be easier said than done, especially if IRA assets represent the majority of retirement assets and an aggressive investment posture is adopted, such as 80% or more in equities. In other words, this suggestion should not be taken to an extreme, that is, all bonds in IRAs and all equities in nonqualified accounts."[1] What does all this mean?

As tax laws change, reallocating assets and asset classes between taxable and nontaxable accounts becomes a new objective. How is that done? When should you begin the process?

To answer, here are a few suggestions you may find useful, as a higher income tax environment becomes a reality:

- In nonqualified accounts, substitute tax-free funds (money market, bonds, etc) for taxable funds. If you do, then these tax-exempt holdings can remain outside your IRAs. You may have already adopted this strategy.

- To the extent that you cannot exchange taxable interest for tax-exempt interest outside the IRA (eg, Treasury Indexed Bonds [I-Bonds or TIPS]), consider re-allocating those to your IRAs where the interest is not taxed currently.

- We already know that mutual funds may declare taxable capital gains even when you don't sell shares. Those can be a nuisance in a 10% or 15% capital gain environment, but as the tax rate on capital gains reaches 20% to 25%, these unwanted capital gain events become terribly inefficient. So, for asset classes outside your IRAs, you may want to consider reducing the amounts you invest in actively managed mutual funds and substituting exchange-traded funds (ETFs). These funds for the most part avoid ongoing capital gain distributions. In short, ETFs resemble index funds; however, they trade like stocks, so only at sale are capital gains (or losses) recognized and realized. For example, if you have all of your $250,000 large cap allocation divided into a growth fund like Fidelity Contrafund (FCNTX) and a value fund like Vanguard Windsor II (VWNFX), you may want to reduce those holdings a bit and add, for example, SPDR Trust-Series 1 (SPY) as a large-blend ETF. When you are finished, it may look like this: $50,000 each to Fidelity and Vanguard, $150,000 to SPDRs. The ETF adds tax efficiency to your nonqualified portfolio by reducing the capital gain exposure in your portfolio.

- Certain asset classes by their nature are tax inefficient generally because of high levels of trading (called "turnover"). Small-cap equity funds and some mid-cap and international funds are good examples. As a result, these mutual funds tend to spin off large capital gains that can wreak havoc on your tax planning. Such asset classes may be better situated inside your IRAs where high turnover, and the resultant capital gain, can be better tolerated.

- Depending on your age and your income level, you may want to fund Roth IRAs rather than traditional IRAs, if possible. If you follow the rules, none of the internal gains will ever be taxable to you.

When should you consider such changes? My original idea back in 2005 anticipated that making changes such as these might not be possible all at once. I summarized my comments on this mistake at that time as follows, "As an example, if you wanted a 50% equity/50% bond allocation strategy, you could consider a 40%/60% split in the IRA and 60%/40% outside the IRA."

In 2005, I was concerned that moving asset classes around might cause high levels of capital gains due to selling in the midst of a bull market. Today that may not be as much an issue as extreme market volatility from late 2007 into 2009 has unfortunately wiped out much of those taxable gains. In fact, many investors find themselves in the position of now having significant tax losses in their nonqualified portfolio, not capital gains. As a result, now may be an opportunity for you to make the allocation changes I've outlined and at the same time harvest potential tax losses in nonqualified accounts, which can be used now or in later tax years to offset capital gains taxed at potentially higher rates.

From an estate planning standpoint, this strategy of more fixed income in the IRAs and more equity classes—with the exceptions I've outlined—in the taxable brokerage accounts makes sense too. When you die, the IRAs are considered "income in respect of a decedent" and the gain is taxed to your beneficiaries under the income tax rules for such assets, and always at ordinary income rates. Capital assets, such as equity mutual funds, ETFs, individual stocks, etc, receive a stepped-up cost basis equal to the date of death value, so the capital gain is forgiven (ie, not taxed). So, keeping equity assets outside your IRAs make sense for your estate as well.

A minor caveat: If you are very near or in retirement, even if you could, you'd not want to carry this allocation strategy to its extreme where you hold only equity assets outside your IRA. Why? Because you need to maintain a certain level of liquidity outside your IRA to cover ordinary expenditures. Thus, your emergency fund and your cash liquidity account to cover 18 to 24 months of income needs should come from your nonqualified accounts, not from your IRA unless you are age 70 ½ or over and your required mandatory distribution can account for your routine monthly expenses. You don't want to be caught with only equity assets to draw down from your non-IRA account as potential capital gains may be a problem. Further, if all of your cash and income-producing assets are in your IRA and you are in your 60s, the only way to access the cash or income is to take a taxable distribution from your IRAs, which you would normally want to avoid as long as possible.

In other words, how you income allocate your assets to avoid income taxes while accumulating your retirement nest egg may differ from the allocation you use near or during early retirement, and then again once you reach age 70 ½. Building the right strategy can be extremely tax efficient. Getting it wrong can be costly.

Planning Pointer

When you tax allocate, you allocate at the total portfolio level such that any given account may be, by itself, out of balance, but as a whole, the "big picture" portfolio is properly dispersed.

MISTAKE #6:
NOT MAKING YOUR
REQUIRED MANDATORY DISTRIBUTION AUTOMATIC

IMPORTANT: Congress has suspended required mandatory distributions (RMDs) for 2009 only. In 2010, RMDs will resume unless further suspended or permanently eliminated by legislative act. However, if you reached age 70 ½ in 2008 and have decided to delay your first RMD until April 1st, 2009, you MUST take that RMD as originally mandated.

When you reach age 70 ½, you need to start thinking about how you want to take your RMD. Here are some thoughts to keep in mind:

- Unless you have a certain strategy for making manual withdrawals during the year to cover your RMD (see below), I have found it helpful to put all IRA accounts on auto-pilot so that the IRA custodian makes the distribution(s) to you automatically. Certainly smaller spousal accounts work well this way. Since the penalty tax is 50% of the difference between what you must take out as your RMD and the amount you actually took out, you want to avoid under-withdrawing at all costs.

For example, if your RMD for 2008 was $64,500, and you only took out $44,500, your 50% excise tax penalty is $10,000 (50% x $20,000). Making the distributions automatic puts the burden (ie, liability) of making sure the proper amount comes out on the IRA custodian. If a mistake is made, you know who to call.

- Conversely, why would you NOT want to make the RMD automatic? Let's say you have 2 IRAs, one invested 100% in the Vanguard Index 500 Fund (VFINX), and the other 100% invested in CDs. The RMD for the Vanguard IRA is $10,000, and for the CD IRA, $13,500. At the time you must take an RMD, the S&P 500 Index fund is down near 50% like it was in mid-November 2008. Not wanting to "sell low," you may want to turn off the RMD from Vanguard and take the total $23,500 RMD distribution from the CD IRA. Is this legal? Yes, because the IRS doesn't care which account you use, as long as the total calculated RMD amount—here, $23,500—comes out before December 31st.

- What if you have only one or two IRAs that contain mainly equity funds, stocks, or ETFs? This was another real-life situation like that faced by perhaps millions of investors at the end of 2008 as the various equity markets plunged seemingly out of control. Since a majority of investors ordinarily wait until the end of the year to take their RMDs (for tax-deferral purposes), they were faced with possibly selling into an extreme down market to fund their RMDs in November or December. What if this happens again? What should you do? Consider an in-kind transfer because the IRS simply says you must withdraw a calculated VALUE from your IRAs, not necessarily cash. So, to avoid having to sell shares in a plunging equity market, you can simply distribute shares of one or more funds, stocks, or ETFs that are equivalent to the RMD amount. This is referred to as an "in-kind" transfer. You transfer those shares in-kind to a nonqualified brokerage account to hold or sell when the share prices return to their former higher values.

As a reminder, if you normally have taxes withheld on your RMDs, you can't do that when completing an in-kind distribution, so you may need to check with your tax advisor to increase your fourth-quarter estimated tax payment to account for the under-withholding from the IRAs.

And a final caveat: be careful in an extremely volatile market environment that the shares distributed in-kind are equal to or greater than the RMD amount. This is especially true with mutual funds as they are valued at the close of the day. On days when the Dow Jones Industrial Average (DJIA) can flip from up 300 points at noon to down 700 points at the close, the end-of-day valuation may fall short of the required distribution amount. So check the value of the shares afterward to make sure you've satisfied the RMD requirement.

- If you continue to work after age 70 ½, the RMD rules say you can postpone RMDs from your 401(k) until you stop working. This rule does NOT apply to IRAs so don't get confused.

- If you've worked at a hospital or other nonprofit organization most of your working life, and you have been contributing to a 403(b) plan for years before 1985, you may want to confirm with your 403(b) representative that some of your account balance is not subject to RMDs until you're age 75. Some specialized rules regarding 403(b) plans that do not apply to IRAs make for special tax planning here.

- A little-known RMD rule has to do with after-tax contributions you may have made to a 401(k) plan that permitted such contributions, usually in a commercial setting. I see this frequently with retiring DuPont executives. At DuPont, like many companies, 401(k) rollouts at retirement must consist of an employee's total account balance, both pre-tax and after-tax amounts. The trick comes when the retiring executive is age 70 ½ or older. The special RMD rule here allows for the after-tax amounts to satisfy RMD amount in that year of distribution. So, if the RMD amount is $25,000, and there's $22,000 of after-tax monies coming out during the rollout to an IRA, the $22,000 satisfies a large portion of the $25,000 RMD, so the taxable portion of the RMD is only $3000. Pretty neat result!

- If you have several small IRA accounts, you may want to simplify your life by using these accounts in their entirety to satisfy early-on RMDs. That way you cut down on the number of IRA accounts you need to track.

- Lastly, Roth IRAs have no requirement for mandatory withdrawals, so RMDs do not exist in Roth IRA language. In fact, you can continue contributing to a Roth IRA after age 70 ½ if you have sufficient earned income.

Planning Pointer

RMDs can be distributed monthly, quarterly, annually—pretty much any way you want. You can combine an automated systematic withdrawal with lump sum withdrawals during the year, especially if you have months when expenses peak, such as during the year-end holiday season.

Mistake #7:
Failing to Elect
Net Unrealized Appreciation Treatment
of Appreciated Stock at Rollout

If you or your spouse now work or worked at one time in a for-profit company like Merck or St. Jude, among others, then you may have accumulated company stock in your 401(k) with a very low cost basis (the gain is referred to as "net unrealized appreciation" [NUA]). Ordinarily, when you leave the company, you roll out your entire pre-tax 401(k) accumulation to an existing or new IRA, including the stock. Later on, all distributions from the IRA will be taxable at ordinary income tax rates.

Let me suggest another alternative. Instead, roll the stock from the 401(k) directly to a separate nonqualified (taxable) brokerage account. You pay income tax only on the cost basis of the stock at the time of transfer. Assuming you have held or will hold the stock for more than 1 year, when you sell, the gain over basis is taxed at capital gain rates, not ordinary income tax rates—a difference of 20% to 25%. That 25% difference on a $500,000 capital gain can make for an enormous tax savings. Further, if you hold the stock until you die, all gains are forgiven due to the "stepped-up" basis your assets receive at your death. So if you own highly-appreciated company stock in your 401(k), make sure you actively consider this favorable NUA tax treatment.

MISTAKE #8:
A POTPOURRI OF IRA MISTAKES SUMMARIZED

Here are a few other IRA planning mistakes in abbreviated mode. This does not make them any less important than those I've already cited. Committing any one can be dangerous.

- Using your IRA as collateral for a loan: Do not do this! It is a "prohibited transaction" and will cause the total amount pledged to be considered a taxable distribution. Further, if you are under age 59 ½, you'll get hit with the 10% penalty.

- Exceptions to the 10% penalty tax rule for IRAs: We all know that IRA distributions prior to age 59 ½ incur the 10% penalty. But in certain circumstances, the penalty may be waived. Among these are taking withdrawals as part of Section 72 (t) "substantially-equal payments" (see Mistake #3 above), distributions on account of the death of the IRA owner, distributions under certain circumstances to pay the health insurance premiums of an unemployed taxpayer, distributions not to exceed the participant's "qualified higher education expenses" for the taxable year of the distribution, and up to $10,000 for "qualified first-time home-buyers." Each of these involves certain rules and should be used only after consultation with tax counsel.

- Leaving your IRA to your estate: This occurs when you fail to name a beneficiary for your IRA proceeds. When this happens and you are not yet age 70 ½, taxes must be paid according to the 5-year rule (essentially, income tax is due by no later than the end of the fifth year following the death of the IRA owner), and the tax deferral benefits of a "stretch" payout to named beneficiaries is lost.[2]

- Use of trusts as beneficiaries of your IRA: Ordinarily it is better to list named individuals as beneficiaries of IRAs. However, estate and tax planning goals may force the use of trusts as IRA beneficiaries. The proper kind of trust is called a "see-through" trust, which has many required details, the most important of which is that all beneficiaries must be people who can be readily identified. Improperly devised trusts can rob your IRA beneficiaries of the tax benefits of the "stretch."

- Using a self-directed IRA to purchase "exotic" assets: If you want to put vacation homes, race horses, airplanes, etc into your IRA, be extremely careful. Establishing and maintaining an account with these investment assets is a challenge at best and a tax trap at worst. How so? Well, such investments within an IRA may cause taxable income along the way. They may also cause complete tax disqualification of the IRA. Therefore, be cautious when using your IRA for unconventional investments.

- Transfers between IRAs: Watch out that you don't roll over the same money more than once in a plan year. Money physically rolled out from your IRA to deposit into another IRA can be done only once per year with the same money. However, money you transfer directly from one IRA to another can be moved as many times in the year as you wish. This is called a "direct" transfer.

- 60-day loans: You have 60 days to return money to your IRA once you remove it if you wish to avoid a taxable distribution. Some people use this provision of the law for short-term loans from their IRAs. That's okay and in fact may be a good planning strategy, but make absolutely sure the money is replaced in the same or other IRA within the 60-day limit. The law clearly states, "60-calendar days". Although the law does allow for a waiver of the 60-day rule under certain narrow circumstances like administrative errors, if you miss the 60-day time limit, you will generally have a taxable distribution on your hands. Avoid this error at all costs.

- "Per stirpes" beneficiary designation: Some custodian beneficiary forms do not permit or fail to stipulate a "per stirpes" beneficiary choice. If at the death of one of your children, you want that child's share to go to his or her children (ie, your grandchildren by that child), then you want to indicate "per stirpes" after the designation, for example, "...to all of my children, per stirpes." Otherwise, in many state jurisdictions, and within many IRA custodial documents, the default is the "per capita" designation. This results in your grandchildren by your deceased child being disinherited as their share is divvied up among your remaining children. Since your IRA beneficiary designation supersedes your wills, those grandchildren are left out in the cold. To avoid this potential family catastrophe, check to see if "per stirpes" has been specifically chosen in the beneficiary language of your IRAs, or if not, that it is the default option in the IRA document.

- Surviving spouse chooses wrong rollover option: Mary Lou rolls IRA assets from her deceased spouse to her own IRA to reduce the number of accounts. When might this be a bad idea? When Mary Lou then needs money from her IRA after the rollover. If she's under age 59 ½, the 10% early withdrawal penalty applies. To avoid the penalty, Mary Lou should keep husband Wayne's IRA in Wayne's name and access the money as his beneficiary. Here the 10% penalty does not apply. Later on, when Mary Lou reaches age 59 ½, she can roll Wayne's beneficial IRA over to her own IRA as the 10% penalty no longer applies.

SUMMARY

IRAs are the big elephant in the retirement living room. Tax laws governing IRAs are constantly evolving. Consequently, mistakes can and do happen frequently. The list I've presented is by no means comprehensive. But remember above all that many of these IRA planning mistakes, like missing the 60-day rollover deadline, can flatline your IRA. I suggest you not take anything for granted when transacting business with your IRAs. Seek competent assistance before you act to avoid making that unintentional, but irrevocable, IRA mistake.

REFERENCES

1. Rudzinski KR. Avoid common IRA planning mistakes. *Primary Care Optometry News.* 2005;10(5).
2. Choate N. *Life and Death Planning for Retirement Benefits.* Boston, MA: Ataxplan; 2006.

4

Planning for Income Disasters

"What would your financial world look like today
if you had become permanently disabled yesterday?"

I had just finished playing one of my best rounds of golf when an emergency text message hit my cell phone from the spouse of a near and dear doctor client-friend. I immediately called back and discovered, from Linda's tearful explanation, that her husband, Brad, age 55, had been rushed to the hospital, diagnosed with a life-threatening pulmonary embolism. He was recovering, but his professional work life as a doctor would forever be altered, as his condition most likely would impair his income-earning potential from that point on.

Linda's call to me that day was personal, as she and Brad were dear friends of 30 years, but it was also partly business. She, Brad, and I had met many times in the past to discuss and implement various risk management items. Fortunately, we had planned for this type of income disaster many years earlier, hoping that it might never happen but expecting that it could. There's always the temptation to believe that serious accidents or debilitating sicknesses only happen to the "other guy." There's always the excuse that statistics are just statistics—until you become one of them. But "stuff happens" whether or not we like it and whether or not we are prepared. Brad and Linda were prepared. What about you? Are you guilty of insuring your golden eggs, but neglecting yourself—the goose?

Disability Statistic

Your chances of dying from hypertension have decreased by 73%, but your likelihood of becoming disabled from that same hypertension has increased by 70%.

Rudzinski K. *The Physician's Guide to*
Avoiding Financial Blunders (pp 57-74)
© 2009 SLACK Incorporated

Brad returned to work about 6 weeks after his disability began but was able to work only about 20 to 25 hours a week. His physical stamina was low, and his mental attitude toward his work was even lower. He just couldn't keep up.

However, financially, Brad did not suffer the economic setback you might imagine. He was able to maintain a reasonable standard of living despite his ongoing partial disability. Brad's partners managed to cover his patient load, but Brad's allocated portion of the office overhead expenses were fully paid by his overhead expense coverage. Brad's portion of the business loan carried by the practice was countered by his specialized coverage for that type of expense. Moreover, should Brad become permanently disabled—which he did—the stock purchase portion of their buy-sell is funded and ready to implement. Lastly, while totally disabled, Brad knows that his 401(k) plan will continue to be funded despite having no earned income to validate it.

Disability Statistic
In the last 10 minutes, 390 Americans became disabled.

All in all, Brad, Linda, and his partners, though wishing and hoping Brad would fully recover someday, were at least grateful for the time and money they had spent previously to prepare for this eventuality. They had acted when everyone was healthy and productive to avoid the income disaster that surely would have taken place but for the risk planning they had completed well in advance. The story of Brad is a true story though I've changed some details.

If you had been Brad last October, could you face such an uncertain future with the same degree of confidence and financial certainty? If yes, you are to be congratulated. At some moment in the past, you thought about this danger of lost income, and you did something about it. But let me ask you, when was the last time you took out those policies, dusted them off, and reviewed what is in them? When did you last sit down with your insurance specialist to make absolutely certain, for example, that your level of coverage is adequate based on today's salary and bonus? When did you last dissect your group long-term disability or association coverage to ascertain where its strengths lie and where its weaknesses lurk? If it's been several years or longer, then your chances of incurring an "income disaster" are building, like in a pressure cooker.

If you said "no," then you may find this chapter especially enlightening and informative. However, my goal is not to just educate you. I am hoping that you will use the information to take action now to plug the gap and protect your income-earning potential. Your future income is not some protected right, owed to you now. You must work to produce and enjoy that income. If you can't work, the income is never actualized. The truth is that at age 35, if you are a man, you are 4.1 times more likely to be disabled before age 65 than you are to die. At age 45, it's 4.4. For a 50-year-old male, once disabled, the average duration of the disability is 50 months. For females, it's even longer. Are you financially prepared for this possibility?

TABLE 4-1

ODDS OF A LONG-TERM DISABILITY

YOUR AGE	YOUR APPROXIMATE ODDS	AVERAGE DURATION
30	1 in 3	32 months
40	3 in 10	42 months
50	5 in 22	50 months
60	1 in 10	54 months

Action Step

Make sure you understand how your policies define "total disability" and make note of any internal coverage limits like a 24-month limitation for disabilities caused by mental and nervous disorders. Be satisfied that you know how your standard of living will be replaced if that dreaded accident or sickness finally occurs.

I'd like to pose the following question: If you could insure only one, which would it be—the goose or its golden eggs? You are the goose. The golden eggs are what you can buy with the income you produce (ie, your house, cars, jewelry, vacation home, childrens' educations, etc). You insure your home, your cars, etc, namely all the eggs. But have you fully insured the goose—you—who creates those things? Think about this for a moment. In the last 20 years, deaths due to the "big three" (cancer, heart attack, and stroke) have gone down significantly. But disabilities due to those same three are up dramatically. Things that used to kill now disable.

What is your potential loss? At age 30, making a salary of $150,000 growing at 5% per year, by age 65, you'll earn over $13.5 million. A 40 year old will earn over $7.1 million. But fall off a ladder and become permanently disabled, then "poof," just like that, all that money is gone, never to be recovered. If you protect the eggs but not the goose, you've got it backwards.

Lastly, if you work in a multi-physician practice, the odds of one of you becoming disabled go up dramatically (Table 4-2).

Whether you are a sole practitioner or a multi-physician practice, when reviewing and purchasing disability insurance, you ought to be asking the following questions I hear over and over again by disabled doctors. Is this the best coverage I could have? How ironclad is my policy? Are there limitations or exclusions that will hamper my collecting benefits or reduce the amount I get? If I come back to work, will my benefits stop? And on and on.

Here's the bottom line: When you become disabled and the reality of the moment hits you hard in the gut, your perspective about your income protection changes dramatically. I know this because I've sat with disabled doctors who by their words and actions at the time of their disability taught me what really matters, and that is the quality of the coverage, not the cost of the premium. Saving premium dollars by creating holes, gaps, and contractual weaknesses hardly matters come claim time. At that

TABLE 4-2

PERCENTAGE ODDS OF A DISABILITY IN A GROUP LASTING ONE YEAR OR LONGER

AGE	NUMBER IN GROUP				
	1	2	3	4	5
25	11.67	21.98	31.09	39.13	46.23
30	11.34	21.40	30.31	38.22	45.22
35	10.98	20.75	29.45	37.19	44.09
40	10.50	19.90	28.31	35.84	42.58
45	9.83	18.70	26.69	33.90	40.40
50	8.83	16.88	24.21	30.90	37.00
55	7.24	13.96	20.19	25.97	31.33
60	4.62	9.02	13.21	17.22	21.04

moment, you want the best and what that "best" will do for yourself, your family, your practice, and your partners. Nothing else matters.

Disability Statistic

In the home, a fatal injury occurs every 16 minutes and a disabling injury every 4 seconds.

In the landscape of disability insurance, the best coverage is the personal disability contract, or PDI as we'll call it. It is without a doubt the kind of coverage you want in effect when you become disabled. Only a dozen or so carriers still write PDI and only a handful among those offer all of the exceptional policy provisions outlined below (ie, those you ought to have).

My intention for the rest of this chapter is to enumerate the common yet important provisions of the best PDI contracts, as well as practice/business disability contracts, so when considering such coverage you will have a better handle on what to ask for, or what to look for in your existing contracts when you conduct your disability "fire drill." Unfortunately, we can't cover everything here. There is, however, a pretty good 36-page booklet you can access online at http://principal.com/insurance/ind/from-heretosecurity/index.htm (on the right, under "Get Started Now," click on "Guide to Disability Income Insurance). Download the guide and use it to better understand your need for disability insurance. Then contact your insurance specialist to conduct your disability "fire drill" not only for your personal coverage but also for all those disability contracts, such as practice overhead and buy-sell disability, that your practice carries or should be carrying.

Planning Pointer

If you do not know a disability specialist, e-mail me at
bookspublishing@slackinc.com and I'll help locate one for you in your area.

Disability Statistic

Nearly half of the 1 million Americans who filed for bankruptcy protection in 1999 did so after being sidelined by an unexpected illness or injury.

PERSONAL DISABILITY INSURANCE CONTRACTS

The foundation of your disability income protection starts with PDI. But this is not always self-evident to medical professionals. Why? Because most doctors belong to their specialty association, and most medical associations offer their members some form of group LTD coverage. As a result, many doctors own—or better said, rent—this limited form of disability income protection. Group LTD is also offered by individual medical practices, especially those with 10 or more employees and by hospitals and other large medical providers for all of their employees.

If you are a sole practitioner or a multi-physician practice, your disability protection might look like any of the following: 1) only group or association LTD, 2) a basic amount of PDI and a large piece of group or association LTD, 3) a major commitment to PDI with only a small portion of group or association LTD, or 4) all PDI and no other coverage. I suppose I should add a fifth scenario, namely, the rare doctor who has no disability coverage at all. The more PDI you have in force at the time of a claim, generally, the better off you will be. That said, group or association coverage is better than none at all, so I'm not bashing such coverage. In fact, like an oncologist client of mine, it may be the only kind you can get if you have one or more medical conditions that prevent you from qualifying for PDI. I tackle group and association LTD briefly later on in this chapter. Right now though let's outline the things you need to know about the PDI contract.

GUARANTEED RENEWABLE AND NONCANCELLABLE (OFTEN CALLED "NON-CAN")

These twin features are usually present in every quality PDI product. Combined, they assure you as the insured that the insurance carrier can never raise the premiums on your policy (unless you add benefits), usually to age 65, and that the insurance company cannot cancel the policy except for nonpayment of premiums, or modify its terms and conditions in any way (except for fraud).

OCCUPATIONAL CLASSIFICATIONS

Insurance companies determine rates and coverages based on a system of occupational classifications. This is especially true for medical specialties. Generally speaking, doctors practicing invasive medicine will be rated slightly lower (ie, more costly and with certain limitations) than those who do not. Surgeons are rated lower than non-surgical doctors even in the same specialty, like cardiology, osteopathy, and ophthalmology. Nurses too face differing rates and benefit limits depending on whether they are RNs working in a doctor's office, LPNs working anywhere, or degreed nurse practitioners. So be careful not to come to a false conclusion about rates your buddy Dr. Jack the noninvasive cardiologist got compared to yours as an invasive cardiologist, all other things being equal.

MONTHLY BENEFIT LIMITS

Though individual insurance carriers may differ slightly, you can obtain disability coverage with a single carrier up to about 60% to 65% of your earned income (see tax issues next), to a maximum of $10,000 to $20,000/month. Some surgical specialties are often limited to the lower end of the range, but we're seeing more and more carriers raise the limit from $10,000 to $15,000. However, carriers may permit higher limits in participation with another carrier. For example, you already have $5000/month coverage with company "A." You want maximum coverage but want it from company "B," which has a monthly benefit limit of $10,000. Are you only able to get another $5000/month from "B"? Perhaps. But "B" may allow for all $10,000 monthly benefits if it accepts participation with another carrier up to $15,000/month. In that case, "B" would issue $10,000 to give you a total of $15,000/month.

There are several items that may impose additional limits on the amount of disability coverage you can obtain. The following is a partial list:

- Unearned income: High unearned income that would be undisturbed during a disability limits available coverage. This includes interest, dividends, capital gains, rents, royalties, alimony, etc.

- Bonus income: Most carriers permit bonuses to count as insurable income if the bonus schedule has been in place for 2 years or more.

- Net worth: Some carriers won't issue disability coverage if net worth exceeds some figure like $10 million. Alternatively, coverages may be limited to less than an age-65 benefit period.

- Retirement plan contributions: Some carriers permit all or a portion of retirement plan contributions made on behalf of the insured to be added to salary as insurable income.

- LLC/S-Corp Profits: Some carriers completely exclude this "income" as unearned income, while some permit a portion to be counted.

- Taxation: See below limits based on taxable or tax-free benefits at disability.

- State limitations: Some states like California and Florida limit the amount of monthly benefit by law. The limit is a lowered limit compared to other states.

- New professionals and dental students: Regardless of income, younger doctors and dentists may be given higher monthly benefits than their incomes might ordinarily allow. For example, with one major carrier, first-year physicians can get $4500/month; residents (including dental), $3500/month; first-year optometrists, $2,000/month; senior medical and dental students, $2100/month. Each carrier has its own allowances, and these change from time to time.

PREMIUM TAX STRUCTURE CAN INFLUENCE PERMISSIBLE BENEFITS

The IRS can tax either the premiums you pay (ie, you pay with after-tax dollars) or the benefits you may receive at the time of disability. It's your call. To the extent that you personally pay taxes on the premiums for the PDI, you can receive benefits tax free at the time of disability. To determine if and when you might have paid taxes on PDI premiums, the IRS now looks back 36 months. So, a last minute, year-of-disability switch will no longer succeed.

TAX PREMIUMS OR BENEFITS?

Should you take the tax deduction for the premiums and be taxed on the benefits or pay the premium with after-tax dollars resulting in tax-free benefits, if and when received?

This is a moot point if you are a sole proprietor, a partner in a partnership, a more than 2% shareholder in a multi-physician S-Corp, or LLC treated for tax purposes as an S-Corp. Your tax status is such that premiums paid on your behalf for disability insurance are fully taxable to you for the tax year in which they are paid. But for doctors who are employees in a C-Corp or are employees in a commercial or hospital setting, you do have a choice generally. For the former, C-Corp doctors, you can choose to be taxed on the PDI (and LTD if any) premiums. For the latter, at the hospital or commercial company, which would provide group LTD benefits and not PDI contracts, your corporate human resources (HR) has generally elected a default taxation mode. First, any part of the premium you pay is considered paid with after-tax dollars, and therefore benefits attributable to that premium are received tax free. Second, for any part of the group LTD premium paid by your employer, HR may have adopted a universal rule that either adds the cost to your taxable income or excludes the cost from your taxable income (ie, a true fringe benefit). Either way, you can ask to sign a waiver that treats your taxation differently from everyone else. For example, if the cost is not includable as income by rule, you can request that in your case, it be added to your taxable income. Your actual cost is only the taxes you'd pay on the included premium.

I almost always suggest that you pay taxes on the premium. It's better to pay a small amount of income tax on a small premium while you are healthy and making a good living than to pay income taxes on a large monthly benefit at a time when your income has stopped and you need every dollar from your policy benefits to pay bills and keep yourself afloat financially. Such was the case with a disabled 48-year old CT surgeon-client in Philadelphia who retired his scalpel due to tremors. He was able to collect $15,000/month tax-free disability payments to age 67 because he had wisely chosen to pay income tax on his $5500 annual premium. That's an insignificant tax on the premium for huge —$180,000 annually—tax-free benefits when most needed. Make this your choice too!

> ## Planning Pointer
>
> Check with your HR department in a hospital or commercial setting, or with your CPA in a solo or multi-physician practice to set up the taxation of your disability premiums in the manner you select in order to receive benefits in the manner you desire. Do not pay for your group LTD through a cafeteria plan or Section 125 plan with before-tax dollars as that negates the tax-free receipt of benefits if you become disabled.

A last point about taxation and disability benefits. If you are to receive benefits tax free, disability carriers will adjust downward the amount of coverage they offer you. Here's why. You live in Los Angeles and earn $20,000/month. From that, you net $12,000 after all federal, FICA, and state and local taxes are accounted for. If you could buy a $12,500 monthly disability benefit that would be tax free when you became disabled, you might have less of an incentive to return to work (at least that's how the insurance carriers see it). As a result, carriers will lower the amount of monthly benefit you can purchase.

ELIMINATION PERIOD
(ALSO KNOWN AS "WAITING PERIOD")

The elimination period in disability insurance is sometimes misunderstood. It does NOT mean how long you've got to wait after you purchase the insurance before it becomes effective. The elimination period, or "waiting period," is the time interval after you become disabled (according to the definition of disability in your contract) before the benefits begin to be paid. It is most often described as the period of "self-insurance" before benefits commence.

Elimination periods are ordinarily 30, 60, 90, 180, and 365 days. Disability benefits are always paid in arrears. This means that benefits under a 90-day elimination period would not be payable until after 120th day, or the end of the month after a 90-day wait.

> ## Planning Pointer
>
> Although carriers permit short elimination periods, I've found the most cost-efficient elimination period to be 90 days in a PDI. Shorter EPs are very expensive; longer ones do not provide enough premium savings. For business overhead expense (BOE) coverage, EPs of 30 or 60 days are not uncommon.

BENEFIT PERIOD

The "benefit period" defines how long benefits will be paid, assuming continued disability, once benefits begin. Benefit length is determined by you when you purchase the coverage. Carriers normally have available a 5-year benefit period, benefits payable to age 65 (or to normal retirement age [NRA], such as 66 or 67), and lifetime benefits. Obviously, the longer the benefit period, the more costly the coverage will be. With lifetime benefits, coverage can extend beyond age 65 or 66/67, whichever is your benefit limit, but the monthly benefit is reduced after the end of your regular benefit period depending on when your disability commenced. Some carriers reduce the lifetime benefit by 10% for each year your disability starts after age 55; for others, it's 5% after age 45. For example, your monthly benefit is $10,000 to age 65 and you've got the age 55/10% per year lifetime benefit. You become disabled at age 60. You get your $10,000/month to age 65, then a lifetime benefit of $5000 for the rest of your life. The lifetime benefit amount was reduced 10% per year since your disability began at age 60, or 5 years beyond age 55.

DEFINITION OF TOTAL DISABILITY

The definition of "total" disability is one of the most critical elements of the policy. It's what will ultimately define whether you collect full benefits or any benefits.

The best definition is referred to as an "own occupation," or simply "own occ" definition of disability. The definition varies by carrier, but ordinarily reads something like this, "Total disability is defined as the inability, due to sickness or accident, to perform the substantial and material duties of your occupation, and you are under the care of a physician." Said another way, if you cannot perform your main duties as a doctor/surgeon/etc and you are under the care of a physician, you are considered totally disabled and are therefore eligible to collect total disability benefits once you have satisfied the elimination period.

"Your occupation" is usually defined to mean the occupation you are working in at the time of your disability. Some carriers will issue what is called a "specialty letter," which further defines your occupation as, for example, a "cardiothoracic surgeon." Thus, if your disability prevents you from performing those "substantial and material duties" required of you as a CT surgeon, then you would be considered totally disabled.

What's important here with the "own occ" definition of disability is that you could return to work in another occupation that does not encompass the duties of your prior occupation, and your monthly disability benefits for total disability would not be affected.

The insurance carrier cannot force you to go back to your prior occupation. Your personal physician makes that determination initially, but the carrier does reserve the right in most disability contracts to have you examined at some point by their own doctor(s). In many cases, they do.

Planning Pointer

I strongly recommend the purchase of the "own occ" definition of disability by doctors. When disabled, you certainly want to know you have the best coverage you could have bought, not the cheapest. This is where the quality of the coverage originates.

By the way, this issue of the "own occ" definition of disability is one of the main differences between a PDI and group LTD. No matter how you slice it, the group LTD disability is not a true "own occ" definition, even with so-called specialty riders available in group LTD.

Don't be misled by sales material that seems to imply that the group or association LTD contract contains true "own occ" language. If you are not sure, ask your broker to explain what you have. It's better to know this before a disability occurs than afterward when all you care to know is "do I have the best coverage possible?"

RESIDUAL (PARTIAL) DISABILITY

Briefly, "residual" disability is a partial disability formula. If you return to work in your previous occupation, and suffer a loss of income greater than 20% to 25% but less than 75% to 80%, you will continue to receive disability payments. The amount of those payments will be roughly equal to your monthly benefit for total disability multiplied by the percentage of lost earnings. So, for example, if you return to work earning only 40% of your indexed pre-disability earnings (ie, a 60% loss of earnings), you will receive 60% of your monthly benefit. It's basically that simple. Some carriers will pay 50% of the monthly benefit for up to 6 months even if the lost earnings are less than 50%.

Planning Pointer

You always want to make sure you have a "residual" disability benefit added to your policy. Ask for it by name.

RETURN-TO-WORK PROVISION

The better contracts will contain a special "return-to-work" provision that covers the following contingency: you've been out of work entirely for 18 months; you are now no longer totally disabled so you come back to your practice but suffer a complete or near complete loss of income because all or most of your patients have gone elsewhere. In that case, the "return-to-work" provision will provide for continued disability payments for a period of time, maybe 6 or 12 months, giving you time to rebuild your patient base.

COST OF LIVING ADJUSTMENT

If you never received an increase in your monthly benefits when disabled, the purchasing power of your monthly benefit would decrease over time due to inflation. So, I advise including a cost-of-living adjustment (COLA) rider to your PDI. Some COLA rider increases are based on increases in the CPI, up to a maximum annual increase such as 3% or 6%. Other COLA riders increase benefits by a stated percentage regardless of the annual CPI. Some will limit the increases to maximums like 200% of the original benefit amount, and some others are unlimited. The more benefits are likely to go up during disability, the more costly the rider will be.

Planning Pointer

If federal budget deficits continue at a record pace, inflation may come back with a vengeance, so I'd suggest that you avoid a COLA rider with a lifetime cap. The unlimited COLA, though slightly more expensive, may be your best friend at claim time.

Most group and association LTD plans will not include a COLA, but if they do, it will usually be a fixed percent, like 3%, and only for a specific time period, like 5 or 10 years. But having some COLA is better than none even if it does have some limitations.

FUTURE INSURABILITY OPTION

It's been said that disability premiums only pay for your insurance; it's your health that buys it. So, obtaining coverage always requires good health when you apply. If your income skyrockets and you want to buy more coverage, but your health has regressed, you might not be able to qualify for any further monthly benefits. That's where a future insurability option (FIO) is most valuable.

Purchasing this option, usually available to age 50, allows you to increase your coverage at various specified ages (or annually) with no medical underwriting. Financial underwriting still applies (ie, you must have increased income to warrant higher monthly benefits).

Your policy may contain another form of FIO, called the "automatic increase benefit" (AIB) and it increases your monthly benefit usually by 5% compounded annually for 5 years. No health or financial underwriting is required. Your premium increases automatically too to accommodate the increasing monthly benefits. I believe this rider is valuable. If it's not priced into the quotes you've obtained, then ask if it can be included.

Planning Pointer

Make sure you add some FIO to your contract at issue to lock in your current health status as your future income increases. You will be delighted you did, especially if your income increases but your health deteriorates.

GRADUATED VERSUS LEVEL PREMIUM SCHEDULE

The premium for most PDI contracts is locked in at the age you purchase it. However, some carriers permit the use of a graduated premium that reduces costs for perhaps 10 years or longer compared with the higher level premium. Later on the graded premium exceeds the level premium but the lower, earlier premiums may help younger doctors better afford the coverage. Sometimes carriers will not allow certain benefits like the "automatic increase benefit" to be added when graduated premiums are selected.

PREMIUM DISCOUNTS

Most disability carriers will discount premiums when you buy 2 or more polices together, like a PDI and a practice overhead expense (POE). Additionally, when 3 or more members of the same practice buy PDIs, a 5% to 10% "list bill" discount is possible. Sometimes a 2-physician office will add an office manager to reach the 3-person requirement. It's normal to get a discount for nontobacco use, which can range from 5% to as much as 20% depending on the type of disability policy purchased. Good health discounts, called "preferred" rates, are also available.

Planning Pointer

When planning to insure your income, always maximize benefits under PDI contract first. Once in place, then you could layer on group or association LTD as available. Why this way? Once your PDI coverage is in place, it can never be cancelled or modified by the insurance carrier. If you superimpose group or association LTD over top of the PDI, and your total monthly benefits exceed 60% to 65% of your income, you can usually collect from both (check your group/association plan provisions to see if there is an offset for PDI—usually there is none). On the other hand, if you start with group or association coverage first, that coverage will count to some degree or entirely against you in determining how much PDI you can purchase. If given the choice, always start with PDI.

GROUP LONG-TERM DISABILITY

Group LTD should not act as a pure substitute for PDI. Group LTD is not a true "own occ" contract, the residual coverage is not as strong, a COLA adjustment is usually absent, and monthly benefits are offset by social insurance and other income items. Further, group LTD may contain limitations like 2 years for disabilities caused by certain outpatient mental and nervous disorders or strictly from self-reported symptoms. However, you may have no choice as group LTD coverage is provided by the hospital or other health care provider where you work, and some type of coverage is better than none at all.

If you have a multi-physician practice and employ 10 or more employees (including doctors), then you can design an effective group LTD plan to complement your PDI coverage. For example, for a higher premium, you can add a COLA benefit and remove the 2-year limitation for mental and nervous disorders. Additionally, you can make the LTD coverage selective, covering only doctors (and maybe key staff).

If you are uninsurable for PDI, you may be able to add group LTD without detailed individual underwriting. Check with your broker about this use of group LTD for larger groups.

By complementing or supplementing PDI coverage, group LTD can significantly raise your coverage limits to a higher monthly maximum. So, for example, a cardiologist eligible for only $15,000/month benefits under a PDI could perhaps add an extra $10,000 to $15,000/month of coverage through group LTD, assuming 10 or more total employees in the practice.

If the group LTD is in place first, however, only a small amount of PDI may be purchased, if any, over top of the group LTD. For example, carriers may issue up to 70% to

80% of income in a "combo plan" if the benefits are taxable. So, if group LTD covers 60% of income, then a small PDI may be possible up to the 70% to 80% limit. If the benefits are to be structured as tax free, then the 70% to 80% maximum may not be allowed.

Planning Pointer

Remember, you can ask for employer LTD premiums paid on your behalf to be taxed to you, thus rendering the benefits tax free when received.

ASSOCIATION LONG-TERM DISABILITY

Association LTD coverage is group LTD. In my experience, association LTD is designed to be cheap to attract members. As a result, the contractual language and benefits of association LTD leave a lot to be desired.

Generally, there's no COLA, no "own occ," limited monthly benefits, and a 2-year limitation of disabilities caused by mental and nervous disorders, among other things, with association LTD. There may be exceptions with certain association plans, and your own association plan may be that exception, but the majority of these plans are fraught with coverage gaps.

You get what you pay for. Association group LTD is cheap, and cheap is not what you want to have as your main source of income protection. It can serve you well as a supplemental plan over top of your PDI insurance, but, given the choice, making it your primary source of disability income may be a decision you'd regret when you go to file a claim.

Planning Pointer

I strongly suggest you get out your association LTD certificate and review what you have. By this I mean the contractual provisions as much as the obvious monthly benefit and premium cost. Call your association insurance carrier and ask if there are any other details they can send you. Know what you have before you need it.

BUSINESS/PRACTICE OVERHEAD INSURANCE

Besides individual planning for income protection, Brad's practice had also taken precautions to insure each doctor for overhead expense coverage.

So, Brad's share of the fixed overhead expenses, excluding his own salary or bonus payments, was covered under a practice overhead expense insurance (POE) policy. Examples of includable expenses would be staff salaries, rent, CPA fees, utility costs, etc. Fixed overhead was $24,000/month. Each doctor had purchased $8000/month of POE. Thus, when Brad went out on disability, his share of the expenses was covered. His 2 partners, despite having to work longer hours to cover Brad's absence, at least didn't have to foot the bill for his share of overhead costs.

The elimination period for BOE/POE should depend on the strength or weakness of accounts receivable. If receivables are collected within 60 days, then a 30-day waiting period could be used for the POE. Recall that benefit payments are made in arrears, so money needed around the 60th day requires a 30-day elimination period. Each practice should gear their POE to its particular needs. Longer elimination periods like 60, 90, and 180 days serve to reduce premiums.

Typical benefit lengths in POE are 12, 18, and 24 months. There's no rule of thumb here; each situation governs its own coverage needs. Select the benefit length that works for you.

Some rider benefits such as residual disability, FOI, or COLA can be purchased. COLAs are not practical due to the short-term nature of the coverage.

Unlike most types of disability coverage, the premiums for a POE policy can be deducted for income tax purposes; the benefits then will be taxable at the time they are paid. However, since the money received from the policy is used to cover deductible overhead expenses, the receipt of policy benefits is considered a "tax wash."

At the time of purchase, on the application itself, you must list the approximate overhead expenses attributable to yourself. Once coverage is issued, should a claim occur, the carrier requires an itemized list of overhead expenses, usually produced by the practice's CPA, to justify the benefits paid. So, if Brad's expenses are $6000/month, only $6000 monthly will be paid as a claim. Since Brad had an $8000/month policy benefit, the $2000/month of unused benefit remains in the policy for later distribution. If money remains in the POE bucket at the end of the benefit period, the benefit period is extended until all monies have been disbursed.

Planning Pointer

POE coverage can be extremely valuable. For the solo practitioner, policy benefits may mean that he or she has an office to come back to and a staff still in place after a period of total or partial disability. For the multi-physician practice, the POE payments mean that the healthy doctors need not work themselves "to the bone" to cover expenses as well as maintain profitability.

RETIREMENT PLAN DISABILITY PROTECTION

Retirement plan disability (RPD) coverage is the new kid on the block. Here's how it works: You must be totally disabled to collect. You can buy disability benefits up to the permissible 2009 contribution limit for retirement plans, currently about $4090/month. When you become disabled, the policy benefits are paid to a taxable irrevocable trust set up by the insurance company. You control the investing of the trust assets. The earnings on the accumulated deposits from the insurance may be taxable to you annually. However, the monthly deposits from the insurance are received by the trust tax free because you pay the premiums with after-tax dollars. The benefit length is usually to age 65.

If you are totally disabled, this coverage may be your retirement savior. It will accumulate assets for you which otherwise would have been nonexistent since you had no earnings and couldn't contribute to a qualified retirement plan. Additionally, if you have little or no earned income over a large number of years, your monthly Social

Security benefit would most likely be minimized as well because it's unlikely you would qualify for Social Security disability benefits. So, ask your broker to investigate this new kind of disability coverage. Only a few carriers offer it, but more are coming on board each year.

Planning Pointer

RPD coverage can be added in addition to normal benefit limits so you can super-impose it over top of your PDI coverage, thus closing the gap between your income and your lower PDI coverage limits. For high-income specialties with low disability income limits, this added coverage could be extremely valuable to you. Be sure to check it out.

BUY-SELL COVERAGE

Many buy-sell arrangements in medical practices take the form of a limited buy-sell entity or cross-purchase event with the majority of the selling partner's per share value coming from a deferred compensation agreement. Provisions are made for the partner's share of accounts receivable (A/R) and in many cases for a form of tax equality since the deferred compensation arrangement favors the remaining partners by being income tax deductible to the practice. The departing partner, in other words, gets compensation payments that are fully taxable. The remedy may be to "gross up" the deferred comp payments so that the after-tax amount received by the departing partner is boosted while the payments continues to be tax deductible to the practice.

It's not common knowledge that the portion that represents the direct buyout of the partner's shares can be funded with special disability insurance should the event triggering the buyout be the total disability of the partner. This is similar to using life insurance to fund a death buyout.

Buy-sell disability insurance is common in commercial businesses to provide the dollars to complete the disability terms of a buy-sell agreement. It is useful in medical practices as well depending on the significance of the buy-sell portion of the buyout relative to the deferred comp portion. The larger the buyout portion, the more useful the funding dollars become.

Briefly, buy-sell disability insurance is written to reflect the terms of the buyout as closely as possible. It can be written as a lump sum benefit, an installment benefit of 2 to 5 years, or a combination of both. It covers total disability only and generally has longer elimination periods to choose from (eg, 12, 18, 24, and 36 months) to match the "triggering event" (ie, the disability buyout). Premiums paid by either the practice or copartners are nondeductible, nonincludable as income to the insured partner, and the benefits are income tax free as received from the policy. Lastly, the insurance can be written before the buy-sell agreement is put in place (but most carriers require the agreement to be in place at the time of the claim).

Planning Pointer

If you have never considered buy-sell disability coverage in your practice, ask your broker to get some sample quotes (this coverage has a limited universe of insurance carriers). Rule it in or rule it out, but getting facts and figures allows you to make an informed decision. If you do not have a disability specialist, email me at bookspublishing@slackinc.com and I'll help you locate one in your area.

SUMMARY

What would your financial world look like today if you had become permanently disabled yesterday? Would your standard of living be destroyed? Would your retirement be devastated? Would your children's education be denied?

At age 40, you have a 3 in 10 chance of suffering a disability before age 65. At age 30, it's 1 in 3. What have you done about it? If standing where you are, you had a 33% chance of being struck by lightning, would you move? In the final analysis, if you say you can't afford the disability insurance, how can you afford the disability? Remember, statistics are just statistics until you become one of them. Act now to get your disability house in order.

5

Protecting Your Assets From Predators and Creditors
The Basics

"What's mine is mine; what's yours is negotiable."

It is Saturday morning, and there is a knock at your front door. You open it and find yourself standing face to face with a nightmare—the local sheriff serving you with papers announcing the filing of a lawsuit against you. Whether it be for malpractice, negligence, tort liability, or something else, the feeling of dread spreads throughout the pit of your stomach. You wonder in a panic if your hard-earned assets are protected from a worst-case scenario, and you sense that it may be too late to protect them now that the legal "cat" is out of the bag.

Fortunately, today is Friday, and the knock on the door is so far silent. Today you can do something to protect some or all of those accumulated assets. Have you already addressed this issue with your estate attorney or other legal counsel? Your insurance specialists? If yes, that's great, but let me ask you how long ago that was? When was the last time you reviewed that plan? Conversely, if you have not specifically addressed the issue of protecting your hard-earned assets, what are you waiting for? When you hear the knock, it's too late.

Is it possible to build a protective moat around your asset "castle," to shelter your assets from those creditors and predators who seek to reduce or eliminate your net worth by enriching theirs? Fortunately, various state and federal laws act as buffers, and insurance protection can offer additional support. These are basic. But beyond that, there are other asset protection strategies you can employ; some simple yet effective, others more complex and costly. The bottom line is that no one strategy is a panacea. In fact, most people of means incorporate several into their overall plan to protect their wealth. According to Peter S. Gordon, an estate attorney in Wilmington, DE, "Effective asset protection is really done on a state-by-state, asset-by-asset basis. There are no shortcuts, and no one suit fits all."[1] In other words, a successful defense against determined creditors may involve the use of several asset protection strategies, not just one, employed together as your complete defense team.

Rudzinski K. *The Physician's Guide to Avoiding Financial Blunders (pp 75-90)*
© 2009 SLACK Incorporated

Writers of "asset protection" articles for doctors often limit their focus to issues of malpractice in patient care. I will touch on some of those throughout, but malpractice issues are only one area of liability problems you may be forced to address in your lifetime. There are other predators out there who, given the right circumstances, may seek to replace you as the owner of your house, bank accounts, brokerage accounts, or A/R. In fact, it may be a family member or next door neighbor who may materialize as your biggest threat. Even while you build up your complex fortifications against potential malpractice liabilities, these erstwhile innocent friends and family members can slip around your defensive Maginot Line to wreak havoc on your carefully laid asset protection plans.

That said, let's examine various asset protection arrangements that, if successfully implemented well before the knock at your door occurs, can build a wall of resistance against those forces potentially aligned against you and your personal and business balance sheet.

To understand how vast your potential exposure to liability issues may be, both professional and nonprofessional, attorneys Gideon Rothschild and Daniel S. Rubin, both recognized experts on asset protection, have compiled an audit checklist that summarizes the steps to take in assessing your risk level. According to attorney Rothschild, the checklist is "...intended to provide a good starting point...to identify issues and techniques that can be applied to...particular circumstances."[2] Generally, these initial steps are as follows:

- Determine the potential sources of liability. Classes of liability might be those of professional liability, creditor exposure, officer and director liability (hospital or otherwise), divorce, etc. Normally, you will need help with this step. Your estate attorney and liability insurance specialist(s) would be your sounding boards to identify the areas of personal and professional liability that may affect you, your family, and your business partners.

- Use simple and commonplace techniques before attempting to adopt complex and costly planning. Typically, the simplest defense is through the use of an adequate insurance "umbrella" such as homeowners, auto, umbrella liability, commercial risk, directors and officer's liability, disability, life, and long-term care (LTC). You may only need a "finger in the dike" instead of the complex and expensive fortress.

- Determine your solvency. Are there assets that can be successfully transferred out of the reach of your creditors? If so, move them away and give up control. What you no longer own may be safe if you plan well enough ahead.

- Review and maximize the creditor exemptions that are available under both federal and state statutes. States can vary greatly in their application of creditor protection, such as in homestead and life insurance statutes. Local counsel can best assist you with local laws, statutes, and regulations.

- Examine estate documents and business organization and documents/agreements to maximize creditor protection. Using trusts, LLCs, disclaimers, etc can aid in keeping predators at bay.

- Consider what sophisticated techniques are still needed and available based on individual circumstances. Complex trusts, including the use of foreign trusts, highlight this list of protection devices. Use only when needed.[2]

Action Item

I suggest you hold an "asset protection" fire drill with your estate attorney and insurance professionals to examine the checklist and to determine what specific risk exposures you currently have and decide how you will address them. Will you take a break from your busy patient load and make the call to set this up? If you don't, who will?

With this checklist as a starting point, let's look at specific examples of creditor risks and possible planning methods to defeat them. The vastness of the asset protection universe does not permit me to provide a detailed analysis of the entire matter, but your investment of time in reading this chapter will be well rewarded with practical, useful information.

Let's first define what we mean by "asset protection." Generally speaking, "asset protection" includes the establishment of as many barriers and obstacles in front of predators and creditors as possible, with the intent to legally and ethically protect your stable of assets from them. Asset protection is not—repeat, not—about committing fraud by hiding assets in the dark of night. Good asset protection is designed to discourage creditors from pursuing your assets by making the process as difficult as possible thereby either eliminating the threat or containing it to the smallest degree where it can be adjudicated by an insurance or other protection mechanism. According to attorney Roccy DeFrancesco, "To put it simply, plaintiff's attorneys will not waste time suing for million-dollar damages if there's little to recover."[3]

Action Item

Since "asset protection" is about "assets," my first suggestion is that you sit down and make a line-by-line detailed listing of all of your assets, those owned by your spouse, those jointly owned, and other assets where you have a beneficial or retained interest.

Your list may consist of items like:

- Your residence(s)
- Qualified retirement plans, IRAs, Roth IRAs, 403(b)s, 401(k)s
- Brokerage accounts, directly-owned mutual funds, stock, bonds, CDs
- Autos, boats, airplanes, motorcycles, other sports vehicles
- Vacation homes, rental properties
- Valuable collections, antiques, jewelry
- Checking accounts, savings accounts
- Life insurance policies, annuities, deferred compensation
- Ownership in your practice, LLC, etc, including C-Corp or S-Corp stock
- A/R in your medical practice
- Income from trusts
- Future expected inheritances to you and your spouse[3]

Your list may be more or less extensive, but it does represent your "castle," which needs a fortified defense around it.

Action Item

List (or look up) who owns each of these assets, specifically. Without these first 2 steps, you really can't begin to plan your protection strategies.

To use a football analogy, comprehensive asset protection is more akin to the development of an "offensive" strategy as compared to a "defensive" one. The reason is that you must undertake and complete your planning well before a lawsuit hits your doorstep. If the doorbell rings, it's too late. So, have you been consistent with regard to newly-acquired assets such as cars, jewelry, real estate, brokerage assets, etc (ie, those assets you acquire on an ongoing basis)? In other words, have you titled those assets according to a comprehensive planning strategy that provides maximum asset protection? Hopefully, you have. If not, your need for an asset protection "fire drill" may be long overdue.

All asset protection planning can be broken down into 2 main components:

1. Maximizing assets that are exempt from the claims of creditors

2. Transferring nonexempt assets into specially designed asset protection vehicles

The remainder of this chapter will enumerate and detail the most common and effective strategies to accomplish the first group of planning steps, creating exempt assets. In Chapter 6, we will finish the asset protection discussion with more complex arrangements.

CREATING EXEMPT ASSETS

Titling of Your Assets

You should now have a list of your assets and who owns them. A basic rule of asset protection is that if you own an asset, it can be confiscated by creditors. So, a simple yet effective device to shelter your assets would be to change the titling, asset-by-asset as needed, to someone else entirely, namely to your spouse or to yourself and your spouse jointly. For singles, this strategy generally has no practical application except if you choose to trust someone else with your property outright or in joint name. Most singles prefer not to do this.

According to New Jersey attorney Greg Klipstein, when considering jointly-owned titling of assets with your spouse, if you live in a common-law state, you should consider titling assets as "tenants by the entireties." This is a special form of joint ownership but only between spouses. It affords assets unlimited creditor protection as long as the joint tenancy exists. Thus, if your spouse were to die, the joint tenancy protection dies as well and the asset(s) formerly protected can be suddenly exposed to creditors. Additionally, the joint tenancy protection can fail if the judgment is filed against both of you jointly by the same creditor. Thus, if you own your car jointly, your jointly owned assets can be attached by creditors in a lawsuit involving that car. Conversely, if just one of you is sued, such as in a malpractice case, the jointly titled assets "by the entireties" can protect those assets from the reach of your creditors.

So, your first order of business is to see if assets are already titled "by the entireties," and if not, to consider changing that titling if joint tenancy is your desired ownership arrangement. Don't be fooled by assets titled as "joint tenants with right of survivorship" (JTWROS), thinking it's the same as "tenancy by the entireties." It is not. JTWROS ownership, like "by the entireties," permits nonprobatable, automatic passing of the asset to the survivor. However, it only provides limited asset protection to either joint tenant.

If the titling is silent as to which type of joint ownership is present, some states assume "by the entireties" while others assume JTWROS. If you check and are unsure, my suggestion is to specifically request the "by the entireties" moniker be inserted in the title of each asset you wish to treat as jointly held with your spouse.

So, listing or relisting assets as "tenants by the entireties" forms your first basic defense against creditors. Brokerage accounts, bank accounts, etc can also be listed as "by the entireties." However, if the property so titled is sold or otherwise disposed of (in addition to the death of one joint tenant as indicated above), the joint tenancy is severed and the creditor can take possession of the property to the extent of the judgment. In some states, judgments can be finite, such as in Delaware, according to Wilmington attorney Peter S. Gordon, where the limit is 10 years, after which the creditor would need to renew the judgment (personal communication, October 28, 2008).

One last point on "tenancy by the entireties." Asset protection specialists might warn that in second or third marriage situations, putting assets that were owned by one spouse only before the marriage into joint name may not be a good long-term idea. Why? Because such individually owned property is not "marital" property as long as it is not co-mingled with marital property or re-titled as joint property, whether in "tenancy by the entireties" or in JTWROS. As marital property, then, it becomes subject to equitable division in the event of divorce. In the end, your divorcing spouse may become your biggest creditor, and with 50% of marriages breaking up (higher for second and third marriages), you should give pause before converting nonmarital assets to marital assets before proceeding. This is not meant to be a disguised indictment of re-titling assets. To the contrary, doing so is highly effective, simple, and fast and recommended in many marital situations. But it can have repercussions later on, and that too needs to be kept in mind since your family situation and asset list are unique to you. The information in this chapter is only your guide; it is not the detailed solution that only a meeting with your estate attorney can produce.

In your asset-by-asset planning, you may determine that not all of your property should be held in joint name with your spouse. Perhaps some specific assets may be better placed in your spouse's sole name, assuming you are the doctor with the high-risk exposure. If you do this, then your wills and trusts would need to be revisited if those assets now owned outright by your spouse are not to revert to you once again if your spouse predeceases you. Also, planning sometimes may involve placing assets into the name of the spouse likely to die to take advantage of the stepped-up basis tax rules.

Is re-titling foolproof? Not really, but it's better than no planning at all. Solely owned property could be attached if the spouse holding title is the spouse getting sued. In this case, the ownership strategy would backfire. This is why asset protection is accomplished on an asset-by-asset basis, from simple to more complex so that exposures can be layered and defeated. For example, for liability purposes, many agents suggest that it usually makes most sense to have a car titled in the name of the person who primarily drives it. Doing so can avoid the other spouse in a liability claim.

Recall too that giving your spouse sole ownership can be problematic if your spouse later divorces you and claims the change of ownership represented a gift from you to your spouse with the corresponding irrevocable loss of its marital nature. Also, as writer Steve Leimberg suggests, when you give up your interest in property by re-titling, you need to make sure that you do not continue to control the use of that property. Otherwise, a good litigator could argue that you still maintained ownership in reality despite the re-titling to your spouse. As an example, if you personally sign for large withdrawals from a bank account that you assigned to your spouse, you may taint that asset in a lawsuit and validate a creditor's claim against you. The bottom line is to make sure assets re-titled to your spouse actually become your spouse's property.

For residents of community-property states (Arizona, California, Indiana, Louisiana, Nebraska, New Mexico, Texas, Washington, and Wisconsin), assets acquired during a marriage are considered "marital" assets and are subject to the claims of the other spouse's creditors, so that all community property assets are in essence at risk. This occurs even if the assets are titled in one name only. There are some exceptions to this rule, such as gifts, bequests, inheritances, and the like, which are permitted to remain as separate property unless co-mingled with marital assets at any time.

But all is not lost! It is possible to create separate property from community property and to enjoy the basic asset protection of separated property as discussed above. To do so, both spouses would need to sign a "transmutation" agreement that effectively severs the previous community-property arrangement.[4] The result is that community property can become the separate property of the nonphysician spouse to help shield that property from the creditor or malpractice claims of the physician-spouse.

Planning Action

To summarize, consider each of your assets, one by one, to determine the proper titling of those assets. Spouses can re-title assets as "joint tenants by the entireties." Physician-spouses may wish to re-title some assets in the name of the nonphysician spouse alone. Community property can be split up by means of a "transmutation" agreement.

Using Qualified Plans and IRAs

Qualified plans have both federal and state creditor protection. On the federal level, as early as in 1990, the US Supreme Court ruled that, outside of bankruptcy or a claim by a spouse or dependents, no creditor could attach retirement plan assets as long as they were protected under Employee Retirement Income Security Act of 1974 (ERISA). Then in 1992, the Supreme Court added bankruptcy protection to ERISA-qualified plan assets.

ERISA-qualified plans include the following: 401(k), defined benefit, defined contribution, profit-sharing, cash-balance, and 412(i)-defined benefit plans. Specifically, ERISA plans do not include IRAs (of all types) and Keogh plans, or a qualified retirement plan consisting of only yourself and your spouse (no other employees), such as a solo-401(k).

Additionally, nonqualified deferred compensation plans such as top-hat plans and excess benefit plans are not protected under ERISA. In fact, these plans purposely avoid ERISA protection, and specifically subject their assets to the claims of the company's creditors, according to Baltimore deferred comp specialist, Michael Nolan (oral communication, October 22, 2008).

Planning Pointer

For a comprehensive overview of ERISA protection, go to http://mosessinger. com/articles/files/protecting.htm. It traces cases involving ERISA plans, and offers a state-by-state chart of pension plan and IRA exemptions. Keep in mind that ERISA as federal law preempts state law.

Those assets in ERISA-qualified plans are sheltered under the most ironclad asset protection umbrella possible. So think about this. You may have been deliberately excluding employees from your qualified plan for financial reasons, but since the ERISA umbrella does not extend to qualified plans that include only you and your spouse, like solo-401(k)s, you may want to consider adding an employee to the plan for asset protection purposes.

Many people erroneously believe that IRAs, including SEP-IRAs and SIMPLE-IRAs, enjoy the same level of ERISA protection. They do not. Each state has regulations stipulating what level of IRA assets are protected and from whom. An increasing number of states fully exempt traditional IRA and Roth IRA assets from creditors (but see bankruptcy on next page). For a state-by-state IRA exemption chart, go to www.asset-protectionbook.com/state_resources.htm. If your state does not provide adequate IRA protection, and you participate in an ERISA-plan in your practice or with your employer (ie, hospital), then consider moving your IRA assets into that ERISA-qualified plan at work. This would have to be approved by the ERISA plan administrator. A typical requirement is that the IRA(s) consists only of money that had previously been removed from a prior ERISA-qualified plan, and that the IRA(s) contains no additions of personal IRA contributions. So, if the IRA monies have been co-mingled, often a rollover back to the ERISA-qualified plan will be denied.

As a corollary, if you live in a state that does not provide extensive IRA creditor protection, if you are leaving a practice, hospital, or other health care facility and you are allowed to keep your ERISA-qualified assets in the practice or company plan, then NOT rolling those monies out to an individual IRA may be preferable. If, on the other hand, you are forced to roll out your account balance when you leave or you decide that the ERISA plan does not meet your investment or other financial planning objectives or that asset protection is not a priority, then at least avoid commingling rollover monies with other personal IRA assets. Set up a new IRA that contains only ERISA-protected assets.

If you maintain a significant IRA account balance in an unprotected state, and you do not have the availability of an ERISA-protected plan, you may be able to create an ERISA plan by first establishing a family limited partnership (FLP) and becoming an employee of the FLP. The FLP can establish an ERISA plan into which you could roll your IRA account balance. Because of the large set-up and ongoing expenses of an FLP, use this planning tool only if you have a significant IRA account balance and you have reduced state protection, concludes Delaware CPA Thomas Shopa (oral communication, October 31, 2008). Moreover, this strategy is also more complex, so you should seek advice from your local tax and estate planning counselors before adopting it as they know your state laws and how they may impact the asset protection of your IRAs.

If you do not currently have an attorney to work with, here are 2 good Web sites to locate a qualified estate professional in your area: www.actec.org (American College of Trust and Estate Counsel) and www.naepc.org (National Association of Estate Planners & Councils).

Planning Pointer

To summarize, fund your ERISA-qualified plan(s) to the maximum because they are exempt from creditors and predators. In states with weak IRA protection statutes, consider rolling IRA assets from prior ERISA plans back into an ERISA-qualified plan. Do not commingle formerly ERISA-protected assets in your IRA with personal IRA assets, and especially do not add ongoing contributions to the IRA which contains formerly ERISA-protected assets.

In *bankruptcy* cases, the treatment of IRAs for creditor protection was enhanced in 2005 with the Bankruptcy Abuse Prevention and Consumer Protection Act of 2005 (the "Act"). While seemingly imposing a limit on the amount of IRA assets that could be sheltered from creditors, the Act actually expanded the amount of money taxpayers could protect.

Therefore, in *bankruptcy* cases, under the Act, IRAs enjoy an aggregate $1,000,000 exemption—not a "per account" amount—from creditors for "contributions and earnings." In reality, though, most large IRA balances are not the result of accumulated contributions and earnings, so for most taxpayers, this new limit of $1,000,000 actually increases prior limits. How is this so? According to national IRA specialist Ed Slott, CPA, it is highly unlikely that taxpayers will exceed the $1,000,000 exemption any time soon. The reason is that since 1975, when IRAs were first permitted, only a bit more than $80,000 of contributions (including catch-up contributions) have been permitted, assuming contributions were made each year to the maximum limit allowed.[5] So, even with earnings on those deposits, the accumulation within IRAs would not come close to the new $1,000,000 limit.

But if you have co-mingled your IRA with rollover ERISA-protected assets from a former employer plan, you've limited yourself greatly. How? Recall that those former ERISA-qualified assets enjoy unlimited protection under federal law while your personal IRA assets have the new $1,000,000 exemption limit in bankruptcy situations. So, suppose you have co-mingled a $750,000 ERISA-qualified rollover with a $250,000 personal IRA. Your $1,000,000 IRA assets are protected under the new Bankruptcy Law. However, any future growth in that co-mingled IRA may be exposed to bankruptcy creditors in those states where IRA creditor protection is limited. Had your rollover IRA been kept separate—in a "conduit" IRA—that $750,000 account balance would enjoy unlimited protection as an ERISA-protected asset, while your $250,000 personal IRA would enjoy a $1,000,000 exemption in a bankruptcy situation.

Planning Pointer

It's my guess that a large majority of readers will face this very situation as they begin retiring soon and roll assets out of their qualified plans, or leave current employment for another opportunity. If you work directly with a mutual fund house, the young adult voice on the 1-800 line may not know about commingling IRA assets and the asset protection that can be lost by doing so. In that case, it will be up to you to remember why that could be a bad idea.

Using Section 529 Education Accounts

Besides being excellent income tax-advantaged vehicles for college savings, Section 529 plans also offer outstanding protection against the claims of creditors. While states may differ, most allow the entire balance in Section 529 plans to be exempted from the grasp of cash-hungry creditors. So, it makes sense to stash as much away in such accounts as possible.

Each state limits contributions to any one child's account. For example, in my home state of Delaware, the 2009 limit per child is $320,000. In Florida, the limit is $341,000. Section 529 plans also benefit uniquely under federal gift tax laws. Ordinarily, you can gift only $13,000 to a single beneficiary annually. Amounts in excess of that limit may be subject to federal gift taxes currently if you have exceeded your $1,000,000 lifetime gift limitation. With Section 529 plans, however, you are permitted to make a single gift of $65,000 to a chosen beneficiary's Section 529 Plan, or five times the annual exclusion amount. In essence, you are pre-funding 5 years worth of gifts. As a result, in the 4 years following the $65,000 single gift you'd be precluded from making any further gifts to the same beneficiary, unless the annual gift exclusion rises due to inflation or new legislation.

Thus, for asset protection purposes, you can shelter significant dollars using the creditor protection of Section 529 plans. How "significant" are those dollars? Let's say, for example, you have 4 children, a lot of cash on hand, and you are in a high-risk specialty. The $13,000 annual exclusion applies to each beneficiary and to each donor. So you and your spouse together can make equal gifts to your children. Using the up-front 5-year allowance, $520,000 can be sheltered for your 4 children. The math is as follows: ([$13,000 x 5] x 4 x 2) = $520,000). A creditor's nightmare!

Be aware though that some states impose a time and dollar limitation on contributions to Section 529 plans for the purposes of the creditor exemption. For example, in Delaware, assets contributed to a qualified state tuition plan more than 365 days before a judgment is filed against the owner of the 529 plan are fully exempt from creditor's claims (10 Del. C. §4916). Assets contributed in the 365 days immediately before the judgment is filed are exempt, but only to the extent of the greater of $5000 or the average annual contribution made by the debtor-owner to the plan account for the 2 calendar years preceding the filing date of the judgment. So, the laws in your home state will govern the extent to which your late contributions to a 529 plan will be exempt from creditors. The Bankruptcy Act also imposes limits on contributions preceding the filing of a bankruptcy petition, so the Act needs to be consulted as well (limits within the Act are similar to the Delaware limit stated above). This state limitation for contributions made in the year before a judgment is filed is consistent with the notion that protection from creditors needs to be completed in advance of any claim and not in anticipation of nor with advance knowledge of a specific claim that is to be filed. For many of the states, a year serves that purpose for Section 529 plans.

In the Bankruptcy Act of 2005, only Section 529 plans for the benefit of the debtor's child, stepchild, grandchild, or step-grandchild are exempt from creditors. Thus, you can't shelter monies from bankruptcy creditors by setting up and funding Section 529 plans for your nieces, nephews, sons- and daughters-in-laws, etc.

Planning Action

If you are planning to fund your child's education and have set up or are contemplating setting up a Section 529 plan for that purpose, consider depositing as much as you can afford up to the amount the gift tax law permits and your state's Section 529 plan allows. Doing this assures that no creditor of yours can deprive your child or children (or grandchild or grandchildren) of his or her higher education opportunity. The Web site www.savingforcollege.com is generally considered the most comprehensive source for Section 529 information.

Life Insurance and Annuities

From the standpoint of protecting life insurance policies and annuity contract assets from creditors, state laws vary significantly. In most states, the death benefit payable to a spouse and/or dependent children of the policy owner is generally exempt from creditors under typical "spendthrift" provisions. This shelter is usually reserved for the proceeds of the insurance policy, assuming those proceeds are being held by the insurance company or some other vehicle such as a trust, but not necessarily for distributions from the proceeds to the beneficiaries.

It's not the same, however, for the cash surrender values within the policy or policies during the lifetime of the owner-insured. States vary greatly over the creditor treatment of policy cash values, from no creditor protection at all (Delaware) to complete shelter of all cash values during his or her lifetime (Texas and Florida).

Annuity contract values likewise receive varied treatment state by state, from full protection to none, with the middle ground being the amount of annuity cash value required to provide a certain amount of predetermined monthly benefit to the family (eg, $350/month as it is in Delaware).

Planning Pointer

For state laws on life insurance and annuity creditor protection, go to www.mosessinger.com/articles/files/creditprotec.htm, scroll for the article entitled, Creditor Protection for Life Insurance and Annuities. Additionally, check http://assetprotectionbook.com/state_resources.htm.

Insurance Protection

Professional Liability Coverage

The state where you practice imposes minimum liability limits on your malpractice coverage. This author assumes you are complying with those regulations and that you meet regularly with your agent or broker to review what limits are recommended to protect you and your practice from malpractice claims. The limits you carry and pay for vary based on whether you are considered a low-risk medical occupation such as a general practitioner or a high-risk specialty such as cardiothoracic surgery. Make sure your malpractice carrier is solvent. Avoid the temptation to save premium dollars by reducing limits or by purchasing coverage from unstable or sometimes even unidentifiable insurance carriers. Generally, having coverage with a substandard carrier may be the equivalent of "going bare" according to your state statutes. And that means the potential of losing the ability to go bankrupt to defeat creditors, as well as the possibility of forfeiting your medical license. Additionally, you may need to post sizable escrow. When changing carriers, make absolutely certain you notify both carriers if you have a potential patient "event" that has occurred, as failure to notify both may result in neither carrier having responsibility should the patient bring a lawsuit against you.[6]

Planning Pointer

According to Norristown, PA estate attorney David Schiller,[7] make sure you are individually named as an insured on your malpractice coverage, and that your professional association is also named. If your employer provides you with coverage, make sure you get a copy of the policy naming you as the insured. Also request that your employer's malpractice carrier and/or broker notify you in writing of a pending lapse in coverage due to nonpayment of premiums.

Umbrella Liability

Imagine waking up to the nightmarish news that your teenage daughter let her inebriated underage jerk-of-a-boyfriend drive your car, and he proceeded to drive through a red light, killing a single mom of 3 young toddlers. Besides the grief you'd feel for the now-orphaned youngsters, can you imagine your unbridled panic as you contemplate your financial future? Suppose you had gone "cheap" on your personal liability coverage by lowering the liability limits. Or perhaps you had put off the decision to add or increase the limits of an umbrella liability policy to your core of asset protection devices. You know the lawsuit is coming and you are not prepared for it. But it could be worse. Imagine the car was owned by your medical practice that consists of an unprotected partnership such that all partners as well as partnership assets are now on the hook as well. For you, a high-limit umbrella liability policy may have been your financial savior; for the partners and partnership, see the discussion in Chapter 6 on LLCs and other advanced protection devices.

So, when planning your asset protection "fire drill," make sure you have reviewed all elements of insured liability protection, such as unowned auto, uninsured motorist, personal umbrella liability, and separate policies, if necessary, for each property you or your spouse own. You should be carrying at least $3 to $5 million of personal umbrella liability coverage which at $250 to $300 per million is quite affordable... and wise.

Why purchase such large amounts of umbrella liability coverage? As your assets grow, your exposure builds. In Delaware, and maybe in your state too, there are special laws dealing with the liability of an adult for a minor driving an automobile. Delaware provides that an owner of a motor vehicle who knowingly permits a minor to drive the vehicle shall be jointly and severally liable (translated: you and your spouse are fully responsible) for ANY damages caused by the negligence of the minor (21 Del. C. Section 6101). That's how bad goes to worse!

CAVEAT: If you have elected to use the "joint tenants by the entireties" option for basic asset protection, then you do not want to co-own a vehicle that is principally driven by a child under the age of 18. If you do, then you may both be liable as the judgment against you as co-owners can be satisfied by assets you own jointly. This is why you should seek competent professional counsel on protecting your assets and review it often as circumstances surrounding your assets change, especially when you have teenage drivers at home.

Planning Pointer

Don't wait until after the doorbell rings to think about these liability issues and coverage; get to this now while you can.

Other Liability Issues

If you are serving on the Board of Directors of a hospital or health care facility involving peer review, hospital privileges, or other hospital matters, attorney David Schiller advises that you confirm in writing with the hospital that there is adequate director's and officer's liability coverage protecting you based on your activities on that Board.[6] Don't take someone's word for it. Request a copy of the policy showing you are a covered insured and the extent to which you are covered.

Do you own the building in which your office is housed? Are other offices located there as well? Your liability insurance "fire drill" should examine the limits of liability coverage that protect you and your assets from any gaps or other exposures. Ask questions about "what if's" on your property. What if there's a fire, a gas explosion, etc? If your entity is a general partnership, do you realize that you have unlimited liability for acts that relate to the business?

Do any of your staff use their automobiles for business such as going out to pick up supplies or even just lunch for the whole staff? If you have not sat down with your insurance professional to discuss issues like these, you may be opening yourself up to future claims of unexpected creditors who will seek to rip away your personal net worth.

Incapacity

Disability

From the time you sat through interminable lectures in med school, you were probably exposed to sales pitches on why protecting your largest asset—your ability to earn income—should be taken seriously. You may have some form of group, association, or individual LTD insurance to continue your income should you be temporarily or permanently disabled.

But what if you don't? Who will write your paycheck if you can't work because of a sickness or injury? Do you have enough in accumulated assets or outside unearned income to take the place of your lost income during a period of incapacity? For example, if you have $500,000 in liquid assets, and your annual expenditures are $125,000, without adequate disability protection, you could effectively wipe out your lifetime of savings in 4 years. In Chapter 4, I outlined the various types of disability insurance. These are the ultimate forms of asset protection in that they create dollars during a disability thus permitting your assets to remain intact.

Long-Term Care

Imagine for a moment having successfully accumulated a lifetime of savings, then watching it get stripped away year after year by the onset and continued ravages of Alzheimer's disease in your spouse. Just imagine. This happened to an 80-year-old client of mine about 20 years ago. Her sons and daughter refused our advice to purchase LTC insurance for mom (claimed it was too expensive at $6000 annually). She was diagnosed with Alzheimer's disease a mere year afterward, then died in the nursing facility six years later just after the family cashed in her last $25,000 CD from her now-exhausted portfolio of nearly $400,000 to pay for her care. Turned out the cost of having the disease was so much more expensive than the LTC insurance.

In my opinion, incapacity or long-term care in retirement or in preretirement years may turn out to be the biggest black hole through which your unprotected assets disappear. You may elect to self-insure against this possible loss, or you may decide to purchase LTC insurance to offset the enormous costs of long-term care. Whichever way you choose to go, make sure you factor those costs into your financial independence calculations.

I'm asked often if people with high net worth need LTC insurance if they have enough assets to pay for care should the need arise. Let me answer a question with a question. Do wealthy people opt out of property insurance, leaving their house uninsured, just because they have enough money to replace the house should it be destroyed? No, they do not, generally. Why? Because they understand the concept of "leverage" (ie, paying a small price today to offset a much larger potential loss later on). Yes, they have the liquidity to self-insure the house, but they opt to insure. As my friend Russ Jones, a wealth management specialist in Denver, Colorado, often says, "Liquidity is a problem only if you don't have it; then it's a matter of simple economics." In other words, self-insurance is okay. But the leverage factor of LTC insurance makes sense as well (oral communication, March 11, 2008).

> ## Planning Pointer
>
> Whether you decide to self-insure or to purchase LTC insurance, be certain to build the element of long-term care into your retirement calculations so you can be ready for the potential expense either way. With insurance, it's the annual premium; with self-insurance, it's a $75,000 to $90,000 annual expense rising at 5% compounded per year. On the low side, use 2 to 4 years of care but for projecting Alzheimer's, better plan for 6 to 10 years.

These then are the basic forms of protection that you should consider employing on an asset-by-asset basis. In the next chapter, we'll up the ante a bit and discover what other asset protection devices you can employ if these basic forms of protection are not adequate enough for some specific assets in your asset base.

REFERENCES

1. Gordon P. Protecting your assets from predators and creditors: Part 2. *IDC.* 2006;19(10).
2. Rothschild G, Rubin DS. Asset protection audit checklist. *Estate Tax Planning Advisor.* 2003;4(6).
3. DeFrancesco R. The prevent defense. *Financial Planning.* 2004;73-75.
4. Lowes R. Protect your assets before you're sued. *Medical Economics.* 2003;4(82).
5. Slott E. Ed Slott's IRA Advisor. 2005;2-3.
6. Gassman A. Creditor protection for physicians-most common mistakes. Steve Leimberg's Asset Protection Newsletter. Available at http://www.gassmanbateslawgroup.com. Accessed June 1, 2009.
7. Schiller D. Protecting a physician's assets takes preparation. *Legal Intelligence.* 2002;M5-M8.

6

Keeping Determined Predators at Bay
Advanced Concepts

"Worry is the interest paid on trouble before it starts."
- Grady Cash, CFP

It is still Friday. The knock on your front door has not yet occurred. The predators and creditors seeking your net worth remain illusory. You still have time to plan if you wish to keep them away because they are always out there lurking, ready to pounce. It's a horror show that need not be.

In the last chapter, we examined basic ways to build a defense around your assets so that potential creditors could be dissuaded from pursuing those assets in court. But sometimes the basics are not good enough, and the moat around your castle needs to be widened and deepened. This chapter will give you some additional and more advanced ways to do that. Speaking of your castle, the first area we will examine here is the manner in which your home, or "homestead" as it is called under state law, can be protected.

HOMESTEAD

Is your home your castle? Could it become someone else's? Most states provide creditor relief for primary residences under an exemption named "homestead." However, the homestead exemption is quite limited in some states while in others it may represent the full value of your house. For example, a full value homestead exemption is permitted in such states as Texas, Kansas, Iowa, Florida, and South Dakota while other states limit creditor protection to a mere $5000 to $10,000, such as in Illinois where the limit is only $7500 limit. Pennsylvania provides no homestead exemption at all.

Rudzinski K. *The Physician's Guide to Avoiding Financial Blunders (pp 91-102)*
© 2009 SLACK Incorporated

> ## Planning Pointer
>
> You can find the homestead exemption for your state at http://assetprotection-book/state_resources.htm.

In those states that provide little or no homestead exemption, re-titling your home to "tenants by the entireties" (see Chapter 5) can provide some creditor relief in cases where only one spouse is the subject of the lawsuit. Recall that joint tenancy will not protect an asset such as a house when both joint tenants are named in the suit.

A fly in the homestead ointment is the effect of the Bankruptcy Abuse Prevention and Consumer Protection Act of 2005 (the "Act"). Referenced earlier, the Act established an inflation-adjusted $125,000 limit in *bankruptcy* cases on the amount that can be sheltered via a homestead exemption, regardless of the state exemption, which may have been larger or unlimited such as in Texas and Florida. In other words, the new federal law trumps state law in a bankruptcy. The 2009 exemption is $136,875. This new limitation does not, however, apply to every homestead. Under the Act, it only applies to those homestead interests that are acquired within a 1215-day period (3 years 4 months) prior to the filing of the bankruptcy petition. But a more restrictive provision of the law requires rollovers of exempt homestead interests, such as in Texas or Florida, to be subject to the 1215-day rule despite the fact that the homestead interests were fully exempt in both states. In other words, moving from Texas to Florida, or vice versa, would trigger the 1215-day period. The main purpose of this section of the law was and is to prevent a last-minute move, on the eve of bankruptcy, to a state where move favorable creditor exemptions preside.

Remember, the current homestead limit of $136,875 applies to bankruptcy situations only. Normal state homestead exemption limits apply to all other judgments.

Other asset protection vehicles such as LLCs (see p. 91) may be contemplated for sheltering your residence. But be especially careful. The section on LLCs shows that sometimes what the law giveth, the law taketh away.

SHELTERING ACCOUNTS RECEIVABLE

Generally, encumbered assets are not as attractive to creditors as unencumbered assets. A/R in a practice may represent a sizable asset exposed to a plaintiff's judgment. Therefore, "Leveraging the A/R asset may act as a sheltering mechanism in an asset protection plan of attack" according to Delaware Attorney Peter S. Gordon.[5]

Wilmington, Delaware financial planner Brent C. Fuchs states, "An A/R leveraging plan should not be attempted without expert advice from your legal and tax counsel along with serious and objective input from your financial planner" (personal communication, November 11, 2008).

This type of planning begins with establishing your A/R account as the primary collateral for a bank loan. Ordinarily, a revolving A/R balance of between 30 to 120 days is used by the bank as the amount of loan proceeds available. Because the bank is the primary lender, it establishes a first lien on your A/R account balance, thereby protecting the A/R balance from the claims of creditors other than the bank itself.[1]

The A/R loan is kept alive until you retire at which time you pay off the loan balance (assuming, of course, that no judgment against you exists at that time). The receivables, when collected by you, are taxable for income tax purposes as they would have been had you been collecting them all along.

During your working lifetime, the loan proceeds from the initial and subsequent borrowings are invested with the intention that they will ultimately be used for supplemental retirement income. Since many states have an exemption from creditors for individually-owned life insurance, the proceeds from the loan can be invested in a life insurance policy for example. In states where life insurance cash values receive little or no creditor protection, an LLC can be used to shelter the cash values.

So, assuming your state provides protection for life insurance cash values, depending on your age at the time the loan is established, either fixed or variable universal life is used, with the latter usually recommended when the time horizon to retirement is longer than 10 to 15 years. Growth within the policy is sheltered from income taxes during the accumulation phase and tax-free retirement income can be distributed at retirement (assuming a non-MEC policy). The bank will most probably demand a collateral assignment of the policy face amount should you die while the loan balance is outstanding. When the loan is paid off at retirement, the collateral assignment is removed and you own the policy outright with full access to the cash values and the retirement income it can produce.

A/R leveraging is just that—leveraging. And leveraging only works when the rate of return on the invested loan proceeds (eg, in the life insurance policy) exceeds the interest cost of the bank loan. Ask your life insurance specialist about the various types of policies that can be used in this manner. Some policies produce very high early cash values that can reduce overall drag on the cash values at the beginning.

Sheltering assets in this manner can be truly effective; however, be aware that using A/R leveraging should be done, as earlier suggested by Mr. Fuchs, only after consultation with your legal and tax advisors and after consideration of all available asset protection strategies. Anyone attempting to sell you on this idea as an instant and isolated remedy to your creditor problems—in the absence of an overall asset protection plan—is probably not someone whose advice you should follow.

Planning Action

A/R leveraging is attractive in multi-physician practices where the actions of one physician can endanger the A/R of the other partners.

Creation and Use of Asset Protection Vehicles

Limited Liability Companies and Limited Partnerships

Doctors, like other individuals involved in a career of personal services, cannot hide behind a corporate veil that fends off creditors and plaintiffs suing for negligence. But they can, by selecting the right business entity, at least shelter those assets contained within the business entity. In today's litigious society, the business entities of choice for doctors are the Corporation, LLC (or family LLC [FLCC]) and the LP (or family LP [FLP]).

Basically, if you and a fellow physician contribute assets to a limited partnership or to an LLC that is properly and legally established, you and your friend no longer own a direct interest in the assets you've contributed. Instead, you own an interest in the business entity—the LLC or the LP—which now owns those assets.

For income tax purposes, the LLC can take on the S-Corp or the C-Corp status. Further, LLCs are treated the same as S-Corps or C-Corps from a corporate liability standpoint except for doctors because there's still the personal liability from personal services. Thus, according to attorney Roccy DeFrancesco, "...they (LLCs) can provide the standard corporate protection to all shareholders and directors for any negligence actions directed against the LLC itself." In other words, actions against the LLC itself may not impact the personal assets of its members. He further adds that, "...there is a major difference between an LLC and a corporation that relates to asset protection. This difference involves the role of a so-called 'charging order.'"[2]

Instead of having direct access to assets within the LLC, a "charging order" limits the judgment creditor's reach only to the distributions that otherwise would have been made directly to the owner of the partnership or the LLC. The assets in the LLC are therefore protected from the judgment creditor. If no distributions are made from the LLC (and none would be), no funds are attachable by the judgment creditor. None!

But it gets worse for the creditor in that any income taxes due on the judgment creditor's proportionate share of the income retained within the entity but not distributed are the direct liability of the creditor.[3] Said another way, according to Delaware CPA George Fournaris, the creditor is required to pay taxes on distributions the creditor did not actually receive. This is why judgment creditors with a charging order often wish to settle a claim rather than pay taxes on what could be called "phantom income," at least from an income tax point of view.

In a regular C-Corp or S-Corp, a judge can demand other remedies to satisfy a judgment creditor, such as demanding the debtor's interest in the corporation be sold to satisfy the judgment, or the debtor's interest could be transferred to the creditor (which can kill the S-Corp shareholder status). In the LLC, the only remedy for the judgment creditor is the charging order, plain and simple.

Earlier, I used the example of you and a friend forming an LLC, with reason. In many states, a single-owner LLC may be pierced since the single owner may stand to lose the argument that there's a legal separation between him- or herself and his or her assets. This is not to say that single-owner LLCs have not been established around the country. However, if another owner, even with a slight minority interest of, for example, 5% can be found, the LLC stands a much better chance of protecting the assets within. Some advisors suggest that in states where the single-owner LLC is deemed to be problematic, an LP or FLP be created as the business entity of choice. Competent legal and tax counsel in your state would be essential to guide you in selecting the right business entity for you.

Now, for asset protection purposes, you can use an LLC to hold assets that otherwise would be left unprotected. Let's say you own 3 office buildings where your medical offices are located. Placing each office building within its own LLC would serve to separate and protect those individual assets from judgment creditors attempting to enforce a charging order against your practice, which could be in a fourth LLC.

You can establish a separate LLC for many unrelated assets, such as a vacation home, rental properties (one LLC for each), airplane, snowmobile(s), boat(s), jet ski(s), investments such as stock, bonds, mutual funds, brokerage accounts, etc. You get the idea. How many LLCs you use will depend on how much money you feel compelled to spend to protect yourself against potential liability. Depending on the firm you use to establish each LLC, the cost could run between $2000 to $3000 or more per entity.

When discussing states that limit homestead exemptions, I hinted that what the law gives, the law can also take away. For example, putting your personal residence in an LLC may cause you to lose your $500,000 ($250,000 per spouse) capital gains tax exemption when you sell your residence. Additionally, you will lose the home mortgage interest deduction when the residence is moved to the LLC. There are other reasons for not putting your primary residence into an LLC, but these 2 alone might dissuade you from going in that direction for your personal residence.

When confronted with the "charging order," what if the debtor decides to become a partner (LP) or member (LLC)? You would not want this to happen so make sure the LLC or FLP agreement contains language that states that the agreement is intended to be an "executory contract," ie, a contract whereby all parties on both sides are obligated to perform certain duties. For example, a capital call would need to be performed by all parties, including the debtor-partner or debtor-member. So, not only would the debtor not receive any distributions, and be taxed on them in the current tax year, but that debtor would be required to add money to the LLC in a capital call. This is another not-so-subtle way to force the debtor to settle rather than pursue the judgment (David Schiller, Esq, personal communication, January 7, 2009).

Planning Action

Examine your asset list and think about using either an LP or LLC for those valuable assets that cannot be protected otherwise. Obtain local legal and tax counsel to determine which business entity works best for each of those assets.

Asset Protection Trusts

The variety of asset protection strategies I've listed so far should give you many ways to remove assets from the grasp of creditors. But for those who wish to take their planning to the next highest level, as necessary, the use of so-called self-settled trusts—otherwise known as "asset protection trusts" (APTs)—may be just what the doctor ordered!

Several states, like Delaware, have always had strong statutes to protect beneficiaries of third-party "spendthrift" trusts. As an example, parents may set up an irrevocable trust for the benefit of their children. If properly established, the trust will prevent the judgment creditors of a child beneficiary from reaching the trusts assets for that child. These trusts are fairly commonplace. However, laws in most states have forbidden "self-settled" trusts whereby an individual sets aside assets in a trust for his or her own lifetime benefit, expecting that those assets would then be creditor-proof. But in 1997, Delaware adopted the "Qualified Dispositions in Trust Act," which may have elevated self-settled trusts to a new level of planning for asset protection.

But not so fast! According to Delaware attorney Peter S. Gordon, "To date, there has not been a court decision ruling on the validity of self-settled asset protection trusts, so don't put all your eggs in this one basket."[5] Also, the previously cited "Bankruptcy Act" created some barriers to the potential successful use of APTs in bankruptcy situations. With these 2 caveats in mind, let's look at the Delaware APT in nonbankruptcy situations as a possible answer for your more complex asset protection needs.

At its core, the reasons why the Delaware APT (or other states' APTs, like Alaska) may be valuable as an asset protection device is the claim that assets in the trust are exempt from all creditor claims against the trustor (the person who sets up the trust [ie, you!]) that arise more than 4 years after the transfer of the assets to the trust, and the trust assets are exempt from all claims that arose before the transfer to the trust 1 year after actual notice to the claimant of the transfer to the trust.

According to Mr. Gordon, what this means is, "It is now possible for a person anywhere in the USA to establish a Delaware APT that provides lifetime benefits to that person, and also insulates those assets from attachment by judgment creditors notwithstanding that the person continues to receive lifetime benefits from the trust."[5] Because of the "more than 4 years" requirement, the APT certainly cannot be used as a last-minute opportunity to bypass approaching creditors. So, advance thought and planning need to be coalesced into an action plan for using an APT.

To understand how the Delaware APT works as a planning mechanism, here's an outline of the inner workings of the APT (with thanks to Peter Gordon):

A. You first execute a trust document

B. The trustee must be either a Delaware resident individual or a Delaware trust company (of which there are several)

C. Delaware trustee must conduct a minimal level of business (eg, maintain records, file tax returns, etc)

D. The trust must be irrevocable

E. The trustor (ie, you) may retain the right to veto trust distributions, to receive income, to receive annuity or unitrust payments, to receive principal distributions, and appoint assets at death to the beneficiaries the trustor desires

F. A person other than the trustor may be appointed as a distribution advisor for distributions to be made from the trust and an investment advisor may also be appointed to direct how the trust assets will be invested.

Implementing an APT may involve several variables based on what you might want and what your needs might be. For example, you might want to first stash an asset or assets in an LLC or LP before you place them in the APT. This provides an extra layer of protection to that asset or assets but also an extra measure of complexity. The desired level of protection should dictate the corresponding acceptable level of complexity.

Attorney Peter Gordon[5] suggests including what is called a "trust protector provision" in the APT, or naming a "distribution advisor" friendly to you. As a result, you can maintain some flexibility in the timing and amount of distributions from the APT, if distributions are necessary. You can also name an investment advisor of your choice to the APT.

Assuming an LLC or LP may have been established to hold assets before transfer to the APT, the trustee holds nothing more than "paper," so annual trustee commission reductions are not only possible but expected. Because of their complexity and extensive hands-on requirement at the outset, the one-time cost to establish a Delaware APT may be as much as $10,000 or possibly more, so these vehicles are not used unless the assets to be sheltered are fairly significant. Further evidencing this financial fact is the cost to maintain the LLC or LP in Delaware and to prepare and file the required tax returns.

It is important to keep several thoughts in mind regarding the use of APTs in particular, within the grand scheme of asset protection devices. First, there needs to be some valid business reason for setting up an APT or other asset protection devices other than just to avoid the reach of creditors. Second, the greater the lapse of time between the planning and the actual filing of a judgment against you, the better off you are in proving that your efforts at protecting your assets were not merely designed to defraud creditors. Lastly, you should not attempt to remove each and every asset from possible loss in a lawsuit. In a court of law, this "planned insolvency" could be perceived as intentional and devious, causing the courts to attempt to disassemble your grand plan of asset protection. Remember, "When pigs become hogs, they get slaughtered."

Is the Delaware (or other state) APT the "final answer" to protecting your assets? Not necessarily. Should APTs like this be considered? Certainly, if your asset protection needs rise to this more complex level of planning. Although they have not yet been battle-tested in court, planning well in advance with APTs is much better than no planning at all. Delaware Attorney Richard Nenno says "a properly designed and implemented Delaware APT will raise formidable obstacles for creditors."[4] Practitioners expect APTs to survive whatever legal challenges creditors throw up against them, but as of this writing, the final verdict is still out.

Foreign Asset Protection Trusts

You may be the one among the many who needs protection beyond what I've outlined previously. This may be especially true if you have relatives who live outside the United States. Trusts established in places like Nevis, Belize, the Cook Islands, Bermuda, and Turks & Caicos, known as "offshore trusts," can insert an even denser barrier against determined creditors because these foreign jurisdictions do not recognize US judgments or US attorneys, require the loser to pay the victor's legal fees, impose a tougher burden of proof, and permit less time between transfer of assets and actual filing of the judgment. Simply put, if you move assets to an offshore trust, even at the last minute, you have no control over distributions from the trust. As a result, it is very difficult for a US judge to demand that the assets be repatriated back to the United States to satisfy a US judgment.

Such trusts though are not for everyone. In fact, most practitioners recommend them only as a last resort and only when the amount of assets to be sheltered exceeds $1,000,000. The reason is that the legal cost to set up an offshore trust can range between $20,000 to $30,000. Attorneys also suggest that the amount of assets to be transferred to the offshore trust be a small portion of your net worth to avoid the "hog" label as referenced earlier. You don't want to appear insolvent by using offshore trusts.

But be warned! The world of offshore trusts includes scam artists and frauds. If your planning gets to this level, you need to consult with an extremely competent legal and tax advisor who has experience in designing and setting up these rather complex legal entities. You do not want to become "famous" in tax court as the result of an inexperienced advisor.

Lastly, it's important to keep in mind that a potential creditor to "your" assets may be your spouse in a divorce proceeding. Statistically, you've got a 50% chance that this will happen. Without thinking ahead about the stability of your marriage, your offshore trust may become your worst enemy. In other words, planning devices to solve one problem can potentially lead to greater problems elsewhere. In the final analysis, you and your estate attorney together will determine if this asset protection shoe fits you.

OTHER ASSET PROTECTION CONSIDERATIONS

You as Beneficiary

You may currently be the beneficiary of estate assets from your living parents or other relatives or friends. In many instances, the assets you will inherit may arrive at your door unimpeded (ie, outright). Should that happen in the midst of a divorce or other perilous event such as a malpractice lawsuit, those assets may be in jeopardy. It's not likely that your mother and father ever intended for those assets to go to your ex-spouse or to a patient of yours via a malpractice suit. So what can you do?

Well before you find yourself in this predicament, you may want to talk to your benefactors about the use of a "spendthrift" trust so that assets do not pass to you or to your spouse outright, but rather in trust to you. According to attorney David Schiller, "...such trusts usually stipulate that a beneficiary cannot assign his or her trust interest nor can a creditor of a trust beneficiary have any right to his or her trust interest." Schiller adds that, "such a 'spendthrift provision' is honored in most states as removing trust assets from the reach of creditors" (personal communication, January 7, 2009). However, it is important to note that once money is distributed from the trust, it then becomes available to creditors. That said, as long as a creditor stands waiting, the trustee can elect to hold back distributions to the affected beneficiary. That does not mean to say the trust couldn't have protective provisions that allow the trustee to make payments "on behalf of" a beneficiary directly to vendors, thus keeping creditors at bay from those payments.

Should you not be successful in getting your parents to change their estate plans, or perhaps they are physically or mentally unable to do so, you can elect not to receive assets from them by filing a "qualified disclaimer" in which you legally refuse to accept the asset(s) left to you by them. You cannot control who the assets then go to. Your parents' estate documents would (it is assumed) specifically state who the next-in-line beneficiary would be, just as if you had predeceased your parents. In many cases that could be your children or a sibling. So, rather than accept the assets then subject to a creditor's judgment (or that of an ex-spouse in divorce), the disclaimed asset(s) can escape to the next line of predetermined beneficiaries.

Dover, Delaware estate attorney Paul Boswell cautions that "...a 'qualified' disclaimer—at least under federal law, as state laws may vary—requires certain steps that must be adhered to specifically or the disclaimer may be voided" (oral communication, January 6, 2009), so if you find yourself in this position right now, immediately check with your legal counsel as to what you must do—or not do—to permit the use of this valuable asset protection device.

Planning Action

Ask (gently) to review your parents' estate documents to ascertain if you are a direct beneficiary of their bounty. If disclaimer provisions are not favorable to your family, ask your parents to consider revising their documents to provide for generational asset protection for your family.

You as Asset Gatherer and Estate Owner

Have you checked your will and trust documents recently to determine if you are leaving your precious assets outright to your children? If so, according to Texas estate specialist Dianna Parker, "…those assets might be held hostage in a divorce, lawsuit, etc brought against your child or children" (oral communication, January 14, 2009) Many documents written 10, 15, or more years ago leave assets outright to children when they reach various ages, like 25, 30, 35, etc. Ms. Parker further warns that, "Some documents don't even do that—they leave assets unfettered to children, and in some instances to minor grandchildren, no matter what age they are."

I recall a family estate here in Delaware where a 22-year-old beneficiary, who had inherited over $1.5 million of mom and dad's hard-earned money directly, was penniless and filing for bankruptcy only a few years later. Poof! The money just disappeared with nothing to show for it because it had landed in financially immature hands.

If asset protection is your goal, then you and your spouse should make it a priority to visit with your legal counsel to revise those out-of-date documents. Instead of leaving assets outright, you should consider leaving them in trust to your children, and then in further trust to your grandchildren, in an arrangement often referred to as a "dynasty trust." Without this added level of asset protection, you may be accumulating a lifetime of savings and sacrifice for the ultimate benefit of strangers and predators. If you are not sure what your documents say, will you get them out and look? If you don't, who will?

FRAUDULENT TRANSFERS

Any discussion of asset protection would be incomplete without at least a cursory mention of the legal concept of "fraudulent transfers."

The term *fraudulent transfer* is legally defined as follows, "A transfer of an asset (or the incurring of an obligation) with the actual intent to hinder, defray or defeat a creditor's claim, or, regardless of intent, making a transfer while insolvent or one which renders the transferor insolvent."[2]

The obvious purpose of this provision of the law is to prevent people from stashing cash or other assets somewhere out of the reach of a legitimate claimant. For example, you provide medical care to a patient who suffers ill effects from the treatment. You find out that the patient is suing you for malpractice and that the papers are "on the way." In anticipation of the lawsuit, you cash in your brokerage accounts, bury the cash in your backyard, and move title to the rest of your assets to an offshore trust. You would most likely be guilty of fraud and your actions deemed "fraudulent transfers." Under the law, your intent was clear (ie, hiding assets to avoid losing them in a lawsuit).

Therefore, as stated earlier, when adopting a plan of asset protection, you must make sure you show as many legitimate business purposes as you can for the re-titling, transferring to LLC or LP, creating an "asset protection trust," etc. Gratuitous transfers with no stated business purpose are subject to defeat especially now in the financial environment of the Bankruptcy Abuse Act of 2005. Additionally, the longer in time a transfer takes place before a lawsuit occurs, the better chances you have of defending your actions in pure business terms as compared with actions designed to defraud a creditor or creditors. Simply put, if you want to protect your assets, you must start the process of sheltering those assets way before the possible judgment materializes.

Summary

Attorney Peter S. Gordon summarizes asset protection this way, "The concept of (asset protection)... is to manage and preserve wealth in a manner that will protect it from the unforeseeable, unlimited threat of a lawsuit. It is the great uncertainty of the unlimited jury award that absolutely terrifies."[5] He adds the important guideline that forms the backbone of the asset protection process, "Asset protection takes many forms. There is no answer for all individuals. Decisions must be made on a case by case basis depending upon the assets owned... and the individual's lifestyle and economic goals."[5]

The process of asset protection is not one for procrastinators. Last minute efforts are doomed to failure. When the doorbell rings, it's too late. It's still Friday. The time for you to act is now. Will you?

References

1. DeFrancesco RM. Help your physician client with asset protection by "leveraging their accounts receivable." *Business Compensation Planning.* July 2004.
2. DeFrancesco R. Protective devices. *Financial Planning.* 2004; 127-130.
3. Revenue Ruling 77-173
4. Nenno R, Wolken JC. Asset protection trusts: a concise summary. Available at http:\\www. Leimbergservices.com. Accessed June 1, 2009.
5. Rudzinski KR. Protecting your assets from predators and creditors: Part 2. *IDC.* 2006;19(10).

7

Choosing the
Right Retirement Plan

"The question isn't at what age I want to retire, it's at what income."
- George Foreman

I cringe every time I hear members of Congress use the phrase "tax simplification" when describing the latest Washington, DC version of "making sausage." Let's be honest. The US Tax Code is not, never has been, and never will be "simple." And nowhere is the complexity of the tax code more apparent than in the sheer number of retirement plans available to businesses and medical professionals as well as to individual taxpayers, whether through their employer or on their own. We have traditional and Roth IRAs, SEPs, SIMPLEs, 401(k)s, 403(b)s, solo-401(k), safe harbor 401(k), Profit-Sharing, Defined Benefit, Money Purchase, and on and on.

Add to these the full array of nonqualified plans, and deciding which plan works best for you and your medical practice becomes a daunting task. Have you been confused as you've surveyed the myriad choices available and attempted to discern which among them best meets your needs? If you have a plan now, are you curious to know if it's still the best one for you?

I am often asked by clients and small business owners to sift through this maze of retirement plans and to suggest the best of the lot for them. Regardless of the type of practice you have—sole practitioner, multi-physician, self-employed consultant, hospital employee—knowing the "best" plan for you is hardly self-evident. The pertinent facts of your office demographics such as employee ages and salaries in conjunction with your overall financial and nonfinancial objectives for the plan you wish to install are among the main criteria to consider. So how do I go about answering your questions when you want to know which plan is best for you? The first thing I do is go through a mental checklist of highly relevant questions designed to eliminate the wrong plan(s) and to arrive at the one or two that make the most sense given your list of objectives. Here are the most important questions on that checklist:

Rudzinski K. *The Physician's Guide to*
Avoiding Financial Blunders (pp 103-116)
© 2009 SLACK Incorporated

- How much money do YOU wish to contribute?
- Would you like to maximize contributions to owners/partners of the practice?
- Would you like to minimize or maximize employer contributions to eligible employees?
- Do you need flexibility over the amount of employer deposits to the plan and the timing of those deposits?
- Do you wish to exclude high turnover employees from the plan as long as possible?
- Should short-service terminating employees keep employer contributions when they leave?
- Should each plan participant control his or her own investment account in your plan?
- How important are low administration costs?
- Would you like your own plan assets sheltered from the claims of creditors?
- Should your plan serve as a fringe benefit to recruit, hire, and retain competent staff?

Here's an example of how the checklist works.

You tell me you want to set up a retirement plan that includes your employees, but not the brand new, untested employees. You want to make personal contributions of around $10,000 to $14,000, you are age 50, you don't mind putting money in for your employees (but only for those who themselves contribute to the plan), and you want to limit administrative costs. Further, you'd prefer to have employer-matching contributions come back to the practice if employees leave for any reason, and you'd like to keep any matching costs to a minimum for the first couple of years to phase in your practice expenditures for the plan. Lastly, your spouse, age 50, works part-time in your practice, making $15,000, and you'd like to maximize her contributions to the plan. Which of the plans works best for you?

We can eliminate individual IRAs because of your desired level of contributions. SEP-IRA is eliminated because you want employees to make contributions of their own. Low administrative costs tend to eliminate 401(k) plans (and profit sharing for this and other reasons) for a practice of your size, and solo-401(k) is eliminated because you have common-law employees. A 403(b) plan does not apply since your practice is for profit. This leaves a SIMPLE-IRA as an ideal choice. You can exclude new employees for a while, start off with a lower matching contribution in the first 2 years, and maximize contributions for your spouse. Unfortunately, you cannot satisfy the goal of recapturing employer dollars if employees leave since they must be 100% vested. This last point demonstrates that no plan may satisfy every objective you have but the one that does so for your most important goals is the one that prevails.

Why the SIMPLE-IRA fits the bill in this example requires a run-through of the main features of each of the more common plans listed above. When finished, you should better grasp the pros and cons of each plan, enabling you to choose a plan on your own or to be knowledgeable enough to ask pertinent questions of your retirement specialist.

But first, for doctors in hospital or commercial settings, your choice is limited to only what your employer has chosen for you (eg, a 401(k) plan [traditional or Roth] or a 403(b) plan). However, you may still be able to fund a traditional, Roth, or nondeductible IRA on the side for yourself and/or your spouse as well as a SEP-IRA, solo-401(k), among others, for "moonlighting" income you derive outside of your main employment. See Chapter 3 for additional information on IRAs. So, although this chapter will focus mainly on retirement plans for independent single or multi-physician practices, doctors in hospitals and commercial settings can find pertinent and valuable information here as well.

Planning Pointer

If you intend to establish a retirement plan for your practice, or want to compare what you have with other plan possibilities, I highly recommend going online to www. irs.gov. This site has many good places where you can find objective and detailed information about the types of retirement plans listed below. In particular, when you arrive at the IRS Web site, click on the tab (upper right hand corner) "retirement plans community," then click on "type of plan" to look at links to the various plans I've cited. Alternatively, if you go to www.dol.gov/ebsa or call 1-866-444-EBSA (3272), you can access a very helpful brochure entitled, "Choosing a Retirement Solution for Your Small Business," which includes a chart comparing the different retirement plans, side by side. This brochure can also be found at the IRS Web site by referencing publication number 399, or catalog number 34066S. If you like to research things on your own, you will find the information at these sites invaluable.

TRADITIONAL AND ROTH IRAS

If you only want to save $5000 or $6000 a year, and no more, then go no further than an individually-established traditional IRA, Roth IRA, or nondeductible IRA. There's no need to involve your practice or any employees. If you already have a traditional or Roth IRA, then you are already where you should be.

To refresh your memory from Chapter 3, for the tax year 2009, you can contribute up to $5000 to your traditional or Roth IRA plus another $1000 "catch-up amount" if you are age 50 or older. However, if you are single and your MAGI exceeds $120,000, or married filing jointly with MAGI above $176,000, then you cannot contribute to a Roth IRA for this tax year. The term MAGI refers to your adjusted gross income modified to include tax-free interest. It applies only to Roth IRAs, not to traditional IRAs, which use AGI instead. You may contribute to a Roth IRA at any age, whereas you must be under age 70 ½ to put money into a traditional IRA. I suggest you refer back to Chapter 3, Mistake #1 for the treatment of IRA availability if you are covered under a retirement plan at work, the nonworking spouse rules, additional phase out rules and contribution deadlines.

If you have the choice, which IRA should you use—traditional, Roth, or nondeductible? The following discussion applies not only to individual IRAs, but also to opportunities in employer-sponsored qualified retirement plans, especially if the employer plan permits contributions either to a pre-tax traditional 401(k) or to a Roth 401(k).

Roth IRAs work well for younger individuals, certainly for those under age 40. For example, if you are age 30 and contemplating an age 65 retirement, you have 35 years for the Roth IRA contribution you make today to grow tax-free. Recall that to obtain the income tax benefits of a Roth IRA, your contributions must remain in the Roth IRA until the later of 5 years or age 59 ½. However, if you remove money earlier, you are still permitted to withdraw your deposits tax-free first, but amounts in excess of your total deposits are considered earnings and are then taxed at ordinary income tax rates plus a 10% penalty. The gain withdrawn, therefore, loses its tax-free growth.

So, assuming you let the money grow, that single $5000 contribution you make at age 30, assuming an 8% compounded annual rate of return, would grow to almost $74,000 by the time you turn 65. Further, if you continue to make only a $5000 contribution each year until age 65, your total accumulation at 8% would be over $930,000 and because you followed the rules, all that money can be removed tax free at retirement. This makes for splendid "income allocation," which I've detailed in Chapter 8. Briefly, just like you diversify, or allocate, your assets among various asset classes on the road to retirement, you want to try to allocate your income at retirement as well, such that some of the income is taxable, some is tax favored, and finally, some is fully tax free.

The bottom line is the younger you are, the more tax-free income the Roth IRA can generate due to compound returns. Roth IRAs are also more favorable if it is apparent that your future income will be taxed at a comparable or higher income tax bracket than it is today. You may not need or want the tax deduction for contributions to a traditional IRA today perhaps because your income is lower now or you have significant tax write-offs like mortgage interest such that tax-savings impact is minimal.

Here's another way to think of it: If you contribute to a traditional IRA, take the tax deduction, and then consume/spend the tax dollars you saved, what you're left with is an accumulation account at retirement that has no income or estate tax benefits (ie, all withdrawals are fully taxable). Conversely, the Roth IRA is funded today with after-tax dollars. As a result, the amount you can consume today is reduced because you have to pay taxes now on the deposit you make to the Roth IRA, and the taxes due now leave you less to consume today. Got it?

For example, if you want to contribute $5000 to a Roth IRA, and you are in a 25% federal income tax bracket, you have to pay $1250 in federal income taxes (plus state income taxes) on that $5000 since Roth IRAs are funded with after-tax dollars. That's $1250 you can't spend today for coffee or at your favorite restaurant. But the big benefit comes later when the whole bucket of Roth IRA money—your savings plus all the tax-free growth—comes back to you fully income tax free. So, unless the traditional IRA owner saves and accumulates the tax savings, the Roth IRA owner will almost always win the accumulation battle.

That said, the opposite would be true if you knew that, come time for withdrawing money from you IRAs, you would find yourself in a much lower income tax bracket. Then, having taken the income tax deduction for the traditional IRA in a higher bracket—and having saved the tax savings—you'd pay taxes later on in a lower bracket.

One last point. Although younger doctors will find Roth IRAs to be extremely powerful, I do not mean to imply that Roth IRAs are not useful for the older crowd. On the contrary, funding new or existing Roth IRAs at all ages can make sense not only for income tax purposes but for estate tax reasons as well. Remember that traditional IRAs require income taxes to be paid eventually by you or your heirs either within 5 years of your death (except for your spouse who can continue the tax deferral) or stretched out over the lifetimes of those beneficiaries. Either way, the tax must be paid. But the Roth IRA requires no taxes to be paid as the accumulation and distribution phases are tax free, assuming you follow the 5-year/age-59 ½ rule. Additionally, Roth IRAs do not require mandatory distributions at age 70 ½ as traditional IRAs do. The bottom line is that the longer the time period you can allow for the tax-free build-up in a Roth IRA to offset the up-front income taxes you pay on your contribution amount, the better the Roth IRA will function. And finally, if you will have a lot of taxable income from qualified retirement plans, having tax-free income from a Roth IRA can make for excellent "income allocation."

Planning Pointer

Beginning in the year 2010, under current tax law, you can convert your traditional IRAs to Roth IRAs without today's $105,000 AGI limitation.

SIMPLE-IRA

If you want to contribute more than $5000 or $6000, the individual IRAs won't cut it. The SIMPLE-IRA may be your next best alternative. It works well in an office environment where you don't mind funding some retirement benefits for employees who make contributions of their own. In this case, the SIMPLE-IRA can be an excellent fringe benefit to help recruit and retain key staff members. Additionally, you can exclude certain employees for up to 2 years, and the administrative costs are nil. Here are the details.

The SIMPLE-IRA must be the only retirement plan in your practice (practice cannot exceed 100 employees). Be careful if you have ownership in another business. IRS controlled group (CG) or affiliated service organization (ASO) rules may require you to include the employees of any separate entity together in the same SIMPLE-IRA.

You can exclude employees for up to 2 years if they earned less than $5000 in each of the last 2 years and are not expected to earn $5000 in the current tax year.

You and your employees can contribute 100% of pay up to $11,500 for 2009, plus an extra $2500 as a "catch-up" contribution if you are age 50 or older. Since FICA withholding is still required, you can really only contribute about 92%, not 100%, of your compensation.

Most importantly, your own contribution amount is *not* dependent on the amounts employees contribute. If no one else contributes, you may still fund your account.

Administratively, the SIMPLE-IRA really is simple. Only one IRS form to complete (5304-SIMPLE) to install the plan, no complex discrimination testing, and no annual administration fees except there may be a small per account fee ($10 to $25) charged by the investment provider.

You must make 100% vested (ie, employee owns the money) matching contributions to employee accounts under 1 of the following 2 formulas:

1. Dollar for dollar match up to 3% of employee's contribution

2. A 2% of compensation nonelective employer contribution for all employees eligible to participate, whether they contribute or not

The first formula can be altered, but only in advance, to provide for a dollar-for-dollar match, up to at least 1% of compensation every 2 years in a 5-year period. This alternate formula, for example, can be used in the first 2 years of the plan to hold down your initial costs. After year 2, you must raise the match to 3% for 3 years. If your goal is to reduce costs in the early years, then the 1% alternate first formula above fits that objective perfectly.

The second formula (the 2% nonelective employer contribution) is rarely used since you must put in 2% of compensation for all of your eligible employees whether the employee

TABLE 7-1

2009 CONTRIBUTION LIMITS

SEP CONTRIBUTION

Up to 25% of compensation, limit	$49,000

SIMPLE ELECTIVE DEFERRAL

Under age 50	$11,500
Age 50 and over	$14,000
401(k), 403(b),[1] 457,[2] and SARSEP elective deferral under age 50	$16,500
401(k), 403(b),[1] 457,[2] and SARSEP elective deferral age 50 and over	$22,000
Annual defined contribution limit	$49,000

[1]Special increased limit may apply to certain 403(b) contributors with 15 or more years of service

[2]A 457 plan participant may be able to double elective deferral to the plan during the last 3 years before retirement to make up prior, missed contributions; however, the catch-up provision for those age 50 and over does not apply during this period.

SEP: Simplified employee pension plan; SARSEP: Salary reduction simplified employee pension plan

contributes or not. This formula would only be considered if you knew in advance that all employees would be contributing at least 3% of their compensation. Then, instead of your match being dollar for dollar to 3% of participating employee payroll, you can reduce the nonelective employer contribution to 2% using the second formula. But this is rare anyway. The bottom line is that you can limit your match to 11% or less over 5 years (1-1-3-3-3) under the alternate first formula, almost as low as the second formula (2-2-2-2-2), at 10%, and future employees who don't contribute will receive no matching contribution.

Employees' investment accounts are self-managed, therefore you have limited your fiduciary responsibility. But refrain from giving employees your personal advice on investing their money as that could create liability where none exists. The advisor who installs the plan can counsel your employees as to which plan investment choices they might wish to choose.

Employees must be given 60 days notice before your plan year to decide whether to participate in the plan. So if you wish to start a SIMPLE-IRA for your employees on January 1st, the employee notices need to be provided before November 2nd. Also, current and new employees must be given an announcement identifying the amount and structure of employer contributions at least 60 days in advance of each subsequent plan year.

Premature distributions from SIMPLE-IRAs (ie, those made BEFORE age 59 ½) are hit with a 25% penalty instead of the usual penalty of 10% if the premature distribution occurs before the end of the second year of the participant's inclusion in the plan (as measured from date of the first contribution).

SIMPLE-IRA assets can be rolled over to another SIMPLE-IRA, but not to a traditional or Roth IRA during the first 2 years (see above) if the rollover assets are subject to the 25% penalty.

Planning Pointer

A SIMPLE-IRA can be an easy-to-understand retirement plan for your practice. It limits administrative costs considerably, gives you higher contribution limits than an individual IRA, establishes a predictable limit on your practice matching contribution costs, limits fiduciary responsibility, and creates a meaningful employee fringe benefit to recruit and retain key staff members (if that is a goal).

SEP-IRA

A SEP-IRA may meet your needs if you wish to set aside more money for retirement than is permitted in the SIMPLE-IRA. It might also be the plan of choice if you "moonlight" from your primary salaried job and bring home self-employed (1099) or salaried income. A SEP-IRA is easy to set up, with little if any administrative cost. However, unlike the SIMPLE-IRA, contributions for your eligible employees may be more significant than 3% of payroll so the SEP-IRA works best where you wish to reward long-service employees with meaningful retirement plan contributions. In addition, you can set up and fund the SEP-IRA after you know how much profit is available to fund for retirement. Lastly, the SEP-IRA is appealing because you are able to exclude temporary, part-time, seasonal, or short-service employees. If your practice experiences high early turnover, then a SEP-IRA could work well. Here are the details.

A SEP-IRA can be established by using IRS Model Form 5305-SEP as late as the time you file your income taxes (including extensions) for the prior tax year. Generally, there are little or no costs to install the plan or to administer it annually. If you maintain another qualified plan besides a SEP-IRA, or you employ leased employees, you cannot use the model SEP-IRA Form 5305-SEP. If you own another business, you may be required to aggregate the businesses together under one SEP-IRA roof. You are not required to make contributions each year and employees do not need to be notified in advance.

Contributions to the SEP-IRA are made by the practice only; no employee contributions are permitted. Employees are 100% vested in your contributions to their accounts.

In 2009, you may contribute up to the lesser of 25% of your eligible compensation, or $49,000, or 20% of your eligible compensation up to $49,000 if you are self-employed. For 2009, maximum eligible compensation is set at $245,000.

Under the most stringent eligibility rule, employees must provide services for you in 3 of the preceding 5 years, be age 21, and make at least $550 in each of those years. Part-timers then can be excluded based on their length of service primarily, rather than on their level of compensation, as is the rule for SIMPLE-IRAs.

You must contribute for each eligible employee the same percentage of compensation that you contribute to your own account. So, if you put in 8% of your own pay, you must contribute 8% of each eligible employee's pay. For self-employeds, your 20% contribution limit actually equals 25% of compensation for employees according to IRS math. Here's how they do it. Let's say you make $100,000; you are limited to 20%, or $20,000 as a contribution. But the IRS says this is really 25% of compensation because they subtract the $20,000 from your compensation of $100,000, leaving $80,000. Then they divide the $20,000 by $80,000, which equals 25%, so, they say, your 20% of pay contribution really is 25% and so requires a 25% contribution for eligible employees to avoid violating discrimination rules for the SEP-IRA. US Government math—go figure!

Participants direct their own investment accounts so your fiduciary liability is limited. Again, as stated earlier, refrain from giving employees investment advice.

If you are "moonlighting," you can have a SEP-IRA for that separate income and still fully participate in your employer plan, such as a 401(k) or 403(b).

Planning Pointer

Choose a SEP-IRA if you want higher contribution levels for yourself, you wish to exclude short-term employees of any sort, and you would like to reward long-service employees with a potentially high level of employer contributions for retirement. Additionally, a SEP-IRA makes sense if you want a simple, easy-to-understand plan with low administrative costs and the ability to decide very late how much, if any, you wish to contribute for yourself and for employees. For "moonlighters," the SEP-IRA can be very useful.

SOLO-401(K)

In smaller medical practices, featuring one doctor or only partners in a partnership-owned practice, or in "moonlighting" situations where you may derive side income from a second job, where you have no employees except maybe your spouse, a solo-401(k) could be just the answer.

Because the plan includes just you and perhaps your spouse or you and your partners, the complicated IRS discrimination testing associated with regular 401(k)s is eliminated. Therefore, the plan provisions can be simplified, and administrative costs, minimized. Further, your goal may be to contribute large amounts into the plan for yourself and partners. You might also want flexibility in how much you contribute year to year. Lastly, you may desire the ability to tap into your investment account in a severe financial emergency. If these plan provisions meet your objectives and needs, then consider using a solo-401(k). Here are the details.

- Eligibility can be immediate, with no restrictions.
- You can make elective deferrals from your eligible compensation (capped at $245,000 in 2009), of up to $16,500 for 2009, just like a regular 401(k). You can also contribute an extra $5500 as a "catch-up" contribution if you are age 50 or over. You may also add a profit-sharing element to the plan to increase contributions to your account. However, employer contributions cannot be greater than 25% of your eligible compensation, since 25% of compensation is the maximum deductible limit under current law.
- Combined elective deferrals and profit sharing cannot exceed the lesser of 100% of your eligible compensation or $49,000 (2009), or $54,500 if you are age 50.
- You may arrange for loans from your account just like in a regular 401(k).
- Vesting is 100%, immediately. You always own the monies you put and the practice puts into your account.

- If your spouse is a participant, he or she can make elective deferrals as well and can also benefit from profit-sharing contributions.

The solo-401(k) has limited use, but in the right set of circumstances, it can be an ideal plan choice. Unlike the SEP-IRA, which can await contributions until the practice income tax return is actually filed, part of the solo-401(k)'s makeup is elective deferrals from your pay, which must come from current salary or earnings even if those deferrals are bunched up near the end of the tax year in question. Profit sharing, however, like the SEP-IRA, can be decided at the last minute before the practice tax return is filed.

At lower income levels, the solo-401(k) may be more efficient in terms of allowing greater contributions. For example, in a SEP-IRA where your compensation is $50,000 from your self-employed side job, the maximum you can contribute is 20% of the $50,000, or $10,000. In the solo-401(k), you can set aside $16,500 for 2009 in elective deferrals and another $5500 if you are age 50 or over. Further, you can make a profit-sharing contribution equal to 25% of $50,000, or $12,500. Total contribution = $34,000 ($16,500 + $5500 + $12,500). So if this is the kind of result you are seeking, then the solo-401(k) might be a good choice for you.

Planning Pointer

Not every financial institution or mutual fund family allows for the establishment of a solo-401(k). If you have a favorite mutual fund family or banking institution or brokerage firm, ask if they have the documents and expertise to establish and administer a solo-401(k) for you. If not, check with your attorney or TPA to see if they can provide you with the documents to set up and customize a solo-401(k) plan for your practice. Lastly, your investment advisor or TPA may have already researched the best place for investments to fund your solo-401(k).

TRADITIONAL 401(K)

You may want to consider a 401(k) plan if you have a sizable multi-physician practice with many staff members, although I do not mean to imply that smaller practices may not find a 401(k) plan useful (see Safe Harbor 401(k) on p. 111). The traditional 401(k) would be attractive where you want to make large contributions for yourself and other partners, where you wish to exclude high turnover or very young employees, where higher administration costs are not a overriding negative factor, and where you may desire employer contributions to employee accounts remain all or partially forfeitable if a plan participant leaves the practice early on.

Also, a 401(k) plan may work well if you expect a high level of plan participation and/or where you want to provide a valuable fringe benefit to recruit, hire, and retain key staffers. Lastly, you might choose a 401(k) if your goal is to limit employer contributions to employees' accounts as determined on a year-by-year basis by you. Here are some featured details:

- Eligibility: Typical eligibility might be any employee with 1000 hours of service within 1 year and who is at least age 21. This is the most stringent eligibility criteria. So, unlike SEPs and SIMPLEs, a 401(k) plan can exclude some, if not all, part-time employees. A typical eligibility provision requires employees to work at least 1000 hours during a 12-month period and attain age 21 before they can join the plan. However, you may make the eligibility requirement more liberal if your goal is to include new employees and part timers.

- Contribution levels: Plan participants may make elective deferrals of up to $16,500 for 2009 annually, plus an additional $5500 if age 50 or older. Elective deferrals are usually stated as a percentage of the participant's compensation.

- Matching: The practice can provide for matching contributions based on a predetermined formula announced before the beginning of each plan year. Although the matching formula can vary from practice to practice, the most common formula I've seen in the marketplace is a 50% match up to 6% of compensation. So, an employee who contributes 4% gets a 2% match, 6% gets a 3% match, 10% gets a 3% match. The match can be made concurrent with the employee payroll deferral or can be made less frequently and as late as the actual filing of the practice income tax return.

- Profit sharing: A 401(k) plan may contain a profit-sharing feature in addition to or in lieu of matching contributions. Monies labeled as profit sharing can be deposited into the plan up to the practice's tax-filing deadline, including extensions. The most common method for assigning profit sharing to employee accounts is by "pro rata allocation" (ie, the percentage of the profit-sharing pie that the employee's compensation bears to the total eligible compensation of all plan participants). So, for example, if your compensation is $150,000 out of a total of $450,000 compensation for all plan participants, you would get one-third of any profit-sharing monies up for grabs. If you wish more of the profit-sharing pool to go to yourself and your partners, you can select a formula that takes into account the Social Security payroll taxes payable by the practice for plan participants. Beyond that, new plan designs are entering the marketplace whereby the allocation of profit-sharing deposits can be tilted even more favorably toward doctors as owners. The concept is called "class allocation" or new comparability. If you have not heard about this, and one of your goals is to maximize contributions for owners and partners, then contact your third-party administrator (TPA) now to learn more about these helpful rules.

- Maximum annual contribution per participant (from all sources): Up to the lesser of 100% of eligible compensation, not to exceed $49,000 (2009), plus any "catch-up" contribution. The practice can deduct amounts that do not exceed 25% of the aggregate compensation of all participants.

- Vesting: The plan may allow for "graduated" vesting so that some or all of the employer contributions to the employee accounts—both matching and profit sharing—are forfeited if the employee terminates in the first 5 or 6 years. The forfeited amounts can come back to the employer to cover future costs or can be redistributed among the remaining participants.

- Loans: The 401(k) plan may allow for participant loans, hardship withdrawals, and sometimes in-service withdrawals that do not require the participant to demonstrate hardship.

- Discrimination: Your level of "elective deferrals" may be limited to an amount below $16,500. How? If non-highly compensated employees (NHCEs) do not contribute much to the plan. For example, if the "average deferral percentage" of the NHCE group is 4%, your contribution percentage will be limited to 6% of your compensation, or just 2% more than the 4% contributed by the NHSEs, on average. There's much more detail here, so check with your TPA to understand the rules (and testing) against discrimination.

- Administration: The complexity of discrimination testing requires that you hire a TPA to keep you out of trouble. Also, changes in the law will need to be implemented. This is where the TPA is invaluable. But with the service comes the cost, which for smaller plans is most likely to be at least $1500 to install a plan and $1000 to maintain it annually, ranging much higher for larger plans.

- Fiduciary liability: You may have fiduciary liability with a 401(k) plan.

- Asset protection: As long as you have one common-law employee in the plan, other than you or your spouse, your plan assets are protected from the claims of creditors under ERISA. See Chapter 5 for a complete discussion on asset protection for qualified plans. Under current law, you may now move certain IRA, SEP, etc assets to your 401(k) account without penalty. Check with your TPA for details. So, if you are in a high-risk specialty, you may want to consider the shelter of your 401(k) from the claims of creditors. The same is true with 401(k) and some 403(b) accounts at hospitals and other large medical providers. Check with your HR department to see what assets your employer plan will permit you to move onboard and whether your plan is ERISA protected.

It's not unusual to see mid-size and larger medical practices opt for the 401(k) plan alternative. If you have a small medical practice, you may also choose to go with a 401(k), but you may find that lower employee contribution levels prevent you from maximizing your own elective deferral amounts. You may also like the 401(k) alternative but not the higher administrative costs. On the other hand, if solid asset protection is high on your list of priorities, then the 401(k) leads the way.

Planning Pointer

To increase participation in the plan, consider adding a more generous matching program or consider the use of a "safe harbor" election as outlined below.

SAFE HARBOR 401(K)

As outlined above, you may like the 401(k) approach to your retirement plan needs. However, low contribution levels by rank-and-file employees may hamper your own contribution opportunity due to required discrimination testing. This may happen if your pay scale is low or if staff members are younger. Or, still, you may hire a lot of part-timers who almost never contribute to the plan and thereby drag down the "average deferral percentage," and therefore your contribution level. That's because, for discrimination testing purposes, a part-timer who works 1000 hours or more is equivalent to a full-timer for the purposes of your 401(k) plan.

If these issues are real for you, then you might want to consider a safe harbor 401(k) plan. Another positive is that the safe harbor plan is also less expensive to install and maintain.

Here are the details (limited to differences from regular 401(k)):

- Elective deferrals: The main difference is that, if the plan provides for several "concessions" as stated below, you may make your entire $16,500 elective deferral without regard to the amounts contributed by your rank-and-file plan participants. This is by far the main reason why safe harbor plans are selected.

- Matching contributions: You may choose 1 of 2 safe harbor formulas, very similar to but not exactly the same as the formulas in the SIMPLE-IRA:

  o Matching formula: The basic formula provides for a dollar-for-dollar (100%) match of employee contributions up to 3% of compensation PLUS 50% of the next 2% of compensation. Thus for plan participants making 5% of pay contribution, the match is 4% ((3% x 100%) + (50% x 2%)) = 4%)

  o Nonelective contribution formula: A nonelective employer contribution equal to 3% of compensation for all eligible employees whether or not they elect to make deferrals.

- Vesting: In a safe harbor plan, all employer contributions must be 100% fully and immediately vested.

- Discrimination testing: Several of the discrimination tests required in regular 401(k)s can be bypassed in a safe harbor plan. As a result, administrative costs are generally lower.

- Profit sharing: Generally, both the matching and the profit sharing contributions are 100% vested in a safe harbor plan. However, your TPA may be able to show you how the profit sharing can have graduated vesting, so ask.

You may want to consider the safe harbor 401(k) as a start-up plan or as a step up from a SIMPLE-IRA, or even as a regular 401(k) alternative, especially where you wish to increase your own level of contributions through higher deferrals and matching as well as the addition of a profit-sharing element. The extra 1% matching for employees contributing 5% or greater of their compensation may matter somewhat, but the larger contribution levels for yourself and for other partners may override that extra payroll expense. So, I find that the safe harbor 401(k) is the classic middle ground of plans for most small to mid-size practices.

Recent changes in tax law (IRS) and retirement plan administrative rules (Department of Labor) have brought into the marketplace new plan designs such as the so-called "New Comparability" plan. Additionally, cash balance plans (a hybrid form of defined benefit plan) are becoming more popular as a result of recent changes in federal legislation. Why is that? The reason is these plans permit greater allocation levels of employer contributions to highly compensated employees, like yourself and your partners, if any. According to Doug Cranage, President of Associated Benefit Planners, Ltd in Wayne, Pennsylvania, "This new breed of plans for small businesses, including medical practices, is rapidly catching on" (written communication, January 23, 2009). Cranage, whose company works with many doctor groups, adds, "Doctors looking to maximize their pension contributions without adding burdensome costs for non-owner staff ought to take a close look at these attractive plan design alternatives" (written communication, January 23, 2009). Such features can even be added to safe harbor plans, making them even more attractive for not only small and mid-size practices, but also for larger groups as well. Make sure you talk to your retirement plan specialist and/or TPA to determine how these new design arrangements can help you better achieve the overall financial and nonfinancial objectives of the retirement plan you currently maintain or seek to initiate.

SUMMARY

The selection of a retirement plan for your practice involves first knowing what you want to achieve, then choosing the plan that best allows you to reach those financial and nonfinancial goals. This is sometimes accomplished simply by the process of eliminating all the other plan alternatives. We saw this earlier with the original example on pp. 102 to 103.

But it's also important to remember that no single plan is perfect for every practice and for every objective you seek. Moreover, since I did not survey here all the qualified retirement plans that may be available to you, just the commonly used ones, I strongly recommend that you seek out a retirement plan specialist in your community to assist you in researching and selecting the best plan for you. Your CPA may know such a specialist or may even have one in his or her office. Also check with other professional practices in your specialty or general community. Lastly, your own financial professional (CPA, ChFC, etc) may work with a qualified TPA as a strategic alliance just as we do here.

Planning Pointer

Here is a list of other useful publications you can get at the IRS Web site (www.irs.gov).

- o Publication 560: Retirement Plans for Small Businesses
- o Publication 590: Individual Retirement Arrangements (IRAs)
- o Publication 4284: SIMPLE IRA Checklist
- o Publication 4385: SEP Checklist

8

Will You Be Ready for the Longest Vacation of Your Life?

"One of the most complex economic calculations that most workers will ever undertake is, without doubt, deciding how much to save for retirement."
-Alan Greenspan, 2002

It's 3 a.m. and you lie awake again with anxious thoughts swirling through your mind about the fate of your retirement. Because you have not pinned down when, where, and how you plan to retire, you can't help but worry about whether you will have saved enough to satisfy those still indistinct yet looming goals. If this is you, when will you begin to formulate a clear and precise vision of whatever it is that you will call your "retirement?" Later is not good enough unless you enjoy those middle-of-the-night anxiety-ridden self-conversations. You need to start now.

I've heard it said that most people spend more time planning their vacations than they do their retirement. Maybe that's why I see too many people totally unprepared for the longest vacation of their life—that day, year, age, whatever the measure, that work life stops, often too abruptly, and "retirement" begins (Table 8-1). What about you? When was the last time you and your spouse completed a retirement "fire drill" where you clearly wrote down together—repeat, wrote down—your joint plans for retirement, the when, the how, and the where? If it's been a while for you, or perhaps not ever, when will you do it?

Studies abound showing that most Americans are not being realistic about their chances of a financially successful retirement, and that many will face premature bankruptcy as their assets die before they do. Many people without a concrete plan merely hope that things will work out. But hope is not a financial strategy. As Tennessee Williams once wrote, "You can be young without money, but you can't be old without it." Yet, as the tired but true saying goes, "people don't plan to fail, they just fail to plan" (Table 8-1).

So then, if planning for retirement is good, strategic, advanced planning is even better. Like most NFL coaches who "game plan" the first 15 offensive plays of each game, you can and should start the process for your successful transition to retirement well before its actual commencement date. Think of it as a "life timeline" (Figure 8-1) on

Rudzinski K. *The Physician's Guide to Avoiding Financial Blunders (pp 117-136)*
© 2009 SLACK Incorporated

TABLE 8-1

SOME ROADBLOCKS TO RETIREMENT

- Inflation
- Social Security?
- Pension?
- Longevity
- Security selection
- Market risk
- Income taxes
- Medical costs
- Imploding life insurance

- Amount of contributions
- Market volatility
- Timing and amount of distributions
- Portfolio concentration
- Decisions based on emotion
- Where to live?
- Lack of certainty
- Cost of essentials
- Long-term care

Figure 8-1. Life timeline.

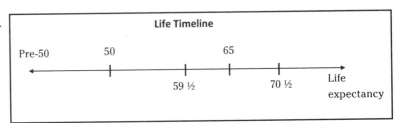

which several ages tend to stand out, like 50, 59 ½, 65, and 70 ½. Let's also add the time zone of pre-age 50 for those younger doctors thinking well in advance about their retirement.

Though not a specific spot on the timeline but more like an age range, pre-age 50 carries with it tremendous financial responsibility as it can effectively or ineffectively tee up the financial success you will enjoy at retirement.

PRE-AGE 50

With all of the financial responsibilities young doctors face, such as student loan repayments, starting a new practice, buying and maintaining a home, raising a young family, paying off other debts, it's not all that surprising that the thought of saving for a retirement 20 or 30 years away gets mentally squashed. In fact, at a recent Fidelity Investments focus group, one Gen-X investor commented, " Many of us have a hard time planning for demands that are years away."[1] Another added "It's 30 years down the road, but retirement crops up as a worry... we'll be relying on ourselves."[1]

It's not my intent here to detail each and every step young doctors ought to be following to achieve financial success at retirement. But a few words on general concepts toward that end can be useful to the doctor who knows that retirement planning is important yet can't quite formulate all of the specifics about it.

"The first basic premise your mind needs to grasp and accept is that someday your accumulated assets will need to replace 75% to 100% of your then-annual income," warns Maryland financial planner Peter Maller (written communication, January 20, 2009). Yet at age 30, you may not be able to define exactly how much income you'll be earning at age 40 let alone at retirement, whenever that might be. What you do know, however, is what you earn now and perhaps what your expenses are now. The difference between those 2 numbers is the amount you can save or consume. If you send it forward by saving rather than consuming surplus dollars in your budget, you can take advantage of the most powerful financial concept created by mankind, according to Albert Einstein.

What is that? It's compound interest. From a purely mathematical point of view, the earlier you start toward that goal of 75% to 100% of your eventual preretirement income, the more successful you will be as the law of compound interest favors those who start early. Go back and look at the examples of compound interest I cited in Chapter 2, Mistake #2. Most importantly, compound interest exemplifies one basic rule of successful saving (ie, using OPM [Other People's Money] to enhance your ultimate savings goal).

Other examples of OPM that you need to keep in mind and take advantage of are matching contributions in your 401(k) or SIMPLE-IRA, and the tax savings by contributing to those plans, otherwise known as Uncle Sam's subsidy. Refer back to Chapter 2 ("leaving free money on the table"), and to Chapter 1, Mistake #8 (OPM). Recall the concept that a 50% match is like getting a GUARANTEED 50% rate of return on your money, or a GUARANTEED tax-free raise. But those free dollars are forever lost to you if you don't grab them while you can. The bottom line for young and middle-aged doctors is this: if you haven't started saving yet for retirement, when will you? How much compound interest are you losing by delaying the savings you know you need to begin setting aside? How many matching dollars are you leaving on the table by not contributing to your employer's SIMPLE or 401(k)? Just remember that with compound interest, nothing happens early. It takes time for the magic to be meaningful.

Here's another financial principle the pre-age 50 doctors need to internalize and follow: managing your debts. Saving for retirement is important and the earlier you start, the better. However, managing your overall debt can be just as critical.

Baltimore financial planner John McCarthy posits that, "Debt can be good or bad. Mortgage debt, debt for higher education or to start your practice are good; excessive credit card debt and gambling debts are bad, the kind that drain surplus and reduce constructive cash flow" (written communication, January 20, 2009). Suppose you carry just $8000 of credit card debt at an average interest rate of 12.93%. Suppose also that you carry that debt over your working lifetime, say, for 30 years. You'd fork out over $31,000 in interest payments. That's almost a 400% mark-up over the cost of whatever you bought using the credit card. If you had been able to invest that $31,000 of interest, at 7% over the 30 years you could have accumulated over $81,000 toward your retirement income goals.

Remember the $300 pizza? The one you bought using your credit card carrying the balance and high nondeductible interest ad infinitum? Your $10 cost today ballooned to over $300 as the interest on the unpaid balance compounded. So, avoid credit card or other bad debt if you can, pay off the balances monthly to avoid interest charges. Use surplus dollars to knock down outstanding balances in those cases where you've already begun accumulating excessive credit card debt.

For those who are or will be setting aside sporadic or systematic savings, your basic concept to remember is to resist any decrease in your savings levels. On the contrary, always seek to increase savings little by little, with big added chunks when you get

Figure 8-2. Potential benefits of waiting to replace a car. A hypothetical constant annual rate of return of 7% was used to demonstrate this concept. All investment returns have been adjusted for a 3% rate of inflation. Investment returns and inflation will vary. Seven percent was not meant to demonstrate the return of any investment or asset class. This illustration does not reflect the impact of taxes.

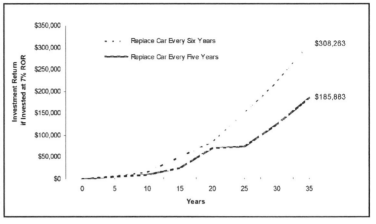

pay increases or bonuses. Remember, if you are going to need 75% to 100% percent of your final annual income to live comfortably in retirement, you need to increase your savings level as your income grows. Otherwise, you'll find yourself scrambling later on to make up the compound interest you could have gained by increasing savings throughout your working years. If you wait too long, you may find that task impossible to achieve. Your standard of living at retirement will suffer drastically or you will need to delay retirement.

Consume or save? It's always a challenge to put off today's pleasures. But by doing so you build for the time when you hang up your stethoscope or scalpel. Ask yourself, do I really need that $5 cup of coffee? Do I need that expensive car every 3 years? What if I paid it off after 4 years and saved the payment amount for 1 or 2 years before buying a new car? What if I did that every 4-year car cycle? How much more money could I have when I retire? Check out the chart above (Figure 8-2).

Former *Wall Street Journal* columnist Jonathan Clements often referred to this concept as "don't sweat the small stuff."[2] He meant that you make decisions every day about expenditures, some you really need, some you don't. If you could save rather than spend those discretionary amounts (some small, some larger), wouldn't they add up to a sizable dollar cache later on? As an example, about 15 years ago, I decided to get some extra exercise in the fall by doing my own yard/leaf clean-up. It's a big job, but I saved about $2000 a year, which I invested in a fund in my SEP-IRA. Not only did I save taxes from the extra contribution, but that fund is now worth over $65,000. By the time I retire in maybe 10 years, assuming a 7% compounded rate of return, that $65,000 will grow to $130,000, supplemented by the continued annual savings from doing the work myself. This equals about $30,000, bringing the total retirement value of my yardwork alternative to over $160,000.

It is obvious then that the "small stuff" adds up over time to become meaningful dollars when invested and compounded. What "small stuff" can you find in the things you buy? Excessive entertainment expenses? Dining out often, at expensive restaurants? Five-dollar book markers for each book you buy at the book store? Save or consume? It's not always the big savings "stuff" that matters. Small "stuff" saved does too, given time to grow.

Now finally we arrive at the timeline. Let's look at each of the ages on the timeline, and briefly summarize what actions you might need to take, or possibly avoid, with regard to your accumulated lifetime savings.

Professionally, if you are outside of a hospital or commercial setting, your plans for further growth and/or expansion of your solo practice, partnership, or multi-physician group may be occurring as well. You may be giving consideration, either passing or perhaps serious, to a possible future exit strategy. Those are important—critical even—but are beyond the scope of this particular book. Maybe in the next one!

For now, though, let's focus on some of the personal decisions you need to make as well as the issues surrounding your personal retirement assets since they are needed to support you and your family throughout the 20, or perhaps 30, years of your retirement or the joint retirement of you and your spouse.

AGE 50

According to recent studies, only a handful of baby boomers feel confident and secure about their retirement. In my experience, at age 50 most have no idea what their standard of living should be when they retire. They cannot come close to detailing their own routine monthly expenditures now. I once called this the "dark side of retirement,"[3] this phenomenon of how totally unprepared many baby boomers are approaching their retirement years. They earn and spend, most times blissfully unaware of their ongoing expenditures for such items as dining out, vacations, clothing, entertainment, leisure activities like golf, skiing, etc. No wonder they feel insecure as a creeping anxiety stirs within that such spending cannot be sustained forever, especially when retirement begins and the clockwork paycheck stops.

Studies also show that among the many concerns boomers have about retirement, 3 stand out as consistent across all levels of wealth. They are as follows:

1. The corrosive impact of inflation on retirement standard of living,

2. The possibility of another extended market decline like 2008-2009, early in retirement, thus decimating invested assets again, when earned income has stopped, and you must rely solely on those depleted retirement investments

3. The need to project a safe but effective withdrawal rate from invested assets to secure a comfortable retirement income for life

Inflation is everyday news as we are constantly reminded of it by the Federal Reserve's battle to fight inflation by raising interest rates and creating or denying liquidity (and therefore credit) in the marketplace. At times, inflation can be tamed but it never seems to go away. Even as we may hear about the possible specter of deflation, the main future risk still seems to be that of systemic inflation as the nation piles up trillions of dollars of deficit spending to survive the current turbulent economy and recession.

Those of us who lived through the late 1970s and early 1980s witnessed the significant damage runaway inflation can inflict on a fixed retirement standard of living. We all remember the teacher who retired on a pension of $3000 a month in 1975 and who saw the purchasing power of that fixed pension decline year after year as prices inevitably rose. Retirees facing such daunting foes as inflation (or perhaps deflation) need to insulate their retirement portfolios. These are certainly legitimate concerns.

The fear of a major market downturn is frightfully real. After suffering through the multi-year market decline in 2000 to 2002, and after a subsequent 5-year bull market, the subprime mortgage implosion led to a serious bear market and deep recession in 2008-2009, tabbed by market experts as the worst since the Great Depression years (well, maybe the worst since the 1980 to 1982 recession!). If you began your retirement

Figure 8-3. Likelihood that you will not sustain a 30-year retirement. (Figure created by author with data from T. Rowe Price Associates.)

Likelihood you will <u>not</u> sustain a 30-year retirement

Stock/Bond Allocation

Rate of Return	100/0	80/20	60/40	40/60	15/85	5/95
4%	15%	12%	14%	15%	29%	63%
5%	32%	34%	42%	58%	91%	100%
6%	53%	59%	72%	90%	100%	100%
7%	76%	82%	93%	99%	100%	100%

◄— Less Likely   More Likely —►

at the outset of either of these bear markets, you would have seriously diminished your asset pool almost immediately with the ultimate loss of significant portfolio assets as compound interest cannot work on assets that do not exist. You and your portfolio would need to be prepared for such an unwelcome financial introduction to retirement. If you are not, you may deplete your assets before you die.

But as my mentor, Tim Johnson, a Nashville, Tennessee investment specialist, says, "… such events are generally systemic and not unusual" (oral communication, January 16, 2009). They happen on average every 5 years, some greater than others (like now), so retirees will experience many bear markets and recessions both before retirement and after. In the decade before your retirement, you'll need to begin planning your retirement portfolio in order to insulate yourself from the worst of these declines. This does not mean sticking your head in the sand and buying only CDs, bonds, money markets, etc. These may be safe from loss of principal, but they are ravaged by inflation, which decimates their purchasing power. Pre- and postretirement portfolios need exposure to equities so your retirement income can maintain its original purchasing power throughout your lifetime.

Finally, study after study has shown that a 4% withdrawal rate from your retirement portfolio, increasing with inflation, combined with a healthy allocation to equity asset classes, makes for a high probability of a successful and secure retirement standard of living of 30 years or more (Figure 8-3).

The problem is how to balance the risk of portfolio loss due to equity exposure with the need to maintain purchasing power over time. I cover this on p. 123.

Another problem is adjusting your thinking to accept and adapt to only a 4% withdrawal rate. That's just $40,000 per $1,000,000! Therefore, to achieve a $120,000 annual income from your accumulated assets, you'll need $3,000,000 to start. If you've just turned 50, and you haven't yet sacrificed the everyday pleasures of "conspicuous consumption," you may find that your retirement savings task is daunting. That's why I stress starting early to permit compound returns to grow your portfolio.

So, if you are age 50 and want to retire comfortably at, say, age 65, you'll need to either continue your ongoing savings if you successfully started early or begin an aggressive program of savings immediately. Working with a skilled financial planner can help you clarify your retirement income goal as well as the savings path to reach that objective on time. If at age 50 you haven't started saving, then face it—you need help!

These fears expressed by boomers are real and need to be addressed. You need to develop your own retirement game plan, beginning at least no later than age 50.

But first, a question you'll need to ask and answer yourself at this early stage in the preretirement planning process is whether legacy planning is important to you (and to your spouse) as an overall financial goal. In other words, should the quality and quantity of your own retirement standard of living be affected (ie, diminished) by your desire to leave significant assets to your children and/or grandchildren at the deaths of yourself and your spouse? Or is your retirement motto to "die broke?" If it's the former, then you have to factor in some amount of invested assets that will need to be retained in your portfolio throughout your lifetime and that of your spouse.

The bottom line is that if you want to retain assets for your heirs, you may need to accumulate more assets since you can't deplete retirement assets beyond the amount you wish to leave behind. In other words, if you have the burning desire to leave $1,000,000 to your children, while you may derive income from that money during your retirement, your legacy goal would prevent you from dipping into the $1,000,000 principal should that be necessary. Sometimes retirees forget that a specific legacy amount such as $1,000,000 can be partially or fully funded with real estate, jewelry, etc. It doesn't have to be cash or invested assets. So, by age 50, you need to grapple with this significant personal issue since it has potential financial implications for your retirement. By the way, from my experience with preretirement clients, I'd advise you to make sure you and your spouse are on the same page since a lack of communication or simple disconnect here may cause relationship problems later on. It's not unusual for husband and wife to be sitting in my conference room discussing legacy planning for the first time and each having a differing point of view. Tackle this topic as early on as you can, at least by age 50, so you can more accurately project the asset base you'll need to fund your retirement standard of living.

Planning Pointer

Another word about spouses. I cannot stress enough to make sure you include your spouse in the planning of your retirement. By "your" I mean both of you. I hinted at this above with the legacy planning issue. But it extends to all aspects of your retirement. I am assuming here, of course, that your spouse will be your spouse when you retire. That said, in my experience, when one spouse dominates the retirement discussion and planning, the other tends to become disinterested, perhaps even resentful, and many a retirement plan done this way winds up becoming a separation plan. So be sure you both get your say about what "retirement" means to each of you and then strike a balance. The earlier you break open the discussion, the smoother the final transition will be.

Here are some additional items to review at age 50:

- What assets are you earmarking for your retirement income standard of living? IRAs, pension plans, 403(b)s, etc are easy. But what about your vacation home? Would you sell it, keep it, lease it, or perhaps sell your current residence instead? What about your office building? Sell or lease? What about the value of your practice or your portion of your multi-physician practice? Have you begun thinking seriously about a viable succession strategy, especially if you are a sole practitioner? Or will all the goodwill you've created over your successful career retire with you the day you walk away? If you are in a multi-physician practice, has the group fully addressed the issue of retiring partners through a buy-sell agreement, deferred compensation agreement, or in specific sections of your employment contract?

What if you became permanently disabled and were forced to retire as the result? What value should be paid to you from the practice? How is "disability" defined? Overall, what plans and timetable(s) do you have in place to convert these and other nonportfolio assets to cash or liquid investments to produce retirement income? To maximize their value? If you have done nothing at all toward that end, when will you start? Now? Later? Never? If you fail to plan, your plan will surely fail.

- Are you maximizing your retirement plan contributions, including the "catch-up" amount that begins at age 50? Do you have outside consulting income? Such part-time professional income is a great source for tax-qualified savings, such as in a separate SEP-IRA or solo-401(k) (see Chapter 7). As college tuitions decrease, then disappear, are you substituting additional retirement savings for those terminating expenditures, or are you rewarding yourself now by spending freely on depreciating consumables that have zero value for your retirement standard of living? To replace 75% or more of your income at retirement, you'll need to save more than is permitted by a 401(k) or 403(b) plan. If you don't save enough for your retirement, who will?

- As Connecticut attorney Bob Appel asks (oral communication, January 9, 2009), "Have you checked the beneficiary designations on all of your qualified plan assets to make sure they reflect your current estate wishes and the needs of your family?" Further, have you perhaps disinherited a child not included under a prior designation? Have you re-done your wills/trusts and perhaps forgotten to coordinate your retirement plan beneficiaries with those revised estate planning documents? This is a mistake I see often. Try to avoid it if you can (see Chapter 3). What if you've remarried and you wish to leave your 401(k) or other pension plan assets to the children of your first marriage? Have you made sure your second (third, etc) spouse has waived in writing his or her ERISA spousal rights under your plan(s)? If not, you may unintentionally disinherit all of your children from those assets as your current spouse exerts his/her ERISA rights to those assets. Please double-check this one as being wrong can have financially tragic consequences for your family, especially for your younger children.

- Do you still have a frozen Keogh account lying around, or perhaps a money purchase, single participant profit-sharing plan? Most of these have long since been abandoned but the accounts may still be alive and invested. If the assets in your account exceed $100,000, have you filed the annual 5500 forms as required, and have you amended your plan documents as needed, under recent pension laws? If not, you may need to revisit these plans to clean them up. Many of the older plans did not permit the tax-deferral "stretch" provision allowing nonspouse beneficiaries to avoid immediate taxes at your death (and your spouse's). Losing this privilege may unnecessarily impose higher taxes earlier on your nonspouse heirs. Work with your retirement specialist to find the best place to move these frozen assets.

- Earlier, in Chapter 3, I referred to the law change allowing conversions to Roth IRAs in 2010 without regard to any AGI limit. Go back and review this—now is as good a time as any to set up and fund a nondeductible IRA for this year.

- Will your plans for retirement be stymied if you become disabled and can't make contributions to your qualified retirement plan, like your 401(k) or hospital plan? In Chapter 3, I explained the new disability kid on the block, the one that makes deposits to a trust when you are totally disabled to take the place of the qualified plan contributions you can no longer make because you have no earned income.

Recall that this coverage can be written in addition to the maximum coverage limits of your regular personal and/or group LTD. Check with your broker or financial planner about this; if you don't have one, email me at bookspublishing@slackinc.com and I'll e-mail you information about this fairly recent type of disability insurance.

- Age 50 is not too early to look into long-term care insurance. This coverage can serve to offset the potential financial ravages of long-term care. Annual costs for nursing care exceed $75,000 nationally. Such an expense could cripple your spouse's retirement if you were the institutionalized one.

LTC coverage is fairly inexpensive at age 50 compared with the asset pool it creates as a substitute for spending down your retirement savings. Financial planner Brent Fuchs, CFP, CRPC, ChFC, CLU, comments, "In many cases you can pay up the LTC insurance during your working years so premiums can stop when you retire and after premiums stop, you are forever insulated from any rate increases."[4]

Further, for those of you in C-Corps, you can even deduct the premiums and not include them as income, so Uncle Sam will subsidize this important retirement asset protection. In my opinion, this is a relatively unknown, and therefore, underused selective fringe benefit. What do you think?

- Is your asset allocation mix still geared for growth? Or are you going "ultra" conservative because you fear losing principal to market volatility? If you've decided on the cash/CD route, you may have simply exchanged one level of risk for another. Maybe you've eliminated "market risk" (markets falling) and "business risk" (one particular stock) from your portfolio by abandoning equities, but in their place you may have introduced "purchasing power" or "inflation" risks to your portfolio. See Chapter 1, Mistake #3 for my explanation of how various risks can affect your retirement income and assets.

Remember that a 4% taxable bond loses purchasing power when first subjected to your 30% to 35% income tax, then to a 3.0% or 3.5% annual inflation rate. At that rate, your "safe" fixed income investment loses purchasing power every day silently but with certainty. So bonds, CDs, and money markets alone are not the answer. Stay focused on the long term (to life expectancy) and maintain a measured allocation in equities to outpace long-term inflation.

That said, as you reach your 50s, you may need to also look at your portfolio allocation from the opposite point of view (ie, are you maybe too heavy into equities?). The market decline of 2000 to 2002, but especially that of 2008 to 2009, took a large toll on retirement portfolios whose allocation to equities was too large, especially those with an 80% or more exposure. In the latter decline, the global recession decimated portfolio values across all asset classes, included many bond holdings. There was literally no place to hide.

However, despite overall portfolio declines, those with 40% to 50% fixed income exposure, especially at the shorter maturities, fared much better than portfolios fully exposed to both domestic and foreign equities. Obviously, this chapter of one book cannot be the detailed guide for every preretiree or postretiree investor. However, it stands to reason that if you lost sleep when the markets tumbled 22% over 7 straight trading days in October 2008, you were probably too heavily invested in equities.

In light of the lessons learned from these recent market reversals, with possible help from an investment professional, you may want to start taming your portfolio as you hit age 50. So, instead of an 80% to 100% exposure to equities, you might reallocate to a 70%/30% split, equities-to-fixed income, reducing further at age 55 to a 60%/40% allocation. By the time you reach your actual retirement age, you might be at 50%/50% or even 40%/60%, especially if you are admittedly loss averse. You need continued exposure to equities to battle inflation, but you can tone down your portfolio to prevent excessive declines in future bear markets and recessions.

Because investors feel differently about risk and loss aversion, not everyone commands the same allocation at the same preretirement age, so my comments are more general in nature. My overall message though is to make sure you begin the process of preparing your retirement portfolio for its proper at-retirement allocation well in advance of that eventual age so as to slowly reduce volatility the closer you get to your official retirement age.

- Financial planner Clark Randall, CFP in Dallas, Texas suggests that in preparing for retirement you give thought to allocating your resources among the various retirement and nonqualified account types which will diversify your "tax burden" at retirement.[5] Randall advises clients that, "Putting all your money in a traditional IRA or 401(k) is risky."[5] He adds that, "You could end up a 'tax prisoner' in retirement."[5] So, to the extent that you can allocate retirement savings to items that produce totally or partially tax-free income, like a Roth IRA or Roth 401(k) (if available), tax-free bonds, and tax-favored annuity income payments, you can, as Randall summarizes,"...help minimize the tax bite in later life."[5]

- The election of Barack Obama as President, along with his pre-election proposals for higher federal income tax brackets for taxpayers/couples earning more than $250,000 (or perhaps some lower income level to be determined), as well as his call for higher taxes on interest, dividends, and capital gains means that tax deferral in its traditional sense may need to be revisited.

Tax vehicles like Roth IRAs and Roth 401(k)s may gain favor in an Obama administration as the goal of saving taxes now on the contributions may be outweighed to an even greater degree by the receipt of tax-free withdrawals later on at retirement. In other words, Roth IRAs are valuable now; they may be even more so under the new administration.

Another traditional vehicle that may gain favor is life insurance, fixed and variable. In the spirit of "income allocation," life insurance offers tax-deferred growth, which can translate into tax-free withdrawals/loans at retirement. Many life policies today can maximize growth over death benefits so the emphasis is on living, not death, benefits. In other words, as internal mortality costs are minimized due to updated mortality tables, more efficient cash value growth ensues, all things being equal. Combined with the tax-free nature of withdrawals from life insurance, this additional growth element makes for an interesting alternative to consider for tax-free income at retirement.

Further, life insurance carriers have on the drawing board life insurance products that offer "guaranteed income for life" riders similar to those offered in variable annuities, so that policy owners can convert tax-favored cash values into tax-free income guaranteed for the life of the policy owner. Stay tuned! As these features become available, your insurance professional may be able to help you sort through the maze to determine which, if any, can be of benefit to you. Make sure you get details as to expenses, fees, limitations, etc, as well as a prospectus and other required materials if the products you're considering are variable in nature. I realize that the mentioning of "life insurance" and "retirement investments" together may seem outdated or even biased to some degree. Historically, the marketplace has not accepted insurance as investment-grade. But with the relentless progression of baby boomers toward retirement, insurance companies have created innovative life insurance products in the retirement income arena. So don't turn a deaf ear to these retirement-oriented features strapped to the traditional life insurance chassis. Otherwise you might miss an excellent opportunity for "income allocation" as espoused earlier by planner Clark Randall, CFP.

- Above all, though, you need to be seriously thinking about a plausible and reasonable answer to the following questions: When am I planning to retire? What about my spouse's retirement? If you can't pin down a specific age or date, work with a couple of planning scenarios, like a #1 scenario of retirement at age 62, and a #2 scenario of retirement at age 65, etc. Build as many "what-ifs" into your planning as you must in order to account for all the contingencies you may want to consider. What if I sell my vacation home? What if we want to move to a 55+ community? What if we need to move to a health-oriented retirement community? Begin to imagine and to visualize the when, where, and how of your retirement. If you don't, how can you plan? And if you can't plan properly, might you be rolling the dice at your retirement goals? Start now.

AGE 59 ½

This age has been burned into our psyche because it's the first normal age after which we can withdraw monies from our traditional IRAs, 401(k)s, etc without the imposition of the 10% penalty. But there are other items of interest that can impact retirement planning at this age, especially yours, such as:

- Many company and hospital 401(k) plans permit in-service withdrawals beginning as early as age 55 or 60. An "in-service" withdrawal means you can take money out of your 401(k) investment account other than as a loan or hardship withdrawal while still working and contributing to that 401(k). What about *your* 401(k)? Your spouse's? If you don't know, you can check in the summary plan description (SPD) the plan must provide to you each year.

  There may be good reasons to remove assets from your 401(k) to invest personally in a separate IRA. Among these are poor or limited investment choices; avoidance of plan-imposed restrictions; the opportunity for a year-2010 Roth IRA conversion; greater estate planning flexibility; the avoidance of the qualified survivor annuity requirement the plan might impose; the opportunity to use restrictive beneficiary designations for certain spendthrift, undisciplined, and special needs heirs; etc. So removing assets from your 401(k) may be appealing if permitted by your plan. Generally, though, if you've rolled assets into the plan from another outside plan or IRA, those assets may be rolled out at any time, even in-service. Just be sure to check it out in the SPD of the plan you are now in.

- While your plan may allow for early in-service withdrawals, and you may wish to do so, there may be other important reasons NOT to attempt an in-service withdrawal, such as lower funding expenses, better investment choices, and—most importantly—the asset protection afforded ERISA plans as explained in Chapter 5 under "qualified plans." This safety net may in fact be the overriding reason to keep your 401(k) plan assets inside your 401(k) plan. However, you may consider an in-service withdrawal for your spouse, assuming he or she is not engaged in a high liability risk profession.

Check with your estate attorney to ascertain your state laws on asset protection for IRAs. The site www.assetprotectionbook.com/state_resources can help you as well. Remember, though, that solo-401(k)s and owner-only Keogh plans, which do not include common law employees beyond just spouses, receive no ERISA creditor protection.

- If you haven't defined your retirement alternatives by now, age 59 ½ ought to be the giant red flag to do so. In my experience working with many doctors, the earlier you begin to formulate the details of your life in retirement—and here I don't mean just money—the easier your transition from Dr. Ultra Busy to Dr. Leisure Time. Waiting too long to plan can cause you to remain defined by what you do rather than who you are, and the early years of retirement may be psychologically rocky, even depressing. So, make the effort now to determine what retirement means to you and your spouse.

- Revisit your asset allocation strategy to continue the process of converting assets to the allocation you wish to maintain in retirement based on your personal experience with risk tolerance, or "loss aversion." Keep in mind, your "time horizon" is not necessarily to the day you retire; it's to your normal life expectancy (and that of your spouse), which may be 20 or 30 years. If you have been at 100% stocks, or 80% stocks/20% fixed income, you should be dialing down equities to inject some downside market protection through fixed income assets such as bonds, CDs, fixed annuities, etc without losing the potential upside of equities in your retirement portfolio.

- In future bull markets, if you feel that equities have cyclically "peaked" and you're concerned about downside possibilities, then consider the various ways to lock in the growth from your equity assets by converting those assets to guaranteed income for life, especially if you are retiring now or very soon.

Traditional immediate annuities are extremely efficient vehicles to convert invested assets to pension-like guaranteed income, with another advantage being a tax-free portion of the monthly payout. The main downside is that you lose control of your money. For example, you buy an immediate annuity with $100,000 of your retirement assets, and the insurance company agrees to pay you and your spouse $525 per month ($425 of it tax-free) for the rest of your joint lives. With such a contract, you've traded your cash for a lifetime income. You no longer have rights to your $100,000 deposit. It belongs to the insurance company. Upon the second death of you or your spouse, nothing is paid to any other beneficiary, although a survivor benefit can be factored in, with a reduced payment to you while both of you are alive.

This loss of principal rights can dissuade potential investments into immediate annuities. However, the marketplace is now seeing hybrid immediate annuities that do in fact give you access to some of your original deposit on a yearly reducing basis. The products also provide a form of lump sum death benefit for a period of time and have a monthly annuity benefit that goes up each year based on the year-to-year Consumer Price Index (CPI). So, some insurance companies are creating useful products designed to capture the imagination (and dollars) of the millions of current retirees and baby boomers.

Other retirement products include the new breed of variable annuities with lifetime income guarantee riders. These riders help insure against longevity and business risks and may suit your investment temperament better. Writer Leslie Scism adds, "More than 22 million variable annuity contracts are currently in force, totaling 1.4 trillion in assets, and the majority include some type of guarantee."[6] With these riders, you are buying downside protection for your retirement income while staying invested to capture potential upside equity growth. For example, a client purchased a $153,000 variable annuity with a guaranteed minimum withdrawal benefit rider in August 2007. By November 20th, 2008, the value of the investment account had fallen to just under $90,000, but the guaranteed income base had risen to $162,000. If the client wanted to start taking income for retirement, the client was guaranteed 5% of the $162,000 income base, or $8100 annually for life.

This "income base" is not a surrender value; you can't remove it or borrow from it. It merely serves as a base value whose sole purpose is to determine the amount upon which the lifetime income guarantee is determined.

Since all income guarantee riders are different and carry varying levels of expenses and fees, make certain you review such information with your investment professional and be sure to get a prospectus as required by law.

Finally, a most attractive feature of these products is that, unlike traditional immediate annuities where you give up your principle to buy a lifetime income benefit, you can purchase the income guarantees within the variable annuity without losing control of your assets. So, if you are seeking various forms of guarantees on your retirement income apart from everyday products like CDs, bonds, etc, consider the various annuity products available in the marketplace—age 59 is not too early to look at such alternatives. Writing about the new variable annuity products, Nick Murray says, "… for the first time… an investor can simultaneously, and inside the same vehicle get meaningful exposure to some equity-based income, and a contractual guarantee of some or all of his capital under specified circumstances."[7]

AGE 65

This has traditionally been defined as "normal retirement age", or NRA. For baby boomers, it can be age 66 or 67 depending on the year of birth. Interestingly, when the Social Security Act became law in 1935, and the NRA was set at 65, the average life expectancy for Americans was age 62 (Table 8-2).

But our timeline moves on and here you are at age 65. Let's hope that you haven't arrived here unprepared and ill advised. If so, "retirement" may be a fiction for you, a "never-land" that forever remains out of your grasp. On the other hand, if you've been future oriented during your working years, you may be quite on target toward reaching those financial goals that clearly define your mental image of a successful retirement. So, your checklist for age 65, if you've completed the tasks earlier in the timeline, may be somewhat anti-climactic, with only a limited number of steps such as:

- Make a determination regarding taking or not taking Social Security benefits. At your NRA, Social Security does not penalize you for income you earn while taking retirement benefits. However, there is a "bonus" of sorts if you delay taking benefits after your normal retirement age, up to age 70. As Table 8-3 shows, this increase varies based on your year of birth, but the increase now is 8% per year, or almost an equity-like rate of return on your fixed government pension. Your spouse, however, does not get that increase if the spouse's benefit is based on your earnings.

TABLE 8-2

RETIRING AT FULL RETIREMENT AGE

YEAR OF BIRTH*	FULL RETIREMENT AGE
1937 or earlier	65
1938	65 and 2 months
1939	65 and 4 months
1940	65 and 6 months
1941	65 and 8 months
1942	65 and 10 months
1943 to 1954	66
1955	66 and 2 months
1956	66 and 4 months
1957	66 and 6 months
1958	66 and 8 months
1959	66 and 10 months
1960 or later	67

*Refer to the previous year if you were born on January 1.

TABLE 8-3

PERCENTAGE INCREASE FOR EACH YEAR OF DELAYED RETIREMENT

YEAR OF BIRTH	YEARLY INCREASE RATE
1937 to 1938	6.5%
1939 to 1940	7.0%
1941 to 1942	7.5%
1943 or later	8.0%

If you really don't need the money, and you both are in good health with long normal life expectancies, you may choose to delay taking benefits beyond age 66. My advice is to work with a retirement planning specialist here to fully understand your options and to build them as "what-ifs" into your retirement planning model(s) before you make a final decision. Delaying the benefits may be good, or not, but check it out.

- Another tip regarding Social Security would be whether or not to take your spouse's retirement benefit before you retire. Here's the scenario. Your spouse, Allyn, age 62, worked for a few years, then stopped to raise your children, yet still qualifies for a monthly benefit based on her own earnings. You are age 64, and you plan to

TABLE 8-4

TAKING SOCIAL SECURITY BENEFITS EARLY

If your full retirement age is 66, your benefits will be reduced:

- 25% at age 62
- 20% at age 63
- 13.33% at age 64
- 6.66% at age 65

retire at your NRA, age 66. Allyn's annual Social Security retirement benefit at age 62 is $400 per month based solely on her own prior earnings. Should she elect to take that benefit now or wait until you retire? Perhaps she should. Here's why.

Allyn's monthly benefit is predicated on her own earnings, so she can begin her benefit at age 62 and that benefit is not reduced because of your continued earnings. It IS reduced because she's taking her own benefit early, before her NRA at age 66 (Table 8-4). But that's moot because at age 66, she qualifies for the greater of her own benefit or one-half of yours assuming you start taking your benefits at age 66. So, if your monthly benefit at age 66 is $2000 per month, Allyn's benefit is the greater of $1000 (one-half of yours) or $400 (her own benefit). Having taken her own benefit early does not disqualify her from getting that $1000 per month benefit based on your earnings.

Action Item

Consider a visit to your Social Security office (or go online – see below) to have them figure out for you whether or not you fit into Allyn's scenario described above. You may even get a clue by referring to your annual projected benefit statement from Social Security. Check to see if your spouse's benefit at age 62 based on your spouse's own earnings is less than one-half of yours at NRA. If it is, then taking your spouse's own benefit early may be a good idea. And while you are at it, make sure they've correctly stated your earnings. Finally, taking your spouse's Social Security retirement income early lets you capture a couple years of "found" income to enhance your retirement portfolio if you save, not spend, the money.

- Social Security has recently rolled out some useful tools online to assist you in determining your retirement benefits. For example, at www.socialsecurity.gov/estimator, you can pinpoint your benefits more precisely. You can even change your retirement age and use your earnings on record. If you want to avoid going to the Social Security office to apply for your retirement benefits, you can now do so online. Go to www.socialsecurity.gov and click on "Applying Online for Retirement Benefits." By answering some questions, you can start the ball rolling. Also at the same site, you can request a statement of benefits like the one you get every year now. Just click on "What You Can Do Online," then click on "Request a Social Security Statement." You will be sent one shortly in the mail.[8]

- If you haven't done so already, you should be making sure your retirement plan beneficiary designations are (still) in order.

- Consider the process of consolidating your assets into fewer accounts to simplify your life. If that means consolidating advisors to do so, then so be it. Pick the one who best understands you not just as an investor, but as a whole person who is someday very soon going to trade a salaried career for a commission job (ie, living off your investments). My advice is don't get "cheap" here. Sometimes the best advice with the most value to you and to your spouse in retirement may not be the least expensive. It certainly will cost more than a monthly subscription to Money magazine or Barron's, or for the cable-TV cost for CNBC or MSNBC. These can certainly be helpful but they are impersonal and fickle. For example, an advisor who charges you an annual 1% management fee on your assets and who prevents you from panic-selling out of equities when they are down 40% as they were in November 2008—thereby preventing you from turning a temporary decline into a real loss—arguably has earned his or her fee. So, your retirement security net needs consistency, objectivity, and a high degree of personal involvement. If you can do this on your own, fine. If not, seek professional help.

- If your qualified plan at work, or your spouse's plan at work, contains highly appreciated employer stock, and you are considering rolling those assets out to a traditional IRA, you may want to investigate "NUA" possibilities. See the "potpourri" section of Chapter 2 for the explanation of how NUA treatment can be extremely tax friendly if this niche scenario fits you.

- If you continue to work after age 65, and your practice employs 20 or more employees, full- or part-time, or you work at a large hospital or commercial venture, your medical plan at work will still be your primary plan and Medicare will be secondary, so you don't need Medicare parts "B" or "D" (assuming your employer drug plan is superior to Medicare part "D"). However, if you employ less than 20 full- or part-time employees, then Medicare becomes primary and your work plan is secondary, so you need to minimally sign up for Medicare Part "B." Don't forget to do this! Check with the broker who handles your health plan for advice here. If Medicare is primary for you and you don't apply for Medicare part "B," you may find unfortunately that you have NO coverage at all. As a rule, if Medicare doesn't pay, your medigap supplemental insurance will not pay. So, if your medical insurance is not properly set up at retirement, you may be faced with a significant unpaid medical liability that could derail your retirement portfolio irrevocably. Professional courtesy goes only so far! When checking, make clear your employee status (ie, true employee or 1099 consultant) because that can make a difference in how you're classified for benefit purposes. Again, watch out for this one!

- By now, unless you are independently wealthy, you should be converting your invested assets to the type of allocation that emphasizes income with moderate growth potential. See my earlier discussion above at earlier ages.

- Is there a "correct" order in which you should spend down your assets during retirement? The nonspecific answer is that retirement distributions and spending should be a personalized matter based on your particular needs for income. But in actuality there is a general pattern of liquidating assets from various parts of your overall portfolio that makes sense in the majority of cases. It's called the "tax efficient order of spending (down)." First, spend down your taxable (nonqualified) assets, including capital gains assets. Second, spend down your tax-deferred assets such as IRAs, deferred annuities, qualified plans, nondeductible IRAs, etc. Third, spend down your Roth IRAs or other tax-free assets such as life insurance cash values for retirement income. There are certainly exceptions to these rules, based on individual circumstances and liquidity needs or family or charitable gifting programs, but this progression is ordinarily the most tax-efficient way to proceed. "Income allocation" as discussed earlier can also be factored in.

AGE 70 ½

George Foreman, the former boxer and current entrepreneur, said, "The question isn't at what age I want to retire, it's at what income." Truly, we can all retire now if we want to! It's just that our standard of living might be less than adequate.

So, at age 70 ½, many of you will be fully extracted from your medical practice and retired; some others may not. Some will be working by choice; others will be working because they did not plan early enough and well enough. Which will you be? Which do you want to be?

One would think that by age 70 ½, there are no major retirement issues left to discuss. But there are, and here's a short list:

- At age 70 ½, you have no choice but to begin removing money from your IRAs and other qualified plans (for exceptions, see #2 and #3 below). The rules are somewhat complicated and space does not permit me to explain all the details. However, suffice it to say that you may delay your first "required mandatory (or minimum) distribution" (RMD) to no later than April 1st of the year AFTER you turn age 70 ½ or you can simply take your first RMD during the year you actually turn age 70 ½. If you do elect to delay your RMD, then in that second year you must take 2 distributions since you can only delay the first year's distribution. So, unless your income will drop dramatically in year 2, take that first age 70 ½ distribution in the year you actually turn 70 ½.

NOTE: Recall earlier that for 2009 only, RMDs have been eliminated, but only for 2009. You may take a distribution but it is not mandatory.

- One exception to the general RMD rule is if you continue to work and have assets in a 401(k) plan at work. In that case, you can delay taking mandatory distributions from the 401(k) as long as you continue to work. This exception does not apply to IRAs or other qualified plans, but only to 401(k)s.

- If you've worked in a hospital or other nonprofit organization, and you've been saving money in a 403(b) plan since before the mid-1980s, you may have some grandfathered amounts in those accounts that permit the RMDs to be delayed for those grandfathered assets only, until age 75. Check with your 403(b) provider for details on this possible tax break.

- If you have several IRAs with different bank custodians or brokerage firms, you may want to sign up for automatic RMD distributions from each account on a given date annually or spread out through the year. This is for convenience and can simplify your life. It transfers the liability for making the proper distribution to each of the custodians. If an account is fully invested in mutual funds, the custodian may sell off shares to raise cash to make the distribution. Check if there's a process the custodian uses to determine what gets sold first, and whether you can have a say in making that determination. Some allow it, most do not.

- RMD rules do not dictate that you take RMDs from each of your IRAs. Let's suppose you have 2 IRAs, one with CDs and cash and the other investing in, for example, an S&P 500 index fund. Let's assume further that the index fund is down 40% for the year. You don't want to sell the index fund to raise cash to cover that IRA's RMD amount. Instead the RMD rules allow you to take the total RMD monies from just one IRA, in this case, from your IRA containing just the CDs. This way you can let the index fund recover without having to "sell low."

- The RMD rules do NOT specifically require that you distribute CASH from an IRA to satisfy the RMD rules. What if you owned only one IRA containing an S&P 500 index fund down 30% for the year? Instead of selling now while shares are way down, you could elect to transfer in-kind as many shares of the fund to an outside nonqualified account as equal the RMD value on the day they are transferred. So, you transfer shares, not cash. Be careful though that the value of the shares at transfer equals or exceeds the RMD amount, as the share price for a mutual fund is determined at the end of the trading day on which the transfer takes place. Price fluctuations can alter the value and cause it to drop below the RMD amount. For exchange traded funds (ETFs) and stocks, the price at sale, whenever that is during the day, governs so you know instantly the market value of the in-kind transfer. Remember, if you fail to make the correct RMD distribution, you must pay a 50% excise tax on the difference between what you were required to take out, and what you actually took out. That's too steep a penalty to ignore or invite.

- A final planning pointer, and a subtle contradiction to the order of distribution (see Age 65, bullet above) of your retirement assets, involves the scenario where you do not need your IRA RMD for living expenses and never will. Further, you have significant assets that surely will cause an estate tax liability and you have heirs you'd like to benefit from your lifelong accumulation of assets. One solution is to use RMDs from the IRA to seed an irrevocable trust funded with life insurance (ILIT). The RMDs are taxable anyway, as is the balance of the IRA payable to nonspouse beneficiaries who elect not to "stretch" out the IRA. But the insurance in the ILIT can escape both income and federal estate taxes at your death. It's a surefire way to convert taxable assets into tax-free assets to maximize the amount of your wealth that your heirs could receive from your estate (and your spouse's).

There are many variations of this tax conversion opportunity, such as the so-called "municipal bond rescue plan," so check with your financial advisor or insurance broker to determine if such a strategy could work for you.

In the final analysis, *Wall Street Journal* columnist Jonathan Clements best describes the concept of retirement. He says, "Retirement is like a long vacation in Las Vegas. It's good to enjoy it to the fullest, but not so fully that you run out of money."[9] Will you be prepared for the longest vacation of your life? If you have not checked recently, when will you?

REFERENCES

1. Improving Retirement Readiness[brochure]. Boston, MA: Fidelity Investments Institutional Services Company;2006.
2. Clements J. Don't sweat the small stuff. *Wall Street Journal Sunday.* April 17, 2005.
3. Rudzinski K. Avoiding the dark side of retirement. *Ocular Surgery News.* 2005;23(20).

4. Rudzinski K. Will you be ready for the longest vacation of your life: Part 1 of 2. *Cardiology Today*. 2007; 10(9).

5. Randall C. Encore [a special report]. Wall Street Journal. December 11, 2006.

6. Scism L. Added value and anxiety – for variable annuity owners. *Wall Street Journal.* February 2, 2009: R1.

7. Murray N. The devil, the deep blue sea, and the variable annuity. Available at http://www.because-money.com/articles/2006/jul/thedevil4.html. Accessed June 3, 2009.

8. Greene K. Social security estimate assumes work until age 66. *Wall Street Journal.* January 24-25, 2009.

9. Clements J. Playing the right retirement cards. *Wall Street Journal.* November 16, 1999.

This chapter is a significantly rewritten expansion of the following previously published articles:

- Rudzinski K. Will you be ready for the longest vacation of your life: Part 1 of 2. *Cardiology Today.* 2007;10(9).

- Rudzinski K. Will you be ready for the longest vacation of your life: Part 2. *Cardiology Today.* 2007;10(11).

Used with permission.

9

"The Death of Equities?"

"The death of equities looks like an almost permanent condition—
reversible someday, but not soon."
—*Business Week*, "The Death of Equities," August, 1979

Who among us was not relieved when the Times Square New Year's ball hit bottom, signaling the end of 2008 and the beginning of 2009? When the lights flashed and the confetti fell, the final chapter in the perfect investment storm that was 2008 became history, soon to be replaced by intermittent optimism mixed with a heavy dose of global uncertainty and doubt for 2009 and beyond.

Market history will show that the Dow Jones Industrial Average (DJIA) fell -31.93% in 2008, the S&P 500 Index dropped -37.00%, and the Nasdaq Composite Index plunged -40.54%. Globally, equities plummeted even farther than the US markets with the Europe, Australia and Far East (EAFE) Index registering a decline of more than -43%.

As I write these words, early in 2009, the country is in the midst of its worse recession since the 1980s. Job losses are surpassing the 500,000 mark almost every month and the holiday retail season was a plain bust. Forecasters predict further unemployment records for 2009 as almost every sector in the economy registers negative growth. The news media hypes the doom and gloom daily with pessimistic stories about the new homeless or the old Wall Street crowd, each beaten down by negative economic forces from all sides. There truly is "no joy in Mudville..." but for many other reasons that Casey just could not comprehend.

But I've been raised with the notion that things are never as bad—nor as good—as they appear to be. At each end of the investment spectrum, one filled with eternal optimism and euphoria, the other besieged by depression and hysteria, emotions of greed and fear dominate the minds of the average investor. According to Maryland investment specialist, Nasser Ali, CFA, CFP, CRPC, AAMS, CMFC, this nurtures the naive belief that when things are great they will always be great, and when they're bad, they will always be bad (oral communication, December 19, 2008).

Rudzinski K. *The Physician's Guide to*
Avoiding Financial Blunders (pp 137-146)
© 2009 SLACK Incorporated

How did you personally handle the extreme market volatility of the October-November 2008 investment storm? As the US markets were dropping 22% in 7 straight sessions in October, did you lose your nerve and sell impulsively, turning a paper decline to that point into an actual and perhaps permanent loss? Or did you hang on by your fingernails, trusting that market history was on your side despite the daily media message that things were "different" this time around and that the eventual recovery may be 5, 10, or who knows how many years from now? Either way, you could not escape the emotional toll the market turbulence dumped on you.

This brings me to the highly fascinating piece, "The Death of Equities" which first appeared in the August 13th, 1979 issue of *Business Week*.[1] Take the time to "Google" information about this article written during another period of major doom and gloom sentiment. According to Business Week, "The masses long ago switched from stocks to investments having higher yields and more protection from inflation. Now the pension funds—the markets' last hope—have won permission to quit stocks and bonds for real estate, futures, gold and even diamonds."[1] The article continues, "Further, this 'death of equity' can no longer be seen as something a stock market rally—however strong—will check..."[1] Lastly, *Business Week* concludes, "Only the elderly who have not understood the changes in the nation's financial markets, or who are unable to adjust to them, are sticking with stocks."[1]

In August 1979, *Business Week* could not see beyond the pessimism of the moment and recommended that investors abandon the equity markets permanently for such diverse investments as gold, diamonds, real estate, etc. In August 1982, the US equity markets began the longest bull market in its history while gold plummeted from its peak in 1980. Though investing in equities in August 1979 was not at the bottom of the markets, it did represent a tremendous buying opportunity for the long term if an investor was able to penetrate the dire doomsday message expressed by notable expert analysts quoted in the *Business Week* article.

The same negative media frenzy occurred in the summer-fall of 1990 as the S & L crisis (when an average of one bank closing per day was not uncommon from 1986 to 1991), a pending war in the Middle East, recession, and bear market all clouded the investment horizon for those investors stuck in the moment with only a daily, weekly or monthly vision of the future. None other than the former stellar fund manager Peter Lynch of Fidelity Magellan fame commented on the "end-of-the-world" picture painted by the entire media community that fall.

It's easy today sitting here looking back in hindsight at the past treatment of market lows by the news media. But it's also highly enlightening. Ask yourself, if you were sitting on your front porch back in August 1979, surrounded by such "expert insight" as portrayed in the *Business Week* headline story, could you, would you have ventured into the fearful market unknown and continued investing in your retirement plan with only a hope and a prayer? Or would you have considered bailing out and going to cash or plunging into gold futures or diamonds? Would a sense of market history have helped you then?

You are now that investor here in late 2008 or early 2009. You either resign yourself to an investment in US Treasuries, yielding a near 0% rate of return or low-yielding money markets and CDs, or you take a step to the future by hiking through the past made crystal-clear by the passage of time. Sitting on your porch today, as an investor, what do you see? Do you think for yourself, or are you guided only by the opinions of others when they tell you that "equities are horrible and are to be avoided—forever!" At the opposite end, in early 2000, did you believe that technology and dot.com stocks were truly a separate economy and could continue forever, disobeying the common sense rules of supply and demand?

Whatever you did or believed, it's important to remember that things are never as bad, nor as good, as they appear to be.

In autumn, 2008, especially in October, I started receiving calls from clients who were becoming frantic about the seemingly unprecedented market decline and its effect on their portfolios. Even clients whose portfolios were over-weighted in bonds were concerned about the future. The newspapers they read and the market-oriented TV shows they watched day after day enumerated reasons why we were "surely" entering the "Great Depression" of 2008 to 2009. Hearing their emotions as well as their words, sometimes panicked, sometimes resigned, I sat down to write out in article form information about market history and investor behavior that I was discussing with my clients in those calls almost daily. Two of those articles were published in various medical specialty publications in January and June 2009.[2] They were written in late 2008 without the benefit of any crystal ball as we headed into the unknown and unclear investment world of 2009. I've reproduced them here in their entirety to give you a look at another perception of the market lows we were experiencing and how to deal with your own emotional investment behavior during such pessimistic times. If the markets of 2008 to 2009 were never to be repeated, then you would be wasting your time going any further? Why worry about the past? But, as we know, recessions and bear markets are all too common, so moving forward we can expect to experience not only the euphoria and excitement of market highs again but also the depression and fear of market troughs. You can bet on it. So keep this book and chapter handy for the next time!

With those thoughts in mind, let's examine another viewpoint of the markets to contrast that with the doom and gloom media that we all seemingly can't avoid.

THIS IS WHAT IT FEELS LIKE TO BUY LOW

Submitted for publication on November 17, 2008

As an investment advisor, I sense things are getting real bad out there, maybe even approaching market bottoms, or so-called "capitulation," when long-time clients who have never been bothered by the vagaries of the equity markets begin calling me looking for "good news" or "words of wisdom." One client in particular called me and said, "I know what you're gonna tell me, but I need to hear it anyway." How about you? How are you handling the extreme market volatility we've experienced throughout 2008? Are you beginning to believe that fear and doom and gloom are justified, that we are approaching, what I heard one TV reporter say, "the end of the world as we know it?" Are you convinced that this global recession we're experiencing is bottomless and that the newly-elected Obama administration is powerless to stop it? If so, you are not alone.

But let me add this to your monsoon-drenched parade, "This is what it feels like to buy low."

Suppose you and I were sitting in your office or at your kitchen table last July 2007 as the equity markets cruised higher powered by a 5-year bull market, and in the course of our discussion about investment principles we verbally espoused that old fundamental truth, "Buy low; sell high." We would have nodded in clear and objective agreement with that statement and with barely an afterthought, rambled along on other investment matters. Now, let's have that same conversation today, when you may be at the point of bailing out of your equity positions (or you've already bailed!), down 45.8% since October 9, 2007,[7] and dropping further. You've got a lot of cash sitting idly on the sidelines from matured CDs and maybe you're even thinking about stopping your 401(k) or other retirement plan payroll contributions in order to "wait until things clear up a bit." Yes, you tell yourself, "it's different this time; not even close to the prior nine recessions we've had since 1957."[7]

"Buy low; sell high!" If that was unabashedly true last July, why isn't it even truer today? Because when we talked last year, we weren't confronted with the "end of the world," highly charged emotional roller coaster we find ourselves on today, that's why. Oh, yes, this time it's different! No recovery in sight; good news has died. We had no emotional ball and chain last year, but we do now.

But I suggest to you that the "low" we talked about before is staring us in the face, maybe not the lowest of the low, but more likely closer to the bottom than to the top. As I write this, the S&P 500 Index has plunged (to use a media "scare word") more than 45% from its high last October 9th.[7] Could it go lower? Yes, of course, and maybe it will. But, borrowing from our conversation of last year, I contend the following: "This is what it feels like to buy low." Do you remember my previous analogy about shopping at Jim's? Well, Jim is throwing a party and offering a 45% sale. He may go lower, but then again he may come to his senses and slowly or abruptly terminate the sale, perhaps returning to his usual 10%, 20%, or 30% markups (see Chapter 2, Mistake #3).

Warren Buffett said it right when he proclaimed, "Be fearful when others are greedy, but be greedy when others are fearful."[3] To that, let me add, "The only people who get hurt on roller coasters are the jumpers."

But, you say, look at those headlines! The "experts" are saying things like:

- "Can Your Bank Stay Afloat?" *U.S. News*, November 12th
- "Uncertainty Reigns for The U.S. Economy", *Wall Street Journal*, December 3rd
- "How The Real Estate Crash Threatens Financial Institutions", *U.S. News*, December 16th
- "The Real Estate Bust", *Newsweek*, October 1
- "Housing Recession That Began In The Northeast Three Years Ago Now Engulfs Entire Nation", *New York Times*, December 16

Can't you see, it's different this time! Is it really? Granted, there are certainly unique facts and circumstances to this market decline and recession that make it appear "different" on the surface. But check this out! As I was researching data for the chapter on investments in my upcoming book for physicians about avoiding financial blunders, I went back to read Peter Lynch's book about his managing the renowned Fidelity Magellan Fund. In it, he itemizes some of the more pessimistic headlines of the year 1990, some of which I cited above.

Yes, 1990! Back then it was the Savings & Loan crisis when banks were closing by the hundreds; it was the United States and its allies on the verge of the first Gulf War with no guarantee that we would be successful; it was the country in the midst of a deep and seemingly endless recession; and it was the equity markets roiled by all of the uncertainty we were facing, all of which, it appeared, were "different from anything else we had ever experienced before." It would not have been unusual to hear people moan in the fall of 1990 that, "It's different this time. We know markets recover in time, but not now, because it's different this time."

As if to echo but defeat that prevalent "end of the world" notion in 1990, on page 44 of his book, Peter Lynch summarizes what happened following the months and months of negative doom-and-gloom media that could be summarized by a headline in Barron's that read, "Suspense and dread cast a heavy pall over the markets."[4] To quote Lynch, "Of course we now know the war wasn't as terrible as some had expected... and what we got from the stock market instead of a 33% drop was a 30% gain in the S&P 500 average, a 25% gain in the Dow, and a 60% gain in smaller stocks. You would have missed it if you paid the slightest attention to our celebrated prognostications."

Yes, it was just as different then as it is right now! My suggestion is to turn off Cramer, and take a ride in the country fueled by gasoline that's now selling below $2.00 a gallon, and which was predicted just a few short months ago, by THE experts, to break through $5.00 a gallon on its way to...?

(Author's note: Gasoline prices have risen to about $2.50 per gallon since last November.)

Although the history of a certain recession or bear market is never exactly like another before it, one thing does remain consistent over time, and that is that the fundamentals of investing do not change. Paramount among those basic rules is this: when markets become overpriced, sell; when markets become over sold, buy. In other words, buy low, sell high. Unfortunately, what the ordinary investor does is this: when stocks become very expensive (market highs), buy; when stocks get very cheap (market lows), sell. In other words, buy high, sell low. I am not advocating market "timing" here as much as I'm stating the way the "average" investor tends to behave.

I recall a line in the movie, "A League of Their Own," when baseball manager Tom Hanks tells his star player after she says the game is "too hard," that it's meant to be hard, and that's what makes the game so great. As many investors have discovered recently again, successful investing is not easy, it's hard. It's difficult to stay invested as markets plunge and to continue automatic investing at market lows when every human emotion is screaming at them to bail out before the market retreats farther and farther until all their money is gone—forever.

But it's that hard part—the staying invested—that makes for successful results over time. It's the tenacity and fearlessness in good investors that overcomes the huge rate of return deficit in portfolio success as measured by the Dalbar Institute (see Chapter 2). It's not an easy task to be like Warren Buffett in the middle of a market landslide and be "greedy when others are fearful."[3] It's much simpler to be humanly frightened like everyone else.

Sometimes just contemplating what another human might have felt in 1931, 1942, 1974, or 1990 as their economic and financial worlds were collapsing, is not only comforting but objectively instructive. It helps to imagine that the facts and circumstances during these times were as different as today is to 1990, 1974, or 1931, and that someone sitting on his porch in 2015 may look back and think about us today in 2009 in the same way we contemplate these past events.

So, past market history can be useful in the storm if for no other reason than to lessen the tug of the emotions that cause investors to make the Big Mistake over and over again (see Chapter 2). It's for this reason that I wrote the second article I titled "What The Past Teaches Us About Investing." Here it is in its unedited entirety.

WHAT THE PAST TEACHES US ABOUT INVESTING

Submitted for publication on December 3, 2008

Since the daily volatility in the stock markets ratcheted up in October to levels rarely experienced before, I've received numerous calls from clients who needed to hear an alternative view to the media's overwhelming 24/7 "end of the world as we know it" mantra. One especially agitated client blurted out as I picked up the phone, "I know what you're going to tell me, but I just need to hear it." Have there been days in the last 2 months where your investor temperament bordered on panic or on emotional distress? If so, you are truly not alone.

Clients expect their advisors to be unemotional about their money even while they can't sleep at night or are afraid to open their monthly account statements. I suspect that the fruited plains are rife with similar investor behavior. As long as that behavior does not get irrational, then fine; if it does, then such investors are prone to make the big mistake, which can be summarized as the following, "Sell low, buy high."

In my last article, I wrote about "this is what it feels like to buy low" and the headlines from 1990, which mimicked those of today's market decline and recession. Today, as the Big Three beg for Washington, DC money, let me give you some more market history to think about. Unemotional facts about similar times can help you cope with the extreme distress you might feel as you flip on your favorite cable show to see how much money you "made" or "lost" today. I'm not saying that a trip through the past will turn the markets around. What it can do though is to change your focus from the daily DJIA bouncing ball to a much broader perspective of the various equity markets as they have repeated themselves over the last 50 years or so.

Let's talk about bank failures. Twenty-two of them in 2008, through December 1st. Big news, right, every time another one goes down the tubes? Why? We're told that only 22 banks failed from 2002 to 2007 , and now, 22 in 2008 alone! But lest we forget, during the 5 years from 1987 to 1991, a total of 1901 US banks and savings and loan institutions either failed or required financial assistance from the government, or more than 1 per day.[5] So, 1901 versus 22—different perspective, different mindset.

Through December 1st, the S&P 500 Index was down 37.7% year-to-date (YTD) (total return). This decline will rival the previous worst annual decline of the S&P 500 Index when it fell 43.3% in 1931. Let's see, 1931 was the Great Depression, therefore we must be heading toward the Great Depression of 2008, as the pundits will tell us. But that's only half the story. The other half is that in the 5 years following 1931 (1932 to 1936), the S&P 500 Index gained +176%, or better than an average annual gain of 22% (total return).[7] Not a bad take-home gain, right?

Do real, pertinent facts like these mean we are surely headed for a bull market rally in 2009? No, not at all. But what they tell us is that the worst of times can in fact be followed by a significant market reversal and the good times we hope for but fear may never return. Remember this: there was no reason a person in 1931 might be optimistic about the markets in years to follow, like now. But those next 5 years taken together were gold!

On November 20, 2008, the S&P 500 plunged to its lowest closing point during the current bear market, or -51.9% from its peak on October 9th, 2007. The magnitude of this decline was the worst since 1942.[7] No reason for optimism right now? No reason for people in 1942 to be optimistic either as the United States prepared for war after a decade of the Great Depression (preceded by the stock market crash), a real estate crash, massive unemployment, credit contraction, plummeting agricultural commodity prices, and the bombing of Pearl Harbor. Seemed then like the future was nothing but doom and gloom. Sorta like now, maybe?

Ponder this for a moment. From April 1, 1942, an investment of $10,000 in the S&P Composite Index returned 54.27% 12 months later. Further, it gained 19.54%, 18.53%, and 17.12% annually over the next 5, 10, and 20 years, respectively, to $236,035 at the end of the 20 years.[6] From the worst of times to the best of times! As Warren Buffet says, "...be greedy when others are fearful."[3]

The same market reversal occurred from the depths of the 1973-1974 recession. We had the OPEC oil embargo, high energy prices (remember the gas lines?), Watergate, a war in the Middle East (1973), high inflation, interest rates, and unemployment. Then there was the Chrysler bailout in the mid 1970s. But if you had invested $10,000 in the S&P 500 Index (you couldn't, but let's pretend), you would have earned an annualized return of 38.13%, 16.86%, 15.63%, and 15.11% over 1, 5, 10, and 20 years, respectively, or $166,942 over the 20-years.[6] But would you have had the courage to do that then? Do you now?

Will such investment histories repeat themselves? Maybe yes, maybe no, because past history is no guarantee of future performance. But the next time you are watching TV or reading the hometown newspaper, and they are both dripping with pessimism, fear, and doubt, remember that a crystal-ball view of the future without a corresponding trip through the past may give you only a distorted and incomplete vision of the reality that the equity markets demand. So, when clients call seeking peace from the storm, my tale to them of the future is a firm glimpse of the past.

A new investment year as well as an entirely new political environment in Washington, DC was ushered in in 2009. It's impossible to say whether the optimism caused by the new administration or the pessimism of the continued recession will prevail when next the ball drops atop Times Square, announcing 2010. But one thing is certain—investors will behave as investors do and markets will behave as markets do. I cannot affect the markets, but perhaps I may have struck a chord with you to examine your behavior as an investor and to make whatever changes you should to achieve true long-term market returns and not those of the "average" Dalbar Institute investor. It's up to you.

REFERENCES

1. The death of equities. *Business Week*. August 13, 1979.
2. Rudzinski K. This is what it feels like to buy low. *Cardiology Today*. 2009;10(11)
3. Buffet W. Buy American. I am. *The New York Times*. October 16, 2008. http://www.nytimes.com/2008/10/17/opinion/17buffett.html?_r=1. Accessed July 7, 2009.
4. Lynch P. *Beating the Street*. New York, NY: Fireside: 1993; 41-44.
5. Higley M. By the number$ newsletter. December 1, 2008.
6. Weldon M. Take a deep breath and consider buying. Jersey City, NJ: Lord Abbett; 2009.
7. BTN Research weekly newsletter. December 1, 2008. Available at http://philbirnbaum.com.

This chapter uses the following previously published articles with permission:

- Rudzinski K. This is what it feels like to buy low. *Cardiology Today*. 2009;10(11)

- Rudzinski K. What the past teaches us about investing. *Hem/Onc Today*. 2009;10(11).

10

Creative Do's and Disastrous Don'ts in Your Estate Planning

"Taxes are enforced exactions, not voluntary contributions."

Author's Note: It is expected that both Congress and the Obama administration will work toward modifying current estate tax laws sometime before the end of 2009. Readers will be able to access an updated version of this chapter after December 31, 2009 along with bonus planning ideas and concepts by sending a request to bookspublishing@slackinc. com.

Can you imagine coming out of surgery and finding out the DJIA had dropped 4500 points that afternoon and could never recover? Imagine further that you were fully invested in the equity markets and that this 45% permanent loss of your net worth could have been prevented simply by having adopted some basic defensive strategies.

Would you be kicking yourself now if you had not fully prepared for that possibility?

Failure to properly plan for the passage of your accumulated assets to your heirs can have the same effect on their value as a 40% or 50% drop in the stock markets. The only difference is that market declines are temporary, even the bad ones; estate taxes are permanent. But it's worse than that. Estate taxes, once paid to the IRS, are forever lost to your family. As an example, suppose you fail to remove a $2,000,000 life insurance policy from your estate. You and your spouse die in a plane crash in the Hudson River, and the estate tax on the policy alone is $900,000 in a 45% estate tax bracket. Your children/grandchildren painfully write the check to the IRS, and the money is gone, gone,

Rudzinski K. *The Physician's Guide to Avoiding Financial Blunders (pp 147-164)*
© 2009 SLACK Incorporated

gone. At 7%, that $900,000 you gifted to the IRS would have grown to over $7,000,000 in 30 years and to over $14,000,000 in 40 years. That's how an innocuous estate planning error can compound itself and deprive your family of significant future dollars.

So let me ask you. When was the last time you reviewed and updated your important estate documents? If you have not yet created those documents, what have you been waiting for? If you don't do this, who will? The answer to the last question is easy. The state where you legally reside will dictate, by law, how your assets will be divided. This is called "intestacy" and applies to those people who die without a will. If that's you, you forfeit the right to say who gets what and when and how they get it.

Except for jointly held property (including community property), beneficiary designations, and business contracts, which all have survivorship provisions built in, all other property in your estate passes according to the intestacy laws in your state when you die without a will. Ordinarily, that might mean your spouse only gets one-third of your property and your children, two-thirds. Other relatives like your wife's lazy brother Biff or your irresponsible sister Susan may get access to some of your property if you have no children. Without a will, your estate is subject to attacks from all sides. It's like walking through a germ-infested preschool classroom in January with your immune system shut down. You invite unwanted and perhaps deadly germs into your bloodstream just like you'd be inviting "in-laws and outlaws" into your estate "plan."

Planning Pointer

You can look up the intestacy laws for your state by going to http://finance.cch.com/text/c50s10d190.asp and then clicking on your state at the map.

I will assume here that most of you have taken the time to visit with your estate attorney to do at least some basic planning so that your lifetime of accumulated assets can and will pass effortlessly and efficiently to the next generation and beyond. So this last chapter will address some classic and creative do's and don'ts that you may wish to incorporate into your estate planning if you haven't done so already. We'll use a Q&A approach to raise the estate issues you should be aware of. But first some basics.

TABLE 10-1

GIFT AND ESTATE TAX—2009

Gift tax annual exclusion	$13,000
Highest estate and gift tax rate	45%
Estate tax exemption	$3,5000,000
Lifetime gift exemption	$1,000,000

Ten years ago, the estate exemption was only $600,000. It has now expanded to $3,500,000 (Table 10-1). Twenty years ago, the concept of having a "trust protector" was relatively unknown; today it is fairly common. My point is that no matter how much planning you have done up to this point, you will most certainly need to revisit each and every part of that plan now or shortly after any comprehensive changes in

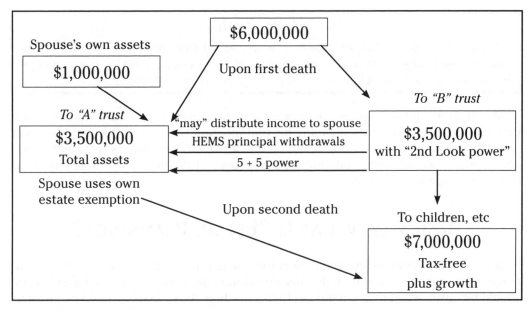

Figure 10-2. Example of a typical A-B trust arrangement.

estate tax law become effective in 2009 or, at the latest, in 2010. Let me give you one simple example of why this is so. Many attorneys in the past drafted two-part wills that permitted estate assets to be divided up in trust such that federal estate taxes were kept to a minimum if not eliminated altogether. This was accomplished by an estate plan that would leave an amount in trust to the children equal to the then-current estate tax exemption. This trust was called the "B" (bypass) or credit shelter trust. The balance of the estate went to the spouse outright or in trust (called the "A" or marital trust). With the exemption rising to $3,500,000 in 2009, many of those wills and trusts contain provisions that will place unnecessary restrictions on the surviving spouse's access to principal in the estate (Figure 10-2). How might that be?

As mentioned above, the "B" trust served to reduce estate taxes to the minimum amount possible. Although the spouse had income and certain principal withdrawal rights in the "B" trust, the "B" trust was designed to leave assets ultimately to the children and grandchildren tax-free. So, if you had $1,300,000 of assets, and the exemption was $600,000, the formula put $600,000 into the "B" trust and the balance, or $700,000, went to your spouse outright or in trust. Now flash forward to 2009. You now have $3,000,000 in assets solely in your name. The trust provisions (ie, funding the "B" trust first) would dump all $3,000,000 there with nothing going outright or in trust to your spouse. Here's the rub! Although your "B" trust may provide for income distributions to your spouse, it may also impose certain restrictions on her right to draw down principal if needed. This is unnecessary today because, in reality, assuming no growth in the assets, all $3,000,000 could now be left to your spouse outright or in trust estate tax free, since the exemption is now $3,500,000. So, at a minimum, a will structured like this needs to be reviewed and possibly revised. How do your documents divide up property in your estate (or your spouse's estate)? When did you last look?

Action Item

Schedule an estate planning "fire drill" with your attorney to determine what, if any, changes need to be made to your estate plans in light of new estate tax laws, changes in your family, asset values, or medical practice structure and value.

At this point, let's consider some questions and answers on other estate issues that may be of use to you in planning for that meeting with your attorney. Some will cover the fundamentals of estate planning for the uninitiated; others will cover some advanced areas, including planning gaps and needed document updates, based on ever-changing estate tax laws.

BASICALLY, WHAT IS "ESTATE PLANNING"?

In its simplest form, estate planning is the efficient passing of your property to the people you wish to leave it to. It defines who should get your assets, what assets they should be given, when they should get them, and how those assets should be given to your heirs. In other words, the first goal of estate planning is to distribute your estate to your beneficiaries efficiently and economically. Beyond that, effective estate planning ensures:

- Your assets will be managed properly if you become incapacitated and cannot legally act with regard to those assets

- You preserve the value of your assets

- You reduce as much as possible estate settlement expenses and transfer costs

- You make maximum use of those lifetime gift opportunities as provided by current gift tax law, such as annual exclusion gifts and lifetime gifts

Over the years, I've seen estate planning where the "tail wags the dog" (ie, where the primary goal was to reduce or eliminate estate taxes at the expense of the heirs). I've also seen where estate values were not maintained such as happens when a prolonged bout of incapacity decimates the asset pool originally destined for heirs. And let's not forget the devastating drain on unprotected estate assets from a liability or malpractice lawsuit, the impact of which could have been prevented with proper planning.

If proper and efficient estate planning involves passing on the greatest amount of assets to your heirs, it is not just a matter of reducing or eliminating federal estate taxes. It involves asset protection, insurance and liquidity planning, survivorship income and specific needs (like education), portfolio maintenance, retirement asset planning, practice succession planning, etc. It also means having the correct and updated legal documents in place to clearly stipulate what you want accomplished, by whom, and when.

> ### Planning Pointer
>
> Your estate planning team should consist of various individuals who can professionally and objectively advise you in all the pertinent planning areas. Among these would be your estate planning attorney, trust officer, CPA, financial planner, etc. Be careful that these professionals do not operate in a vacuum, or in competition, as can happen. Someone needs to be both the catalyst and the coordinator of the various independent efforts. In my experience, many advanced estate planners in the financial services arena serve this purpose very well. Without this "quarterback," it is not unusual for planning gaps and/or for lost opportunities to occur. For example, you may have a brilliant estate attorney who has drafted the best estate documents but if all of your assets are not lined up with those documents, the documents may become useless at best and counterproductive at worst. So, when you draft your estate team, know who your quarterback will be first.

WHAT ESTATE DOCUMENTS SHOULD I HAVE IN PLACE?

At a minimum, you should have a basic will; a financial durable power of attorney (FDPOA); an advanced medical directive (AMD), which consists of a medical power of attorney (MPOA), living will, and health care proxies; and perhaps a single or joint revocable trust. With larger estates, your will would contain most likely a "pourover provision" whereby the largest portion of your assets pours over to a revocable trust, which then acts as the document to designate who gets what part of your estate, when, and how. Lastly, your attorney may suggest a qualified terminable interest property (QTIP) trust for assets designated to your spouse, especially in a second (or more) marriage.

When you are young and single with minimal assets or married with or without young children, a simple will may be all you need. However, when you have young children, you should think about who should act as "guardian" for your kids if you die prematurely. There are 2 forms of guardianship here: for the "person" of your children (ie, physically taking care of them) and for the "assets" (the money you leave to your kids outright). You can name different people for each of these needs or the same guardian for both. For example, you may have a sibling who would be wonderful raising your children and another who is financially astute, so you split the guardianship.

> ### Planning Pointer
>
> Make sure you ask permission of the person or persons first before you name them as guardians, especially the one who will act as guardian of the person. They may or may not be agreeable to the task. Also, should you be thinking about a will provision that provides monetary support to the guardian(s) where adding your children to their family may cause some expensive changes in their lifestyle such as, for example, a larger house or an addition to the current house? Maybe you can provide for a financial "stipend" to the guardian(s) when your youngest turns 18 or older for having acted as your surrogate(s) while your children were growing up.

Your FDPOA authorizes someone (usually your spouse, or if single, a highly-trusted individual or institution) to act on your behalf should you be declared "incapacitated" and cannot legally perform for yourself matters such as signing tax returns, buying or selling real estate, etc. The power may be effective immediately or it may be "springing," meaning it becomes effective only when you are declared "incompetent" by law. Usually spouses act for one another, then one or more of the children may act, usually a child or children either who live nearby or who are financially astute.

Your AMD, briefly, contains the powers you clearly bestow, in advance, on one or more people to determine what medical treatments you should have and which you do not need in the event you are incapacitated and cannot make those decisions for yourself. These are actions required to keep you alive. On the other hand, the living will designates one or more people to make the "final" decision (ie, to "pull the plug") if all else fails. You name your spouse first, generally, then one or more children. You may grant the power to a specific child for the "keep me alive" decision where one child has a medical background, or has suitable personality traits, while naming all of your children for the "pull the plug" decision, not wanting to put that "life or death" decision on one child.

Many clients ask if a "revocable" or "living" trust is necessary for every estate. Generally, the larger an estate, the more the need for a revocable trust. Briefly, it works like this. You establish a revocable trust that you control as your own trustee. You re-title your assets into the trust. You can change the provisions of the trust anytime during your lifetime. The trust contains the provisions that divide up your assets at death and determines who inherits what, where, how, and when. Also, your will would be set up to pour over into your revocable trust assets still in your name at your death. The revocable trust has lifetime distribution provisions as well, but these are not the primary goal of the trust. Lastly, because you are your own trustee and control your revocable trust, the assets are still part of your estate when you die. So why do it?

Well, smaller estates may not need this complexity. But the revocable trust does accomplish 2 other things: 1) it allows for privacy and 2) it enables assets contained within to bypass your probate estate and thereby saves probate costs. These vary state by state. In Delaware, for example, probate costs are about 1.75% of probatable assets. As for privacy, because the assets in the trust pass outside of your probatable estate, the contents of the trust are not part of the public record. So, the revocable trust may have a place even in smaller estates where privacy as well as lower administrative costs are desirable.

WHAT IF I LEAVE ALL OF MY ASSETS TO MY SPOUSE, CAN I AVOID ESTATE TAXES?

In a word, yes. But attorney Bob Appel adds (personal communication, January 27, 2009), "...that may not be a good idea!" Spouses have an "unlimited marital deduction." They can leave everything they own to each other estate tax free at the first death. "It's at the second death, though, that the tax problem arises," Appel cautions. Here's why (Figure 10-3).

Under current law—as this book goes to print—you and your spouse can each leave up to $3,500,000 to beneficiaries other than your spouse's estate tax free. Refer to Figure 10-2. Let's say you leave your entire estate of $4,000,000 to your spouse, Lori. There's no estate tax due to the unlimited marital deduction. Lori adds that to her own $3,000,000 then passes shortly thereafter (common disaster car crash). She now has an

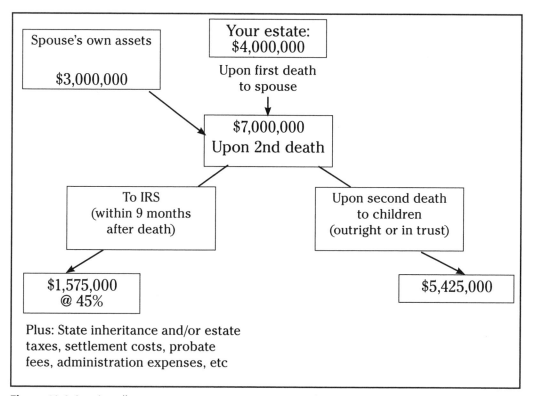

Figure 10-3. Leaving all your assets to your spouse: an example.

estate valued at $7,000,000 but only has a $3,500,000 deduction available to her estate, leaving the other $3,500,000 subject to tax at 45%. That's an unnecessary federal estate tax bill of $1,575,000, not counting state taxes and administrative and probate fees. Why "unnecessary"? Because, in your revocable trust, if you had set up a "B" trust, funded it with $3,500,000 of your assets at your death, giving Lori your other $500,000 to add to her own $3,000,000, you would have eliminated the $1,575,000 estate tax and other settlement costs. How? Assets placed into the "B" trust eventually go to your children tax free when Lori dies because she didn't own those assets, the "B" trust did. Her own estate is only $3,500,000. Therefore, her own exemption eliminates the tax on her assets. Bingo—the $1,575,000 tax disappears!

Lori would normally be able to access all of the income generated from the "B" trust (but she should take it only if she needs it [see p. 152]). Ordinarily, she'd have rights to access principal according to an "ascertainable standard" (for her health, education, maintenance, and support, or "HEMS" for short), perhaps additional rights to access principal not requiring the HEMS standard, and, lastly, she might have what is called a "second look power," or the right to change the amount of money going to the ultimate beneficiaries. Lori can't add a new beneficiary or even eliminate a beneficiary you name, but she can, for example, change a 50/50 split of assets to your 2 children to a 90/10 or even a 100/0 split. This might be useful if one child is getting divorced, is being sued, hits the lottery, or perhaps has been cruel or nonsupportive of Lori after you died. In other words, she can be given the power of the trust "purse strings."

Planning Pointer

In the past, many attorneys split assets into a pile for you and a pile for your spouse so that the "B" trusts could be funded in each estate. Doing so, however, may have been counterproductive in a malpractice liability situation as assets you own or those your revocable trust owns are assailable by predators and creditors (see Chapter 5). Nowadays, splitting up joint property, for example, is not absolutely necessary as joint revocable trusts have come into common usage. But it's still important to make sure that actions that are good for estate planning purposes do not degrade the highest level of asset protection that you need as a doctor.

WHAT IS AN IRREVOCABLE TRUST AND WHEN IS IT USED?

Unlike a "revocable" trust whose provisions can be changed at any time by the trustee, an "irrevocable" trust when established cannot be changed, altered, or modified in any way by the grantor of the trust (ie, the person who sets up the trust). So, for your irrevocable trust, you are the grantor. You name a trustee (cannot be you) to carry out the trust provisions, one of which may be to terminate the trust someday. See p. 159 for a commentary about a "trust protector" you might wish to include in your new irrevocable trust.

Spouses normally name the other to act as trustee, except in a joint irrevocable trust where a third-party trustee is needed. Assets (ie, money or an insurance policy) in the trust cannot revert to the grantor, but they can be distributed out to the trustee-spouse as trust beneficiary (and to other trust beneficiaries) if and when the trust is ever terminated. Spouses can be given other "access" rights to trust values if based on the HEMS standard (see p. 159). Your estate attorney can advise you on the feasibility of including those means of access as they are not advisable in all cases.

So when is such a trust called for? While there may be other uses such as for a special needs child or incapacitated adult, the main reason an irrevocable trust is established is to provide instant liquidity to an estate that lacks cash to cover estate settlement costs, including inevitable estate taxes. For example, your estate is valued at $12,000,000. You own IRAs and other assets, but the main assets are a 6000 sq ft. beach house on Malibu Beach, which you inherited from your parents, and a piece of land you bought years ago overlooking the ocean at Laguna Nigel. You want your family to keep these valuable assets, especially since real estate has been devalued, but at the second death of yourself and your spouse, the estate tax bill may be $2,250,000 ($12,000,000 − ($3,500,000 x 2) x 0.45% = $2,250,000). And this does not include state estate or inheritance taxes, as well as other administrative settlement costs.

Without extra liquidity in this case, your heirs might be forced to either sell one or both of the properties at exactly the wrong time or to liquidate all the other cash assets in your estate, leaving nothing for survivorship income or other cash needs like education. Additionally, if one of the cash assets is a $1,000,000 IRA, then it might have to be liquidated to cover the estate tax bill generating income taxes that will need to be paid as well.

Faced with large liquidity needs like this, many people will create an irrevocable trust and fund it with a life insurance policy, the combination being referred to as an ILIT, or "irrevocable life insurance trust." The reason for the life insurance is that the cash needed to cover taxes at the second death of yourself and your spouse becomes available exactly when it's needed. The "leverage" of life insurance makes it ideal for such use (ie, a small premium relative to the death benefit creates and maintains the policy).

So, in an ILIT, you as grantor (or you and your spouse in a joint survivorship ILIT) make a "gift" of the annual premium payment to the ILIT. The trustee then takes the money and pays the insurance premium. When you die (or when your spouse dies), the insurance proceeds are paid to the ILIT tax free and those tax-free dollars can be used to provide liquidity to the estate, via loans to the estate or the purchase of estate assets. The ILIT doesn't eliminate federal estate taxes; it merely provides the dollars to pay the tax, those dollars purchased with so-called "discounted dollars" via the low leveraged premium.

A word about gift tax issues in an ILIT. Money deposited to the ILIT ordinarily represents what is called a "gift of future interest" since the beneficiaries get no immediate benefit from the ILIT today. As a result, the gift of money to the ILIT does not normally qualify for the $13,000 annual exclusion. Instead, it reduces dollar for dollar the $1,000,000 lifetime gift exclusion you have been given under gift tax laws. This is usually not the result you want. So, to qualify the deposit to the ILIT for the $13,000 annual gift exclusion, you can give the trust beneficiaries the right to withdraw their pro rata share of the deposit temporarily, usually for 30 days. This is called a "Crummey" withdrawal right, from a court case decided in the taxpayer's favor. Your estate attorney can assist you in making this administrative requirement a simplified process. The bottom line is that the ILIT can help your family overcome liquidity needs in your estate in order to retain valuable illiquid assets that would otherwise have to be sold to cover the tax bill, which, incidentally, must be paid within 9 months after your death.

IN GENERAL, WHAT ARE SOME OTHER METHODS I CAN USE TO REDUCE ESTATE TAXES?

In the broadest sense, methods that help to reduce or even eliminate the federal estate tax, after taking into consideration the $3,500,000 exemption for yourself and your spouse, fall into 3 major categories: 1) removing assets from your estate, 2) using leverage, and 3) discounting of estate assets. In many cases, estate taxes are reduced by a combination of one, two, or three of these working together. Let's examine these.

Removing Assets From the Estate

Gifting is the best example of removing assets from your estate. Examples include the following:

- $13,000 annual exclusion per beneficiary; $26,000 per beneficiary for couples
- The $1,000,000 lifetime gift exclusion
- Gifts for education and for health care for one or more beneficiaries
- Gifts to Section 529 plans for children/grandchildren
- Gifts to charities

Annual exclusion gifts are simple yet effective ways to remove assets from your estate. At $13,000 per beneficiary per person ($26,000 for couples), you and your spouse could give away $260,000 annually to 10 beneficiaries. What's even better is that once the money is gifted, all future growth of the gifted amount is removed from your estate. So, over 10 years, gifting $260,000 per year, at 7% would remove over $3,800,000 from your estate, saving almost $1,730,000 in estate taxes in 45% estate tax bracket.

Planning Pointer

Because of the recent stock market declines, outright gifting can be so much more efficient. If a stock has declined 50%, you can pack twice as much value into a $13,000 gift now, allowing the future recovery of the stock value to take place in the name of your beneficiary, not in yours.

Gifts you make that do not qualify for the annual exclusion may still be sheltered by the $1,000,000 lifetime gift exclusion every taxpayer has. Use of this exemption during your lifetime can be powerful. For example, you own $1,000,000 of stock in a private company that you are certain will be purchased by a large public firm. You give away the stock to your grandchildren now at that current value. The company is in fact purchased and the stock value increases predictably to $5,000,000. All of the growth now, as well as all future growth, is outside of your estate – forever. Leveraging and or discounting the $1,000,000 exemption can make it even more efficient (see p. 155).

Often overlooked are gifts for education such as tuition, room and board, and for health care, including premiums for health insurance. If, for example, you make tuition payments directly to the education institution for your grandson, those payments are gifts, but they are not subject to the $13,000 annual exclusion limit. The key is to make the payments DIRECTLY TO the institution. Thus, you can give your grandson $13,000 and make his $30,000 tuition payment directly to the college as well. The same goes for gifts of health care costs paid directly to the provider of the medical services for a beneficiary, as well as premiums for health insurance. You can effectively remove tens or hundreds of thousands of dollars from your estate using such planned gifts.

You may recall from Chapter 5 that you can lump together 5 years' worth of gifts to fund a Section 529 college plan for your children/grandchildren. Therefore, you and your spouse can gift up to $130,000 ($13,000 x 5 x 2 = $130,000) in a single year per beneficiary into a 529 plan. However, if you die during the 5 years, the gifts made for years beyond the year of your death are brought back into your estate for tax purposes. So, if you put $65,000 into a Section 529 plan for your granddaughter and you die in the third year, $26,000 is brought back into your estate.

Planning Pointer

Gifts to Section 529 plans are effective as a method to remove assets from your estate and also as a means to remove those assets from the claims of predators and creditors. In effect, if you have 10 grandchildren, you and your spouse could gift $1,300,000 every 5 years to Section 529 plans and remove those assets (subject to state limits) from the reaches of potential creditors and predators.

Gifts to charities can be of many varieties. See the Q&A on p. 159.

Leveraging/Discounting Estate Assets

The best example of the use of leverage in estate planning is life insurance, as indicated in our previous discussion on ILITs. A small premium creates a big death benefit.

Another common example is the qualified personal residence trust (QPRT), where you gift your personal residence or vacation home to a trust. You retain the right to live in the house for a specified number of years. At the end of the term, if you are still alive, ownership of the house passes to your heirs, tax free. If you die during the term of the trust, the value of the personal residence or vacation home is brought back into your estate. In other words, it's a "heads I win, tails I break even" proposition since if you die before the end of the QPRT term, and the asset is brought back to your estate, you would have been taxed on it anyway. But don't forget, with a QPRT, you give away not only the value of the house at a discounted gift tax value, but also the entire future growth of that residence or vacation home, assuming you survive the term.

The discounting of the QPRT gift occurs because you retain the right to live in the house for a term of years. That right reduces the value of the remaining interest, along with the potential gift tax. Here's an example. You're age 65 and you own a $500,000 vacation home. You set up a QPRT, put (gift) the house into the QPRT, and retain the right to live there for 15 years. The federal discount rate is 2.4% (changes monthly). Your probability of living 15 years is 59.21% so the remainder interest is valued at $350,325. The amount of your taxable gift today is calculated at only $207,431. Bottom line: you made a gift valued today at $500,000 for the gift tax cost of only $207,431. If you chose to use some of your $1,000,000 lifetime gift, you only needed $207,431 instead of $500,000. And when the house passes to your children after 15 years, at whatever its appreciated value then, it passes tax free. Lastly, if the QPRT is set up as a "grantor" trust, you will get the mortgage interest and property tax deductions along the way.

A similar concept to the QPRT is the grantor retained annuity trust (GRAT). In a nutshell, you create an irrevocable grantor trust for a term of years into which you place an asset or assets, such as stock, bonds, etc. You retain the right to a fixed income payment from the GRAT, for example, 6% per year, and at the end of the term, if you are alive, the trust assets (called the "remainder interest"), including all future appreciation, pass tax free to your beneficiaries. Similar to the QRPT, your right to receive income from the GRAT produces a discounted gift value of the assets you put in the GRAT. Also, if you do not survive the term of the GRAT, like the QPRT, the assets in the GRAT are brought back into your estate. Here's how powerful a GRAT can be. You set up a GRAT and gift $1,000,000 of assets into the GRAT. You are to receive a 6% fixed income payment (based always on the original value put into the trust) at the end of each year for 10 years, after which the trust corpus, plus all appreciation, passes to your named trust beneficiaries. For our example, the federal discount rate is 2.4%.

As a result of this input, the remainder interest is valued at $527,848. Therefore, the gift tax value today of that remainder interest is only $472,152! In essence, you removed $1,000,000—and all its future growth—from your estate for the discounted gift tax value of only $427,152.

Another discounting technique is the use of the FLP or LLC. Briefly, you create an entity called an FLP and you transfer assets to the FLP. You retain all control rights as the general partner, and your beneficiaries are named limited partners with no control rights. Each year, you give away units of the FLP to your beneficiaries (ie, you transfer value to them). But because they hold only minority interests in the FLP usually subject to certain restrictions, and because they cannot sell their interests to anyone else outside the FLP (ie, lack of marketability), the value of the gifts are discounted sometimes as much as 35%.

```
┌─────────────────────────────────────────────────────────────────────────┐
│                           Planning Pointer                                │
│                                                                           │
│   The use of FLPs, LLCs, GRATs, etc present many areas of complexity that │
│   should involve only expert professional advisors. But these techniques  │
│   can be extremely useful in serving to reduce the size and scope of your │
│   estate, thus lessening the amount of federal estate taxes and other     │
│   transfer costs.                                                         │
└─────────────────────────────────────────────────────────────────────────┘
```

If My "B" Trust Exists to Pass Money to My Children Tax Free, Why Does It Contain Language That Requires Distributions to My Spouse During Her Lifetime? Isn't That a Self-Defeating Provision?

It very well may be, especially if your spouse does not need the income. Many trusts contain wording that dictates how income created in the trust is to be handled. It is either accumulated within the trust or it is distributed out to the beneficiaries at least annually. Taxable trust income paid out to beneficiaries is taxable to the beneficiaries. Accumulated income in the trust is taxable, tax deferred, or tax free depending upon the asset that produced it. However, trust income tax brackets become very high very fast, reaching the highest marginal bracket of 35% at only $11,150 of taxable income. So, paying out trust income to a spouse can have its income tax advantages, assuming the spouse is in a lower tax bracket than the trust, which would not be unusual. Remember though that tax-free or tax-deferral vehicles in the trust can almost eliminate taxable income if it is to be accumulated within the trust.

That said, many trusts in existence today, especially those written 10 or more years ago, may state the spouse's right to income in the following manner, "...the trust shall distribute income....at least annually...", with no other contingency. That means that there is no choice but to distribute income at least annually to the spouse. If he or she doesn't need that income, then the "shall distribute" provision forces income out of a trust that was created to grow estate tax free over time for the benefit of the children or grandchildren when the spouse dies. In other words, let's say that you fund your "B" trust with the 2009 exemption amount of $3,500,000. If the income in the trust is 5% annually, then the trust must distribute $175,000 out to the spouse even if she doesn't need it. What does she do with it? Maybe accumulates it, thus adding this annual income to her own estate. If she has assets of her own that equal or exceed the $3,500,000 exemption in her estate, then all that income from your trust will be taxed when she dies, assuming she doesn't gift it away (one solution) during her lifetime. What's the tax problem? Well, the additional federal estate tax at 45% on the $175,000 accumulated annually over 20 years at 7% would be over $3,228,000 (($175,000 x 20 x 7%) x .45) = $3,228,394). That's the problem your children will face eventually because of this drafting language used in your trust! Just one word—shall—caused a bigger tax bill.

This result can be avoided by substituting the phrase "may distribute" for "shall distribute." That change allows for income distributions but does not mandate them. Thus, where income taxes are an issue for the trust, the income can be distributed. Where the spouse wants and needs income, such as if the "B" trust is over funded at the expense of the "A" trust (see previous discussion), income can be distributed. When income is not needed or the goal is clearly to maximize the amounts passing to the children estate tax free, and where the income accumulating inside the trust can be rendered tax free or tax deferred, then the trust income can be accumulated.

As indicated earlier, dollars can be removed from the "B" trust under other provisions such as a HEMS-related withdrawal and the 5+5 power. These are usually regarded as rights to withdraw principal, not income, from the trust, and they are voluntary in nature. Figure 10-2 shows a typical A-B Trust Will/Revocable Trust setup.

Planning Pointer

What does your trust document say about income distributions? "Shall distribute" or "may distribute"? Attorneys sometimes use the "shall distribute" language followed by an "or" statement that allows income to be distributed "on behalf of" the spouse or other beneficiary. The latter provision helps prevent distributed trust income from being attached by creditors as the income is not given directly to the spouse. It is used to pay for expenses "on behalf of the" spouse by an independent trustee within the trust. In the final analysis, you should consult with your estate attorney to discuss the various pros and cons of the spousal distribution rights within your trust.

How Can I Use Charitable Gifts to Reduce Estate Taxes?

For many people, charitable gifts involve cash donations to their favorite charity, like their church, former college, the United Way, Boy Scouts, firehouse, etc. But it can be much more than that for the purposes of estate planning. Think of it this way: when you and your spouse die, your estate assets can go into one or more of 3 major buckets:

1. Your family's bucket—for your children and grandchildren

2. The IRS bucket—up to 45% of your taxable estate can wind up here

3. Charity bucket—for reasons and to places that warm your heart

That's it, just these 3 buckets. It's a zero sum equation—in other words, increasing the amount in one bucket directly reduces the amount in one or both other buckets. Every cent the IRS takes reduces the amount available to your heirs. Now, the question is how much do you want to leave in each? Your instincts would be to direct assets mostly to #1 and maybe some to #3, but certainly none to #2. Can there be a "zero tax" equation that effectively leaves out the IRS? Yes. To the extent that your total estate does not exceed $7,000,000, it is possible with proper planning—and the correct estate documents—to lock out the IRS as a beneficiary of your estate. The $3,500,000 estate exemption per spouse gives you that opportunity if fully and correctly utilized.

You can even do so if you have a $100,000,000 estate. Simply leave $7,000,000 to your children and grandchildren and, assuming you are the second to die between spouses, give the rest to charity. This is called a "zero tax" plan, no IRS involvement. But it is one rarely used because it obviously requires you to divert some of your hard-earned assets away from your natural bounty—your kids.

What is the middle ground, the way you can accomplish your first and foremost estate planning goal (ie, to leave the bulk of your assets efficiently and economically to your family), followed by your second goal, which is to reduce or eliminate the cash confiscation the IRS wishes to inflict on your ultimate asset pool? This is where basic and advanced charitable planning can help.

Generally, charitable gifts fall into at least 3 major categories: 1) outright gifts, 2) charitable bequests, and 3) gifts of a split interest.

Outright gifts are the kind you and I are normally associate with charitable gifting. We write a check to our church or synagogue or we donate clothes to Goodwill. In other words, we give cash or property directly to the charity. Besides the immediate gratification we feel for making the gift, we usually claim an income tax deduction for some or all of the gift value. The IRS limits these income tax deductions to a percentage of your AGI depending on what type of property was given away and to what type of charity—public or private—it was given. For example, we can only deduct an amount up to 50% of AGI for gifts of cash to public charities (most churches, hospitals, colleges, etc). Capital gain property valued at fair market value is generally limited to 30% of AGI. Other limits apply to other types of property given to charity. Excess deductions can be carried over for up to 5 years. Outright gifts to charity can also take the form of a charitable gift annuity or a pooled income fund.

With a *charitable gift annuity*, you enter into a contractual obligation with the charity. You give assets to the charity and the charity agrees to pay you a predictable income for the rest of your life (or the joint lifetime of yourself and another person, presumably your spouse). You get a current income tax deduction, actuarially calculated (not necessarily the amount you donate) at the time you make the donation, and the annuity payment to you is considered partially taxable interest and partially a tax-free return of principal. When you die, the gift annuity is not includible in your estate for federal estate tax purposes. For example, let's assume you are age 65 and you want to create a charitable gift annuity of $100,000. Let's further assume a 5.7% lifetime payout to you, and a federal discount rate of 3%. With these facts, you would receive an upfront charitable deduction of about $28,000 and almost $3700 of the $5700 annual payout would be excluded from current income taxation. When you die, the annuity payments stop as the charity has no further obligation. Annuity payments can be factored for your survivor as well.

A *pooled income fund* (PIF) is a trust maintained by a charity. You make a donation of cash or other property (can be nonincome-producing property) to the PIF. You then receive an income interest from the charity in the form of shares of the fund. The shares generate income to you for life or to a beneficiary (-ies) named by you. Income from the PIF paid to someone other than you constitutes a gift, which can be made to qualify for the $13,000 annual gift exclusion. A formula determines the amount of current income tax deduction you receive at the time of donation. All income though is taxable when received and, unlike the charitable gift annuity, the income from the pooled income fund is not predictable. When you die, the remainder interest goes to the charity and is therefore not taxed as part of your estate.

Charitable bequests are those gifts made at your death, through your will or trusts, consisting of a specific amount, a particular asset, or a percentage of your estate. The gift is generally revocable during your life if you change your mind. It becomes irrevocable only at your death. There are no current income tax benefits for naming a charity in your will, but the entire amount given to the charity when you die is deductible against the federal estate tax since the estate charitable deduction is unlimited.

Split interest charitable gifts are among the more complicated of the forms of charitable giving yet they can be extremely powerful. They consist of 2 parts: an income interest and a remainder interest and both charitable and noncharitable beneficiaries. Generally, they are set up as irrevocable trusts.

If a noncharitable beneficiary receives the income from the trust with the charity getting what's left over at the end (remainder interest), the trust is called a "remainder" trust (CRT). If it's the opposite, it's called a "lead" trust (CLT). If the income derived from the trust is a fixed percentage of the original amount invested, the trust is referred to as an "annuity" trust (CRAT). Annuity trusts cannot accept further contributions after the initial donation. On the other hand, if the income is a fixed percentage of the trust assets valued at the end of each year, it's called a "unitrust" (CRUT). Future contributions can be made to a unitrust. For example, you set up a trust that will pay you a 5% fixed income for life with the charity getting the trust corpus when you die. That's a CRAT. Alternately, if you set up a trust that pays a 5% fixed payment for 15 years to your church based on the value of the trust assets each year, with the remainder going to your children, that's a CLUT.

In a remainder trust, the trust corpus passes outside your estate as it goes to the charity; in a unitrust, the trust corpus can pass to your heirs as noncharitable beneficiaries. Either way, the size of your ultimate taxable estate is reduced, as well as the taxes attributable to those assets. In other words, you've enhanced your family's bucket and the charity's bucket at the direct expense of the IRS bucket.

These types of charitable trusts, in addition to even more complex charitable opportunities such as private and community foundations, have complicated rules. They are not for the average person.

Planning Pointer

When CRTs are employed as an estate tax reduction strategy, the charity rather than the estate beneficiaries receives the remainder interest. To replace the value lost to heirs, the donor will often establish an ILIT, commonly called a "wealth replacement trust" with a policy face amount equal to the amount of the remainder interest given to the charity. In many cases, the premiums for the insurance can be generated from the income tax savings of the CRT. Done this way, both the remainder interest and the insurance proceeds are outside of the taxable estate, thus generating both an estate tax savings as well as a highly-leveraged philanthropic gift.

I'VE HEARD OF SOMETHING CALLED A "TRUST PROTECTOR." WHAT IS THAT? HOW CAN IT HELP ME IN MY ESTATE PLAN?

Trust planning, especially the so-called "dynasty trusts," most often establishes income and principle provisions for several generations of beneficiaries. A complicating factor, according to Texas estate specialist Dianna Parker (personal communication, January 28, 2009), "…is that these trusts become irrevocable at the grantor's death, if not already irrevocable during the grantor's lifetime." Ms. Parker adds, "A future concern has always been the continued competency of the trustee(s), the possibility of a fractured relationship of the trustee with future beneficiaries, poor decision making of the trustee, tax law changes, etc." So, in order to make the management of a trust more flexible regarding not only trustees but also with regard to future law changes and other factors, the concept of a "trust protector" was adapted to domestic trusts from their use with offshore trusts.

According to Boston attorney Alexander A. Bove, Jr, "A trust protector can introduce flexibility and response to future needs and changes that a trustee could not or would certainly be reluctant to do. In this context, a trust protector can be uniquely useful and should definitely be considered in any trust where such flexibility and outside consultation are indicated."[1]

The powers that can be given to a trust protection are numerous. The following are some examples:

- Remove, add, and replace trustees
- Veto or direct trust distributions
- Add or delete beneficiaries
- Change the situs and governing law of the trust
- Veto or direct investment decisions
- Amend the trust as to administrative or dispositive provisions
- Terminate the trust[1]

So, if future laws change that require changes in the trust, the laws of one state become more favorable than the state where the trust is first established, or a beneficiary needs to be added or removed, the powers given to the trust protector can permit the necessary changes to be made. In other words, the trust protector can render revocable items of a trust that were formerly considered irrevocable.

Planning Pointer

The concept of the trust protector is fairly new in domestic trusts. It may be a good point of discussion with your attorney if you need to review your wills and trusts or if you are first establishing them. However, it may be a cumbersome process to try to change existing trusts to adapt the trust protector provision. Generally, a new trust is needed so there is an expense factor to consider. Lastly, specific powers that can be granted to a trust protector may vary from state to state.

Estate planning can be simple or complex. But above all, it is personal and laudable. To quote Judge Learned Hand, "Over and over again, the courts have said there is nothing sinister in so arranging one's affairs as to keep taxes as low as possible. Everybody does so, rich and poor, and all do right, for nobody owes the duty to pay more taxes than the law demands. Taxes are enforced exactions, not voluntary contributions."[2]

REFERENCES

1. Bove AA. The trust protector: trust(y) watchdog or expensive exotic pet. *Estate Planning Journal.* 2003.
2. Hand L. Case of Gregory v. Helvering 69 F.2d 809, 810 (2d Cir. 1934), aff'd, 293 U.S. 465, 55 S.Ct. 266, 79 L.Ed. 596 (1935).

Epilogue

Today, as I sit here at my computer and write these final words, the world is celebrating the 40th anniversary of man's first steps on the moon, July 20th, 1969. It is interesting to note as well that today, with the DJIA closing up +104.21 points, or +0.82% for the year 2009, all the major equity market indices—the DJIA, S&P 500 Index, Nasdaq, NYSE Composite, MSCI EAFE (Europe, Australia & Far East) and others—are now in positive territory for the year.

Just as many so-called experts said we'd never fly to the moon, especially after the three Apollo astronauts died in that terrible launching pad fire early in the moon program (January 27, 1967), as spirits were crushed and that straightjacket called failure seemed to paralyze the dream that President John Kennedy articulated, so too it seemed we'd never arise from the doom and gloom of the market decline of 2009. As if the pain of the market plunge of 2008 was not enough, by March 9, 2009, the equity markets were in freefall and no one could see an end to this disastrous trend with pundits predicting a 5,000 DJIA or lower (on March 9th, the DJIA closed at 6,469.95). But like the rise of the Apollo program through the late 1960s until it's culmination on July 20, 1969 when Neil Armstrong first set his feet steadily on the lunar landscape, the equity markets of 2009 have fought back as they normally have done through all previous recessions, and have now displaced former unbridled pessimism with cautious optimism.

Too late to be included in Chapter 8, I wrote an article in early February 2009, that appeared in *Hem/Onc Today* on March 25, 2009, that reflected my attitude toward the market decline of 2009 in a rather personal way. In Chapter 2, I related how the subject matter for my articles in many cases comes from real life situations I experience. As the markets were falling off the cliff earlier this year, I had an "aha" moment as I pedaled the stationary bicycle at a physical therapy session while recovering from knee replacement surgery. It quickly became the central theme of the article I called, "Where in the Game Are You?" I can think of no better way to end this book than to share with you this piece that I so much enjoyed writing and for which I received such enthusiastic feedback from readers who needed to read my thoughts at that moment in time when they were ready to panic and to sell off their equities at the very bottom of the markets.

Rudzinski K. *The Physician's Guide to Avoiding Financial Blunders (pp 165-168)*
© 2009 SLACK Incorporated

So, here it is as I originally wrote it.

WHERE IN THE GAME ARE YOU?

In discussing market movement with clients, I try to provide examples in everyday living to illustrate the frame of mind investors need to maintain during these volatile and uncertain times. Readers of my articles know that I espouse the long-term view and eschew the day-by-day roller coaster that can cause investors to make fatal mistakes with their invested capital.

So, I was at physical therapy in early February when one of the young therapists, Matt, age 31, told me he was waiting for the 8,200 DJIA to decline to 7,000 before investing his 2008 and 2009 Roth IRA contributions. He was trying to time the markets at the low end. I advised him to hedge his bet by investing his IRA money now (in case of market rally), and his wife's money later on (in case of market decline).

But as I continued pedaling on the stationary bike, it occurred to me that Matt is so young and has many years of investment time horizon yet to go. I reasoned that even investors in their 50s have a much longer time horizon than they think—maybe 35 years to normal life expectancy, or to age 90 jointly with their spouse. So I imagined I was watching an Eagles football game (substitute your home town favorite), and we were getting beat by two TDs after 5 minutes of the game. What do you and I say to ourselves when this happens? Game over? Pack it in? No way! We remember the times our team came back from deficits before—some worse than this—and we tell ourselves, "It's a 60-minute game." Some though—the pessimists in the group—give up, sell out and turn the channel. So when the Eagles win a thriller in the last 30 seconds, those people miss out on the seemingly impossible comeback. They're busy watching "The Dog Whisperer".

In the investment "game", all of us are in it at various points in our life's timeline. Those of you who stayed invested throughout this market decline are getting your monthly statements, or going on-line daily, weekly, to witness the bad news that you know resides on those pages or computer screen. You know you did the right thing by not capitulating at the market bottom, but bad news is hard to take. We want to rid ourselves of it, so some people "turn the channel" and sell out, all the while knowing they ought not to. They are perhaps forgetting that it's early in the game, and that rallies happen as they've happened before turning losers into winners. It's a 60-minute game.

Think for a moment about YOUR timeline. Think about now and how many years you have until your expected retirement, and then beyond that to your single or joint life expectancy. If the current market decline takes 3 or 5 or however many years to reverse itself completely, where does that put you on your timeline? Are you still in the first 5 minutes of the game? First quarter? First half? If you're down at half, do you show up to play the second half or do you invoke some rule that concedes "game over; go home"?

Pessimism, fear and uncertainty are our constant companions today. We can't escape them. Whether we read the newspaper, watch TV news or Jay Leno, it's "in our face" everywhere and all the time. It's like it was as a kid watching the game with my father. He never had an optimistic moment before or during the game. I had to stop watching games at home. I went to a friend's house instead. The result of the game was the same but I was able to handle the momentum shifts and emotional moments much better. What do you do when the media paints the news as overwhelmingly bad with nothing good interspersed? Always half-empty; never half full? I suggest you turn it off, like I did when I watched the game elsewhere. Seek out other sources of financial information that offer an alternative point of view—the half-full portrait—that balances off the negativity of the half-empty crowd and keeps you from reacting badly to the wave after wave of panic headlines.

I remember in August, 1979, *Business Week* ran a cover story that in essence threw in the towel early in the game. It was called "The Death of Equities." *Business Week* told us all to desert equities forever, that "...only the elderly who have not understood the changes in the nation's financial markets... are sticking with them." The article advised investors to blindly sell equities and buy gold, diamonds, rare antiques, among other things. This was the "glass fully empty". Shortly thereafter gold reached its peak then plunged, and a few years later the greatest bull market in US history emerged from the ashes of those "dead" equity markets. Back then, do you think you might have followed *Business Week's* advice and sold out low or held on, keeping a long view of the markets? If the latter, you would have been tested and tested hard but in the end you would have succeeded because you had realized you were still in the first quarter of a 60-minute game that you fully expected to win.

Equities didn't die in 1979. Or in 1987 or in 1990 or in 2001. Before you think about halting your systematic monthly investments into your 403(b) or 401(k), or bailing out of the markets when fear and uncertainty become your sole guides, stop... think about your timeline, where you are on it and how far into the game you are right now. My friend Matt the therapist is barely beyond his opening kickoff. Where are you in your 60-minute game?

We still have a long way to go to make up for the decline in 2008, and we may still be in for some rough market waters in 2009. But the fall then rise of the markets in 2009 may serve as a limited-time example of how the bigger market decline can be overcome given enough time and patience. Just like the Apollo moon program rose from its fire and ashes to achieve the goal that John F. Kennedy set for it—to reach the moon and return successfully before the end of the decade. The full recovery of the equity markets may still be a ways off, but at least with today's market results we're on the right path.

I hope this book has challenged you to "get under the hood" of your financial plan for life. If I've helped you find things in your plan that aren't right, then fix them. If I've given you ideas to improve your plan, then implement them. Above all, remember my queries to you throughout this book—if you don't do what needs to be done for yourself and for your family, who will? If you haven't gotten to it yet, when will you?

Bibliography

Books

Beam Jr BT, O'Hare TP. *Health and Long-Term Care Financing for Seniors*. Bryn Mawr, PA: The American College Press; 2005.

Cady DF. *Field Guide to Estate Planning, Business Planning & Employee Benefits*. Cincinnati, OH: The National Underwriter Company; 2006.

Cady DF. *Field Guide to Financial Planning*. Cincinnati, OH: The National Underwriter Company; 2006.

Cash G. *Spend Yourself Rich*. Kalamazoo, MI: Financial Literacy Center; 1998.

Choate NB. *The 100 Best and Worst Planning Ideas for Your Client's Retirement Benefits*. Boston, MA: ATaxplan Publications; 2003.

Choate NB. *Life and Death Planning for Retirement Benefits*. 6th ed. Boston, MA: ATaxplan Publications; 2006.

College for Financial Planning. *Asset Management & Investment Strategy During Retirement*. Greenwood Village, CO: Author; 2007.

College for Financial Planning. *Employer-Sponsored Plans*. Greenwood Village, CO: Author; 2007.

College for Financial Planning. *Estate Planning*. Greenwood Village, CO: Author; 2007.

College for Financial Planning. *Personal Savings: Investing for Retirement*. Greenwood Village, CO: Author; 2007.

College for Financial Planning. *Planning for Incapacity, Disability & Long-Term Care*. Greenwood Village, CO: Author; 2007.

College for Financial Planning. *Retirement Plan Distributions*. Greenwood Village, CO: Author; 2007.

College for Financial Planning. *The Retirement Planning Process & Meeting Multiple Financial Objectives*. Greenwood Village, CO: Author; 2007.

College for Financial Planning. *Sources of Retirement Income*. Greenwood Village, CO: Author; 2007.

Fenton JH. *All About Medicare*. Cincinnati, OH: The National Underwriter Company; 2009.

Holton L, ed. *The Encyclopedia of Financial Planning*. Denver, CO: FPA Press; 2006.

Hurley JF. *The Best Way To Save For College—A Complete Guide to 529 Plans*. 8th ed. Pittsford, NY: BonaCom Publications; 2009.

Rudzinski K. *The Physician's Guide to Avoiding Financial Blunders (pp 169-172)*
© 2009 SLACK Incorporated

Leimberg SR, Allen JR, Hayes JR, et al. *The Tools & Techniques of Charitable Planning*. 2nd ed. Cincinnati, OH: The National Underwriter Company; 2007.

Leimberg SR, Kasner JA, Kandall SA, et al. *The Tools & Techniques of Estate Planning*. 15th ed. Cincinnati, OH: The National Underwriter Company; 2009.

Leimberg SR, LeClair RT, Doyle RJ, et al. *The Tools & Techniques of Investment Planning*. 2nd ed. Cincinnati, OH: The National Underwriter Company; 2006.

Leimberg SR, McFadden JT, et al. *The Tools & Techniques of Employee Benefit and Retirement Planning*. 10th ed. Cincinnati, OH: The National Underwriter Company; 2007.

Leimberg SR, Satinsky MJ, Jackson MS, et al. *The Tools & Techniques of Income Tax Planning*. 3rd ed. Cincinnati, OH: The National Underwriter Company; 2009.

Leimberg SR, Satinsky MJ, LeClair RT, et al. *The Tools & Techniques of Financial Planning*. 8th ed. Cincinnati, OH: The National Underwriter Company; 2007.

Littell DA, Tacchino KB. *Financial Decisions for Retirement*. Bryn Mawr, PA: The American College Press; 2005.

Lynch P. *Beating The Street*. New York, NY: Fireside; 1994:41-47.

McGlaughon HK, ed. *Charitable Giving Applications—Selected Readings on Financial and Estate Planning*. Bryn Mawr, PA: The American College Press; 2004.

Miner DH, Wagnerm WJ, Stenken JF, et al, eds. *Tax Facts on Insurance & Employee Benefits*. Cincinnati, OH: The National Underwriter Company; 2009.

Miner DH, Wagnerm WJ, Stenken JF, et al, eds. *Tax Facts on Investments*. Cincinnati, OH: The National Underwriter Company; 2009.

Murray N. *The New Financial Advisor*. Self-published; 2001.

Quadagno J. *Understanding the Older Client*. 3rd ed. Bryn Mawr, PA: The American College Press; 2005.

Schilling D. *Financial Planning for the Older Client*. 6th ed. Cincinnati, OH: The National Underwriter Company; 2006.

Slott E. *Parlay Your IRA Into a Family Fortune*. New York, NY: Viking Press; 2005.

Slott E. *Your Complete Retirement Planning Road Map*. New York, NY: Ballantine Books; 2007.

Stenken JF. *Social Security Source Book*. Cincinnati, OH: The National Underwriter Company; 2009.

The Trial of the Century—Avoiding Probate Court: Planning Techniques to Protect Your Client. [video] Bryn Mawr, PA: Society of Financial Service Professionals; 2001.

Upson W. *Long-Term Care Alternatives and Solutions*. Walnut Creek, CA: St. Bernie's Press; 2007.

ARTICLES

The death of equities. *Business Week*. August 13, 1979.

Cassel A. The death of equities: is it any truer in 2001 than in 1979? *The Philadelphia Inquirer*. April 9, 2001.

DeFrancesco Jr RM. Help your physician clients with asset protection by 'leveraging' their accounts receivable. *Business & Compensation Planning*. July 1, 2004:1-4.

DeFrancesco Jr RM. Protective devices. *Financial Planning*. September 1, 2004:127-130.

DeFrancesco Jr RM. Guarding the fortress. *Financial Planning*. March 1, 2005:102-103.

DeFrancesco Jr RM. The prevent defense. *Financial Planning*. August 1, 2005:73-75.

Gassman AS. Asset protection planning—the 10 most common mistakes. *Steve Leimberg's Asset Protection Planning Newsletter*. November 1, 2002.

Gassman AS. Creditor protection for physicians—most common mistakes. *Steve Leimberg's Asset Protection Planning Newsletter*. July 17, 2006.

Gassman AS. 8 common LLC planning errors. *Steve Leimberg's Asset Protection Planning Newsletter*. May 16, 2006.

Gassman A. Primary asset protection planning rules: a general overview and summary. Available at www.gassmanbateslawgroup.com. Accessed June 1, 2009.

Gassman AS, Gomez AF. Avoid catastrophe. *Trusts & Estates*. October, 2007.

Gordon PS. The Delaware Asset Protection Trust. Excerpts from Presentation at Delaware Tax Institute; Newark, DE; November 21, 2002.

Greene K. Social security estimate assumes work until age 66. *Wall Street Journal*. January 24-25, 2009.

Lowes R. Protect your assets before you're sued. *Medical Economics*. February 21, 2003.

Rothschild G, Rubin DS. Protecting your assets from malpractice. *Cataract & Refractive Surgery*. 2002.

Rothschild G, Rubin DS. Asset protection audit checklist. *Estate Tax Planning Advisor*. May 15, 2003:15-16.

Rothschild G. Asset protection planning—current strategies & pitfalls. *Tax Management Estates, Gifts and Trust Journal*. September 1, 2005:251-254.

Rothschild G. The United States of asset protection. *Trusts & Estates*. January 1, 2008:38-41.

Rothschild G, Rubin DS. Creditor protection for life insurance and annuities. *Journal of Asset Protection*. 2003.

Schiller DJ. Protecting a physician's assets takes preparation. *The Legal Intelligencer*. October 1, 2002:M5, M8.

Slott E. The Supreme Court rules that IRAs are protected in bankruptcy. *Ed Slott's IRA Advisor*. May 1, 2005:5, 6.

Slott E. Bankruptcy law grants new level of IRA creditor protection. *Ed Slott's IRA Advisor*. June, 2005.

NEWSLETTERS

Leimberg SR. Stephan R Leimberg E-Mail Newsletter. Available at www.leimbergservices.com.

Slott E. Ed Slott's IRA Advisor. Available at www.irahelp.com.

Index

Rudzinski K. *The Physician's Guide to*
Avoiding Financial Blunders (pp 173-184)
© 2009 SLACK Incorporated